NEVER DIE WONDERING

The Alistair MacLeod Story

This book is dedicated to the people
Of the Australian bush.

Never Die Wondering

First Edition 2009 / Second Edition 2020

Copyright © 2020 Alistair Macleod
All rights reserved. No part of this publication may be reproduced, stored in a retrieval system or transmitted in any form or by any means, electronic, me- chanical, photocopying, recording or otherwise, without the prior written per- mission of the publisher.

The information, views, opinions and visuals expressed in this publication are solely those of the author(s) and do not reflect those of the publisher. The publisher disclaims any liabilities or responsibilities whatsoever for any damages, libel or liabilities arising directly or indirectly from the contents of this publication.

Author: Macleod, Alistair, -
Title: Never Die Wondering
ISBN: ISBN 978-0-6488065-0-9 (pbk.)

CONTENTS

CHAPTER ONE: 1965 – 1982
A journey of a thousand miles must begin with a single step 1
   Introduction 1
   - Stories of influence – 2
   - High Country Icon – 6
   - Maribynong River - 11
   - Show Time Spruiker - 14

CHAPTER TWO: 1980 – 1985
Embrace your fears and turn them into positive energy . 18
   - The Swy - 18
   - Jackeroo Years - 21
   - In for a flogging - 33
   - Strathbogie Ranges - 35

CHAPTER THREE: 1985 - 1986
I have everything in life I need, what I want is only a bonus. 44
   - Sales Retail - 44
   - Desert country - 47
   - Aboriginal Land - 50
   - The Centre of Australia - 52
   - The Kimberley's - 55
   - Across The Top - 68

CHAPTER FOUR: 1986 - 1989
Success is a journey not a destination 73
   - On The Wallaby - 73

CHAPTER FIVE: 1989 – 1992
The biggest regrets in life are the things we don't do, : not the things we do. 87
- 'Wangarra', my first property. -........87
- Fruit Picking Strike -........89
- Horse Injury - 95
- Hardy's Mill - 99
- Pack Horse Trek -........101
- Defacto relationship claim - 104
- Knocking around the mountains - 106

CHAPTER SIX: 1993 – 1994
What would life be like if we did not have the courage to attempt anything? 110
- Exploring New Zealand - 110
- Wangarra High Country Retreat - 113
- The Shooting – 117
- Court Proceedings - 122
- Snow Country - 127

CHAPTER SEVEN: 1995
Successful people make quick decisions and rarely change their minds. Unsuccessful people delay making decisions and always change their minds. 147
- Injustice of the legal system - 147
- Birth of a son - 150
- Across the Alps - 151
- Standing Trial -........152
- In the prison dock - 154
- On A Crusade -........163

CHAPTER EIGHT: 1997 – 1998
A great sailor does not become great by sailing on calm waters........165
- New Year 1997 - 165
- Old Clancy - 167

- Near Drowning - 168
- Rogue Brum Stallion - 169
- Union Strike Action - 171
- Three Days In The Snow - 176
- My Second Property - 178
- Trade Cattle - 181
- Buster on Brum Run - 184

CHAPTER NINE: 1998 – 2000
A pessimist sees difficulty in every opportunity; An optimist sees opportunity in every difficulty 187
- Development of a Timber Mill - 187
- Evils of the Family Law Court - 197
- Sales Consulting - 201

CHAPTER TEN: 2000 – 2002
Fear is temporary regret is permanent 208
- Family law Case - 208
- Nick the Rat - 213
- Frog and the Scorpion - 220
- Running My Own Legal Case - 221

CHAPTER ELEVEN : 2001 – 2006
Happiness lies in the joy of achievement and the thrill of creative energy 231
- Property Consultant - 231
- To beat a conviction - 233
- A. J. MacLeod Property Development - 237
- Belted Galloway Cattle - 241
- Out Back Trip - 242
- Buying Up Grazing Country - 244
- Father and Son Pack Horse Adventure - 245
- Cattle buy up - 248
- My Son with Me - 250
- Ballarat Property - 251
- The Catch - 253

CHAPTER TWELVE: 2005 – 2007
Money will not bring happiness but bad stewardship of money will steal happiness..257
  -Utopia -..257
  - Winter Drought - 2005 –...260
  - Final Court Case - 261

INSPIRING SAYINGS 273
ABOUT THE AUTHOR..281
  Son of a Highlander 283

CHAPTER ONE
1965 – 1982

A JOURNEY OF A THOUSAND MILES MUST BEGIN WITH A SINGLE STEP

Introduction

When is the right time to write your memoirs, and how do you start? In recent years, many people have asked me to write down my life experiences but recently my son's attitude to life has prompted me to do so. I look at him and all I see is a copy of me; a young kid burning with a want for knowledge, a want of adventure. What more can a father wish for, as long as he lives life with integrity and respect for others? I have been fortunate to experience a few pinnacles in my life, but the ultimate would have to been my son and I, mustering several hundred head of our own cattle on our own grazing properties at 1,000 meters above sea level in the Snowy Mountains. Riding horses that have had years of experience with us in the high country; our dogs barking, moving the mob of cattle along, stringing out for a kilometre; the crack of our stock whips, echoing through the crisp mountain air, and the both of us in our element. **It does not get better than this.**

To me, this moment was the result of 30 years of hard work, many of which were filled with anxiety, despair and failure. Now I know the asset pool is heading towards the millions but the dollar figure isn't the success **Wealth is created a long time before any money is made**.

When I was a boy, my father would take me into the mountains to catch trout. I remember the first time I caught my first fish, a rainbow. It was not the fact it was my first trout that made this so strong in my memory, it was all the dreaming beforehand, the excitement of the planning of the day ahead, the excitement early in the morning heading up the track towards the fishing hole. It was the grass hopper I put on the line, the casting out to the right spot, waiting for a bite. Having that adventurous spirit and a passion for life, I would eventually get to live a life of passion and real adventure; trying to turn all the negative aspects that life threw at me to positive ones, to have a successful life. This is my story.

- Stories of influence –

I was born in Melbourne, on the 8th of July 1965, at the Essendon hospital. For 17 years I lived at 17 Archer Avenue, Ascot Vale, a middle class suburb, and was schooled at Ascot Vale West Primary and then Footscray Tech. Though my younger years were spent in Melbourne, three months out of every year were spent in the bush. My father, Harry MacLeod, was a public servant at the ordinance factory in Maribynong. I was fortunate to have a father who spent every spare moment he could with his son. My mother Edna [nee Hamid] MacLeod, followed in tow to some very remote regions of the Australian high country for many weeks of the year. Trout fishing was the biggest lure for my father to visit these places, but I know now that it was just an excuse to be in the bush. Trout fishing, duck shooting or just camping out, as a boy it seemed to me that my home was the Australian bush and Melbourne was a place to just go to school. My family from both sides had been traditionally Footscray identities. I was in fact a fourth generation on both sides of my family. The Hamids and MacLeods had all spent most of their lives in the Maribynong River precinct. My grandfathers, Jack MacLeod and Alby Hamid, were renowned pugilists, and very successful boxing trainers. I did a bit of gym work as a kid, sparring and so on, at the Footscray Youth Club. My father would always tell me, "It's a mugs game". But as a young feller, I loved the yarns and stories of the old timers, hearing about how they had made a bob slogging it out. The tales of their hard lives were folk lore: to me growing up I found it fascinating, listening to the stories of what men would do to feed their families in the hard times, my grandfather Alby Hamid was a well known boxing trainer, who had fought the Australasian Flyweight Champion and had won, he had close to sixty fights, only 11 being amateur. The notorious gangster Squizzy Taylor paid him as a youngster after he won a fight at Fitzroy stadium. Grandfather Alby also ran an illegal bookmaking business, S.P. (starting price) and a two up game in the Latrobe Valley. He would sit me down and yarn about the traveling boxing shows that he was involved with, such as those run by the famous Jimmy Sharman and Puck Evans.

My grandfather was a half caste by virtue of his father being Casim Abdul Hamid, a Sri Lankan jewellery dealer. He was sometimes believed to be one of the many Aboriginal fighters at that time, some of whom he had sparred with. To the beat of the drum, the spruiker would call out to the crowd, "Who is game enough to take on these fellers?" The fighters stood in their weight division, waiting for any takers and for the bets to be made. On one of these occasions, the showman told my grandfather, "This man is only a mug Alby, so jab him towards where I am, and when you get up close, I will nod a few times. Just start upper cutting him and get in close and make sure you're only inches from me." The bell rang and it was on. My grandfather reckons he jabbed this feller right over to the showman who was standing right on the ground ropes. As the mug was punched back up against the showman, he nodded. Then the Grandfather got in close and started to upper cut. The feller just dropped to the ground, stone cold knocked out. They lifted up Grandfather's hand and after collecting the takings, they escorted him into the adjoining tent. The showman was counting the money and said: "Well done, Alby! That was a great fight!" My grandfather was totally bewildered and said to the showman, "But I never hit him!" The showman replied: **"I know you never, I did."** That was one of the many tales my grandfather had told me over the years as I was growing up. He also had a motto: **fight clean, live clean and try to be a gentleman.** Although I was extremely close to my grandfather and loved listening to his stories, there were times in his life where fairness was not in the equation. One day he showed me the double headed coin that he had used in his two up school that he was running in the Latrobe Valley. If he had been caught, he reckons he would have not left there alive. At no stage do I condone his ways but I understand them. They were different times, those Depression years, and people did desperate things to feed their families. My other Grandfather, Jack MacLeod was involved with a variety of business ventures and had friendships with the likes of John Wren, ["Of Power Without Glory" fame), author Frank Clune, ex - Bulldog Norm Ware, world heavyweight champion Freddie [Red] Cochrane, and jockey Ron Hutchison. He also trained fighters like Mal Appleby, who was later gunned down in Footscray in a gangster related incident. He also trained Franky Flannery, the Australian light weight champion, and Al Basten, the

Australian middleweight champion. Jack MacLeod was into betting on all fights, to running roosters [bird fights] and dog fights. He owned and operated a fish mongers business and owned a fleet of taxis, and was known to be fighting the Australian Tax Office for many years. At seventeen years of age, he had joined the Australian Infantry Forces in the 1914-1919 First World War. He had boxed in England and won a lightweight championship as a fly weight, with 36 fights for 32 wins, two draws and two losses. Jack MacLeod also saw action at Passchendaele, in the Battle of the Somme, where the western front claimed tens of thousands of Australian lives. He was wounded in action twice, and suffered for years with shrapnel wounds and the legacy of mustard gas.

Because of his small size, he was given the job to relay messages in the trench. On one of these occasions, with only his bayonet for protection he was travelling to his mate with whom he transferred authorities' messages. Upon hearing the familiar whistle which was their identifying signal, he crawled around the corner on his belly to find that a German soldier had just killed his mate. As the German was trying to lower his rifle to shoot him, Grandfather MacLeod was able to quickly cut the throat of the advancing German soldier with the bayonet that he had cradled over his forearms. Over the years he told my father that living with the memory of shooting people during war was one thing, but taking another mans life up close was a horrible thing to be forced to do. The depression that thousands of Australian soldiers experienced for the rest of their lives was horrific. They referred to it as 'shell shock'; their nerves gone from the blasting of bombs. We now know this was depression. During a shooting trip with my father some 30 years after the war, Grandfather MacLeod quickly returned to the camp site after passing a rotten animal carcass. My father walked over to him and asked what was up. His father was very emotional and told him, "When you have mates that looked and smelled like that rotting carcass then you will understand." Let's hope we never will, lest we forget.

I have been very fortunate in life to know what I wanted to do in life and I can only blame my father for that. Even as a very small child my family would spend up to three months every year chasing the trout in the Snowy Mountains of New South Wales as well as across the Victorian Alps. We started camping in a large old canvas tent, with a Coolgardie safe for a fridge, travelling around in a Holden station wagon. My father had a huge love for the bush. He was born in 1920 at home, at Wearing Street in Footscray where three generations of MacLeod's had lived. He would tell me of the days when thousands of head of cattle would be driven by horse past his home, on the way to the Newmarket sale yards; and of the days when people camped in ghettos by the Maribynong river, buying and selling rabbits as the main source of diet in the tough times, ('ground mutton' as it was called). My father would tell me how he would shoot hares and sell them to the Braybrook Hotel, and a week later see them still hanging up with their fur falling off. This was 'jugged hare': a so-called delicacy. As a boy, he had seen the shame of their next door neighbour's son, brought home by police after being arrested for stealing a pair of shoes. Kids with bare feet were common during those times. The next morning, the father of the boy was found dead, hanging in the backyard. The shame of not being able to provide shoes for his son had overwhelmed him. Although Jack MacLeod was successful with his business ventures, my father spent 45 years of his life at one job - the Maribynong Ordinance factory - and all his spare time was in the bush fishing, shooting and camping.

- High Country Icon –

It was on one of these family camping trips that we met Herb Hain, a mountain cattleman, from the Monaro district of NSW. He himself held more grazing rights in the High Country than anyone else, taking up mobs of cattle or sheep in the summer months to graze on the high plains. I can recall, as a small boy of six years of age, camping with my parents on the Eucumbene River, and seeing bellowing cattle being driven past our camp by whip cracking stockman on horse back, the cattle being taken to better grazing country during a drought. I recall that moment like it was yesterday and that's when I decided I wanted to be a cattleman, a property owner, a grazier. It was to be a long struggle to achieve this goal, as the fulfilment of that dream was to take 34 years.

My father, who was friendly with Herb, would head off with him fishing, and once Herb took me up to a hut were he was staying with his Hereford cattle. I remember him saying to me, "What do you want for lunch, young Alistair? Spaghetti or baked beans?" I said, "Spaghetti thanks, Mr. Hains," and he then would knock off the top of a can with his pen knife and say, "There you go: cold spaghetti!" After that, he fed his dogs with the legs of the kangaroo he had recently shot. At this age I was collecting all sorts of bones and he gave me a large kangaroo paw: it was my pride and joy. I was able to smuggle it back home to Melbourne, only to have my father explain to me when I found it missing, "It must had been one of those bloody stray dogs who took it". My cousin Shaun MacLean would come away camping and fishing with us, and on one of these trips I rode my first horse in the Snowy Mountains. Herb would lend us horses he was using for horse trekking and we would ride all of the upper reaches of the Eucumbene River. I was about ten years of age and I thought how great it would be to operate a horse riding business in the mountains; something that I would eventually do 19 years later.

Herb Hain was a mountain legend, a large man who had spent a life time in the mountains. He was very well educated, and a great showman and story teller. He would get me to place a gum leaf in my mouth and start cracking the stock whip; with three cracks he would have it removed from my mouth. I admit I had to shut my eyes as the last crack was only a couple of inches from my face. He would also wrap a river pebble in the end of the stock whip and with a swing and - crack - the pebble would fly through the air for a great distance with a whistle. He would then send one of his kelpie dogs off to fetch it and the dog would return with a pebble in its mouth, although sometimes it was a larger stone!

He told me that in the 40's they were up on the main range at Dead Horse Gap, where they grazed horses they had taken from the plains of the Monaro to the high country in the summer months. They brought the horses out before the first snow fall to be sold as remounts for the Indian Army. On one of these trips, he and another stockman had several hundred head of horses out from Dead Horse Gap on the southern side of the main range near Mt Kosciusko. The herd had mingled with the brumbies and the mustering of the horses had taken much longer than was expected. As a result of this, they had nearly run out of food and the snow was falling, covering the ground. They awoke one morning in the hut to find they were snowed in. The cattleman who had stayed at the hut before them had shot two brumbies, cut off the hind legs and hung them up on a tree near the hut for dog food. This is what the two survived on for a week. The old stockman working with Herb was writing his last will and testament when there was a break in the weather and the two rode out with their horses. The horses had also been trapped in the snow for a week, and had eaten the tails off each other in desperation.

When he was running his horse treks, Herb camped next to my parents under a huge tarp placed up over the trees. I remember a jillaroo he had working for him was preparing lunch under this tarp: the leg of ham was fly struck, but she just scraped the protein off and made the sandwiches.

Once when we were riding along the flats of the Eucumbene River I asked why my horse was called "Flip". The horse then lay on the ground and started to roll over, hence the name!

We were camping in this region one year when three men came along, firing guns at anything that would move with no consideration, and camped not far from where we were.

I had removed a Joey kangaroo from the pouch of a dead female kangaroo they had shot, and had it in a moccasin. At this stage we had upgraded our canvas tent to a roll out sided caravan. The next thing we knew, the police and National Park rangers were all over the place. These fellers ran to their boat on the foreshore of Lake Eucumbene and away they went, only to have another authority boat collect them. We were told later by the police that they had been in all sorts of mischief and to beware of them, as they were being charged with a variety of offenses but were able to stay at the camp site. With these undesirables hanging around, my mother wanted to leave but my father was catching lots of trout and was not planning to move on as yet. That evening, just on dusk, two of the three men started to surround our camp site. There was long grass all around and these fellers were obviously drunk and started to claim they might have some fun and burn us out. My mother was quite frightened at this stage, but my cousin and I thought it all very exciting as my father put together his double barrelled shot gun from the car. As one of these fellers walked towards our camp with his box of matches threatening to burn us out, my father produced his shotgun, quickly placed two cartridges in the barrel then lifted the gun upwards. My excitement turned to horror as I saw my father, cool calm and collected, lift up the firearm. This person then fled and dived under a log, and that's where he and his two mates stayed. We took my mothers advice, packed up and left. My father simply commented to me: **"No one will harm my family"**. Thank God for the shot gun as a deterrent, but 20 years later I would be in a similar situation; unfortunately forced to use a firearm in self defence.

We would spend months camping at areas throughout the high country, such as the Eucumbene or the Pinch River (just off the Snowy River), Paddy's River, Tumbarumba, Yarringobilly, Buckland River, Rose River, the Buffalo in Victoria and The Gibbo at Benambra. Every year, we would head off on duck shoots, mainly to the top marsh in the Kerang district. I loved those times; up before dawn, wading out into the swamps, taking a position as the dawn started to break, the whistle of ducks above on the morning flight, the camaraderie of shooters. I recall hundreds of men with guns in these areas, and never heard of anyone stealing gear. There was the odd idiot who would get a verbal lashing if he started to fire upon the wrong birds or begin shooting too early before the birds could be recognized; but most shooters were conservationists. The funds from the duck stamps (an annual fee) would go towards protection of the wetlands, and so thousands of acres of wetlands then were protected because the only lobby groups around at the time were shooters. I wonder where we would be today if it was not for the shooting fraternity. I myself gave away the duck shoots in my early 20's; not because of the pressure from the green groups but because I did not have the passion to hunt anymore. Coming back with a bag of ducks, and eating duck for weeks was the true meaning of hunting: to eat your catch. My father was a conservationist. He had passionate belief in protecting wet lands and I have known him to spend days just camping in the wet lands and not even take out his gun. It was the same with trout fishing; I knew him to throw back most of the ones he caught back. Sometimes we would smoke the trout: this process was carried out on an embankment where we had a fire below and a smoke box built above the fire via a hole in the ground. The trout lasted longer after being smoked; an essential practice back then in the days before the mobile gas fridge.

- *Maribynong River* -

I spent a lot of time as a boy on the Maribynong River. I had an inflatable dinghy and used to paddle it up the river. Sometimes I was gone for the whole day with mates and my trusty dog Terry, a yellow stray bitch that looked like a dingo, which would also come away with us on every trip. Up the Maribynong River lived this hermit feller called Nick, a refugee from Russia. He lived in an old water tank on the junction of the Maribynong and Steel Creek. The tank was built on stilts to protect him when the floods came. The old hermit also wore a helmet to protect himself from the odd idiot kid who would throw stones at him from the steep cliff opposite.

I recall there were dozens of cats that he had befriended, many of them suffering from some sort of eye disease. Old Nick would share his apple cider drink with us and yarn around his fire, built with the wood he would collect floating down the river. Many years later I was saddened to hear about how the old hermit was found in the garden of a nearby resident. He had been bashed by a mob of thugs, then dragged himself across the creek and crawled up a cliff to a house garden, dying shortly after.

At 10 years of age I wanted a motor bike and was told if I saved 50% of the cost, my father would put up the other 50%. My ownership of a Honda XR75 began, and we took that bike all over the countryside in the back of the Holden.

My first business deal was about to take place, but prior to this I did odd jobs like selling papers at Flemington Race Course. I had been told of the great money you earned selling papers. A dozen kids would gather on Flemington race day, and be handed these huge bags for the papers. With 'Herald' written on our red hats, we would stand at various locations throughout the race course, and yell out: **"Herald, read all about it!"** I think the papers were five cents and people might give you 10 cents - that was a great tip - but most would just give you the right coin. After a whole day selling papers, there was a midday and arvo addition, and then we all met to hand in the takings. Shock, horror, we only got our tips! That was the first time I was exploited and nowhere close to being the last. It seemed fate that I would do a stint as a union delegate in the future.

The Melbourne Show was close to home and I got a job carrying the large cattle signs around in front of the cattle in the grand parade for a whopping amount of fifty cents a parade. I also got a job in the milking pavilion, assisting a dairy farmer milk and shovel shit. That's right: shit shoveler. I watered cows by leading them to the pavilion troughs a few times a day, and on one occasion I led his prize heifer around the grand parade. I also assisted in delivering calves; and for that entire two weeks work I received another whopping payment, this time $20. I learnt early about compounding interest and investment. Back then banks were paying good interest and I had a State of Victoria Bank account, so all my savings went into it: tips from races, payments from carrying signs, shit shovelling money. I remember staying at Ocean Grove with my mother and getting a job stacking tiles for a roof tiler, helping out on the garbage run and caddying at the golf course.

The capitalist spirit came to me early when I saw our neighbour John Wilson who had been a jockey, horse trainer and was a well known racing identity, throwing out old saddles. I went over and asked why he was chucking good saddles away and he told me they had no value, so I said to him, "You don't mind then if I take them?" I got them home and as mum had saddle wax from her stint at making leather bags, I went to work cleaning and making the saddles shine. Once they were in what I thought was good order, I took them to school where I asked my school mates if they knew of kids with horses. A few did, so I offered a 20 % commission if they would get a buyer for the two saddles. They knew girls with ponies and I sold both the saddles for more than I made working for two weeks in a cow pavilion.

Ascot Vale was a horse suburb with the Flemington race track near by, the show grounds holding the trots every Saturday night, and the practice trotting track close on the banks of the Maribynong River. With stables galore throughout Ascot Vale, it seemed most streets had stables for gallopers or trotters. Every morning you would hear the hoof beats on the asphalt as the horses headed off for training. Alex Wilson, a legendary horse breaker, would ride his young starters through the streets, and lived just up from us. An Aboriginal originally from northern Queensland, he would stop and yarn, discussing the horses he rode. He was reported to be 80 years of age and stayed 80 for at least 20 years! The milk horse and cart was still active at that time and the famous Carlton United Brewery's Clydesdale horses were stabled just up the road. As kids, we would get a ride back from school when they were doing their Melbourne delivery.

I was not one for team sports, but I did like football. Although I would attend the Western Oval to watch Footscray play, I was not very good playing the game. That's were I met Tony DiGrande, a mate of mine whose been around since I was eleven years of age. Tony wasn't any good at the game either and we met while both on the bench waiting to get a run. Later on, we both did boxing gym work at the Footscray Gym on the banks of the river. The boxing was more practical for me, as I have to admit that I loved a good fist fight as a kid. School was also a place to sort out your disputes, and believe me, there was a few of them at Footscray Tech. I can not recall Tony ever taking a pen to school let alone use one, and today we both laugh, still trying to understand what logarithms and algebra are and if they have assisted us in life. Today, Tony has a multi million dollar property portfolio and a successful hay producing business; a self made millionaire and another road scholar. That's 'road', not Rhodes.

- *Show Time Spruiker* -

When I was 13 years old during one Melbourne show, a mate of mine - Jeff Mullenger - and I walked the side show areas as they were preparing for the two week carnival, and asked showmen for work. We got a job scrubbing bottles and spent the morning scrubbing in preparation for painting them for use in the "rings over the bottle" side show. A distinguished old gentleman wearing a little tweed hat rode his push bike past us. He was Ron Potton from Potton's Amusements. I approached him and his son John for work and I would work four Melbourne Shows for this legendary showman. Ron was an Englishman, and I was told he was also a leading clown in the renowned Barnum and Bailey circus. He came to Australia and started the side show alleys along with many other early showmen. My first job was on the clowns where the crowds would place ping pong balls in the moving clown's mouth. After you added up the numbers, they won their pick of the prizes. Later I worked the 'rings over boxes' that had watches on the boxes; if you got a ring over the box you got the choice of watch or ten dollars or whatever the box contained. The 'knock 'em down tin cans' was where I spent most of the time. **"Two shots for a dollar, come on fellers, win your lady a prize!"** is what I would spruik out to the crowds. There were three shelves: a one dollar, a five dollar, and the prize of them all, a ten dollar shelf. After paying a dollar for two balls, you had two shots to throw the balls at five tin cans in a pyramid shape. If you knocked them all down with the two shots, you won the biggest prize of them all, a koala worth about two dollars. The 'spotto' was where I spent my final Melbourne Show. The crowds would throw twenty cent pieces onto a board and try to get them into the box that contained either sixty cents or a ten dollar note. Over the years, I watched people seemingly determined to throw away hundreds of dollars just to win ten dollars. I learnt the biggest lesson in sales while working the 'knock 'em down tin cans'. I had been pulling incredible money in from the usual drunken crowd and I was feeling a bit guilty about this when the old showman came up to me and said, "You haven't been spruiking tonight as much as you do, and I think you're feeling guilty for taking people's money."

"Yeah, Mr. Potton, I do feel guilty," I said. He then took me over to the centre of the side show road way, and asked me to look along the alley. "What do you see young Alistair?" he asked, looking up the side show alley "Only side shows, Mr. Potton," I said. He said, "That's correct, and **if you don't take the money, the next bugger will**." I had no trouble selling after that, and that simple lesson was to be with me for the rest of my life, while selling everything from livestock to properties.

I loved the whole carnival atmosphere, and the showie label that came with it. The Potton's paid me incredible money compared with working in a cow pavilion but I worked long hours for it and banked every cent into that interest earning account. I planned to invest the money later in a fixed term that was going to earn me more return from my investment.

The whole side show thing comes with a bad element, or should I say attracts a bad element. At the end of one Melbourne Show, there was an attack on two showies between my 'knock 'em down tin cans' booth and the 'Ferraris', a dodge 'em type car. For whatever reason, gang types would come to a show and try and fight the showies. Two fellers got a quick hiding and it was all over within a minute. After a couple of hours about thirty gang type fellers turned up, calling out to these showies who had flogged them earlier. People started running to get away from this potential danger. One showie was a huge man of Maori origin, who had recently assisted me when a crazed drunk had started saying he was going to flog me. The drunkard had been greeted by this huge feller, who told him that it would not be in his best interests if he struck me as he would retaliate and hurt him severely. The crazed drunkard quickly left, thanks to him. And again this showie kept his cool in front of the crowd of attackers. He said to the gang, "Just one on one mate, just one on one" They agreed, and a feller stepped forward and went the showie, but he quickly just grabbed him and punched him to the ground. With this, one of the gang appeared with a piece of wood and smashed the showie over the back of the head. From then it was all on: showies from everywhere came with pipes and large spanners for weapons that they took from their amusement rides. I had never seen so much blood. There would have been at least fifty people fighting. I could hear the thud as pipes were swung into people's bodies. I had this nutter swinging a bar at me that he had ripped off a show stand. There was nowhere to go and as a fifteen year old, it was pretty scary. A woman who worked the next show up, a walk-through ghost walk, jumped from her ticket box, rolled up her sleeves to show the cartoon tattoos over her arms and launched into another feller with fists and kicks. She was quickly punched out. A police officer, the only one there, swung his baton over the head of the pipe wielding nutter which finally brought him to the ground. As more police arrived, the gang dispersed and a lot of the showies were taken around the back of the tent I was working on, away from the police and questions.

CHAPTER TWO
1980 – 1985

EMBRACE YOUR FEARS AND TURN THEM INTO POSITIVE ENERGY

- The Swy -

During my teenage years, the gambling scene was the biggest lure; either the races or the trots at Moonee Valley on Saturday night. I have always loved the races and having a punt on the gallopers or trotters, and it seemed that most people in the Ascot Vale area did also. Every Saturday I would head off to the trots with others who where older than I was but keen on the punt. My parent's home would be the venue for Kelly pool or snooker tournaments for the neighbourhood kids that I knocked around with. When I was fifteen, after a night at the trots, a couple of blokes I knew who were a few years older persuaded me to attend Nappy's two up game in North Melbourne. It was referred to as the Swy, and was usually conducted in a warehouse but the site was moved around to avoid the constant police raids. We hailed a taxi outside the Moonee Valley trotting complex and Tommy said to the taxi driver, "Do you know where the Swy's at, mate?" Tommy, who was heavily tattooed and had a nearly shaved red head, directed the taxi driver to the isolated warehouse area of North Melbourne.

Big Vinnie and I sat in the back and Tommy said to the driver, "Just a bit further, mate." The driver was asked to drive up dark back streets, down this street here, then: "No, this is no good, head up that street." We were heading down a laneway between the warehouses and Big Vinnie, who was a huge feller, leaned over and said to the driver in a serious voice, "Have you ever been rolled, mate?" The driver said, "Never" in a very scared voice. Then Tommy said, "You've never been rolled?" The taxi at this stage was just moving very slowly up a dead end lane when Tommy finally said, "This will do." The taxi driver stopped the vehicle and turned on the light and there was sweat pouring down his face. Tommy and I stepped from the taxi and then Tommy said, "You fix him, Vinnie." The driver was literally shaking with fear by then as Big Vinnie leaned over from the back seat. He handed him a twenty dollar note and told him, "Keep the tip, mate."

There was what was called a 'cockatoo' on the door of the Swy, who would stand guard and only let in known identities. Now and then he would ask the others with me, "Is he old enough?" as I was much younger in years. "Yeah, he's eighteen," they would reply.

It was an exciting place, the two up game. You would knock on a door in a deserted warehouse late at night or the early hours of the morning and the cockatoo would open the door and then quickly close it behind you. As you walked into a cigarette smoke filled room, there were men from wall to wall, either standing or sitting in a large circle placing thousands of dollars on the ground. The words of the two up king: "All bets done, come in spinner" directed a person to spin the two pennies balanced on a batten up in the air where an Australian flag hung on the ceiling. There were all types of people at this place; from putty nosed exboxers and wharfies to well known underworld figures. I would only make bets of five dollars at a time and would love to spin the coins. The spinner would 'back the heads', placing the head side of one coin with the tail side of the other opposite as he stood in the centre of the ring waiting for the two up boss to declare: **"All bets done, come in spinner."** At this moment there would be silence from the usually packed crowd. If the coins didn't spin, the spinner was stopped and made to spin them again until they did. No drunks were allowed on the premises and I never saw any type of aggression from anyone, and I frequented the games on many occasions.

On one occasion, I was there with Vince Macri on the second floor of an abandoned warehouse when there was a smashing at the door and people yelling, "Raid, raid, Vice Squad!" The police had axed their way through the door and came barging in. The Vice Squad had a large lock up prison truck backed up against the lower floor with ladders up to the second floor where the game was played. It was pretty hairy stuff for a young feller, especially when this old timer, a putty nosed type, sitting next to Vince, told us:

"It's going to be a cold night in the cells at Russell Street tonight and not enough blankets to go around." Although illegal, two up is considered Australia's national gambling game and in a lot of cases the two up operators were well respected. The police would do a head count of those caught and then the operators would pay the fines at the Magistrates Court without the attendance of those patrons. I believe the place was raided once a month and it was a way that 'the powers that be' could receive their share of taxes through fines. I felt that telling my parents that I had been 'out for a pizza after the trots' was not a lie; I just left out the part about the two up game. I knocked around with a lot of different types of people and some of them have stayed great mates of mine for my entire life; people with the same values, of fit and proper character. But others who I knew during my teenage years chose a different path.

My ambition in life was to own my own cattle property. I would read books about great men, such as the cattle king Sidney Kidman; who at 13 years of age set off on a one eyed horse called Cyclops on a lifetime journey to eventually become Australia's wealthiest man, and the world's largest land holder. I had great role models, listening to stories about my grandfather's adventures and having mentors such as the great showman I was working for or the well known and respected high country cattleman I knew as a boy. My father also played a huge role, as for me to have done anything that would shame the family name would have been of too great a consequence to carry. **Integrity is everything.** Others I knew had very different role models and different ambitions to me. They idolized the Melbourne underworld, and eventually became well known gangsters. I have known several people who had become part of Melbourne's underworld and ended up spending time behind bars, or worse, murdered. There is no question to it; **we all decide what path we go down in life.** I just chose the right path to travel.

- *Jackeroo Years* -

At seventeen years of age, I had just completed fifth form at Footscray Tech. I admit to being a bit of a rebel at school. I recall my teacher asking us all what we wanted to do in life, and I said I was going to get a job as a Jackeroo and then eventually own my own cattle property. She told me, "You're living in a dream world". I learned early not to allow other people's negative attitudes influence me. In fact, I turned other people's criticism of me into determination to prove them wrong. **If you can dream it, you can live it.** I had bought the Weekly Times rural newspaper every week since I was twelve years of age, looking up the property section, studying land and cattle prices, finding out what was on the market and dreaming of which property I could own one day. I looked up the employment section and there was a position for a first year Jackeroo on a beef and wool growing property in the western district of Victoria:

"Must be able to ride horse." I quickly applied for the position and was able to get an interview with James [Jim] Alston, the co-owner, who, with his brother Pete, ran the 6,000 acre property. My father drove me to the property which was near Beac and Lake Corangamite. As we drove over the first cattle grid, there were rocks galore; the reason why the place was called 'StonyHurst'. My father muttered:

"If you came off a horse mustering here, that would be the end of you". He wasn't very impressed, but I don't think I could have picked a better place to spend my first year as a Jackeroo. The Alston brothers had picked up the property of then 3,000 acres in the 1970's beef crash and had gone to work developing the operation. With an Aberdeen Angus breeding herd of some 300 head and running 6,000 merinos as wool producers, they had extended their operation to 6,000 acres.

I got the position and commenced in January 1983 with another Jackeroo, Chaz, for the huge payment of $40 a week. My mates in Melbourne had been receiving weekly payments of up to $200 a week, and that was for a forty hour week. There is no such thing as a forty hour week on the land.

Jim, the boss, and I got along after a bit of a shaky start. There were sheep in the yards that we had to move quickly to a holding paddock on motor bikes. It was a windy day and he left a gate open for me to close as he rode on up the road to the next gate. As it was so windy, my hat was flopping over the front of my face. Because I was trying to see where I was riding without losing my hat, I was travelling with my head tilted down, looking only a few paces ahead. The next thing I knew there was the boss – whack! I just rode over the top of the boss! Jim had stopped his bike right on the road up in front of me and was standing next to it. Before I knew it, I just rode straight over the top of him and could only turn to watch him sitting in the middle of the track after being knocked down. I thought to myself: there goes the job, but as Jim got over the shock, he made light of the whole thing. We had a pretty good relationship for the entire year I was there and I could not have had a better mentor in life. Throughout the year, I was going to learn not only about the workings of station life but also the opportunities Jim and his brother Pete took to acquire their empire; the mind set of a millionaire.

One of the first things Jim Alston said to me was: **"There is a right way, and there's a wrong way in life, and then there is also my way."** Over the many years to follow, I was to be very fortunate to learn this way of life from many people. The attitude and mind set of successful people is far more important than the money they have made. As the old statement goes: **Never measure a man by the destination he has reached, but by the journey he has made along the way.**

As first year Jackeroos, we were accommodated in the Quarters all year. They were large lodgings with six bedrooms, with an ample lounge and an open fireplace. On the mantle piece was a set of large horns from a buffalo that Peter Alston had shot in Arnhem Land in the Northern Territory. Both the bosses had gone through the Jackeroo system - usually a three year stint - living and working on stations throughout Australia. As Jackeroos, we would have our dinner in the huge old homestead, a magnificent two storey weatherboard with a part marble floor on the veranda. It even had servant's bells in the kitchen from a by-gone era. Jan Alston, Jim's wife, was the cook and the four of us – the Alston brothers and the two Jackeroos - would work out on the station. Once a week there would be a formal night where we would dine in the dining room of the homestead and be required to wear a woollen tie during the meals.

The drought of 1983 was on us, and we were out feeding livestock every day amongst the dust. We had a couple of old Holden utes that would tow a bin trailer full of grain, and we had set feeding programs for the cattle and sheep in the paddocks. The place was littered with rocks and the Alston's would say: "We never knew there was one rock on the place when we bought it", referring to the amount of vegetation that would grow in a normal season. They had bought the property back in the '70's during the cattle crash. People had told them that they were mad to buy, but the Alston's had watched as the value of the property increased. What an opportunity the Alston's had seen when others had not. I knew what they had paid for the place and how much it was worth per acre back then, and I quickly learned that property would grow in value more than anything else. Besides that, the return from the production of either cattle or wool that graziers would expect was fairly good back then. A cocky would only have to hang on through the drought years to be in clover after the drought. Horses were used for all the mustering on StonyHurst. We all had our own farm horses: Chaz was given this chestnut gelding called Marmalade. It threw him the first morning out, and then somehow I got lumbered with Marmalade. It was discovered

Marmalade was head shy, so as long as you never waved your hat near his head you were safe. I recall mustering one day near the properties air strip, where the Lands Board, (a farming organization) was loading a plane to drop out 10/80 poisoned carrots for the rabbits. As we were talking to the pilot, he asked: "Is that horse plane shy?" I was mounted on Marmalade as I asked: "What do you mean?" With that, the pilot yelled, "Well, hang on!" as he started up the plane. Marmalade was immediately spooked. I was to ride him for the entire year, and he never threw me once. He was called Marmalade by virtue of the colour of his coat. I would crack a whip on him and beat Chaz in any horse race we would have around the property, as Marmalade could get some pace about him when forced to have a go. But mostly he just wanted to plod along.

I learned to shoe horses at StonyHurst. We would have to have every horse shod prior to heading out and I can recall the length of time it took me to shoe my first horse; worrying about drawing blood from hammering in the nails. But as with everything, it only takes practice before you get the hang of it, and now, many years on, I have shod horses over a thousand times.

Every morning I would rise well before dawn, have breakfast and head out and milk the homestead cow. This chore would require the cow's calf to be locked up the night before so the cow would provide us all with a sufficient supply of milk. During winter, it was extremely difficult to find her in the morning, as everything was pitch dark and it was hard to locate her just with a torch. I would then walk her up to her pen and she would place her head in the bail, coaxed in with a biscuit of hay. I would secure her head in the bail, and then tie her back leg up so she was unable to kick the bucket over and away I would go, working on her teats until the bucket was full of milk. Before I knew it, this chore became a quick process as I got the hang of it.

StonyHurst was full of natural lakes but they were an unreliable water source for stock so we would erect windmills throughout the property. This was done by assembling the large windmill stand over the bore, lowering a pump connected to mill rods and then assembling the blades on top of the windmill stand. The water would be then pumped into a large tank, and from there to the watering troughs. It would be a twice weekly occurrence to check the bores to make sure they were still working. We would refer to this as the bore run. On one occasion I remember getting into an enclosed tank to block the outlet from the inside so we could repair the outside fitting. It was a case of swimming underwater and sealing the outlet, then swimming back down later to removing the plug when it was repaired. You don't realize how cold underground water is until you spend time in it.

It was February 1983 when the Ash Wednesday bush fires broke out. We had knocked off work and had just sat down in the Jackeroo quarters when black smoke covered the property. There was a fair bit of panic as we did not know where the fire was coming from. It took a while to learn from news reports that it was on the western side of Lake Corangamite and we were not in any immediate danger. Within a few days, Jim and I would go down to one of the burnt out properties and help re-build fences as part of the charity appeal. At a later date I would see the aftermath in the Otway Ranges and other places.

We had wondered if there would be any danger if the fires came over the place as there was nothing to burn, just dirt and rocks. But in the autumn the drought did break;

up came lots of feed and the cattle and sheep became fat. During lambing and calving we would have to ride out on horseback to check the ewes and cows. There was plenty of trouble with lambing as the lambs were well oversize in a lot of cases and the poor old ewes could not lamb down. This was a phenomenon we were not familiar with as the onset of green feed meant that they had produced an over size lamb. We pulled lamb after lamb from the ewes and when we could not remove the lambs we had to bring the sheep back, carrying them astride the horse. We would carry a .22 calibre rifle with us for the ones we were forced to put down. With a bit of wind and rain behind it, the cold would hit and would cut through you.

Once during this time we pulled up our horses on the socalled protected side of a hill and were rolling a smoke. At this stage in life I was buying aromatic Bank 'roll your own' cigarettes. It must have been for the stockman image as rolling your own astride your horse was the done thing. At this moment, head shy Marmalade pushed his head at my chest into my 'Drizabone' oil skin coat, so it must have been cold.

It was very early in life that I decided never to go shearing. The four of us did all the crutching on the property and each of us would try and compete with the others. After penning up the sheep, you'd go into the pen and turn over a ewe, dragging her backwards as you came out of the swinging gates. Then pulling down the cord of the Sunbeam gear, you started your machine. With the hand piece held in with your right hand, you shore the behind of the ewe and the 'top knot' *head area+ in order to have a clean area around the arse end so to limit fly strike, and around the eyes to prevent the ewe going blind. It was one of the jobs I hated; lying on my back during lunch, I dreaded the start up of the machines. Shoeing horses was in no way as hard on my back as this shearing caper. So I decided then and there never to go shearing. When the shearing did commence on StonyHurst, they contracted a team from the Murray River area. Most of the shearers used wide combs but this was taboo to some people in the Australian Workers Union at this time. The Union would argue that as the influx of New Zealand shearers used these wide combs, that it was not fair: these new tools of trade appeared to be an unfair work practice. Why this was so is beyond me, both then and now, but during the early '80s it was a very touchy subject. There had been strike action taken around Australia: men had been bashed, shearing sheds burnt, and shearers openly fired on as they left some sheep stations.

We were asked to keep quiet about the coming of this particular shearing team as they used the wide combs. Ironically, now nearly every shearer in the country is using wide gear.

It was all action during shearing; heading out on horse back, mustering large mobs of sheep, bringing them into the yards, drafting them up, then taking the shorn sheep back and mustering the next mob. On one occasion there were a couple of dead sheep in the yards and we threw them into the back of the ute and drove over to a dead sheep pile to drop them off. This pile was not the most delightful place one could visit and as we drove back, the ute went right over the top of it leaving this horrible substance all over the tail end. We decided the best thing to do was drive to the water tank at the shearing shed and get a bucket to wash off the substance. It was a Monday morning and the shearers had been on the beer and boozing all that previous week end. As we pulled up, there was the sound of the smoko bell and out walked a shearer. Well, he took one whiff of this awful substance and a pale look came to his face. He shouted all types of abuse at us and we kept away from the shearing shed for a while after that.

During the shearing, the shearers would stay in the quarters and we would stay at Peter Alston's house, about 5 kilometres away. We got on the grog one weekend with the shearing team and went back to the quarters where they had the shearer's cook put on a huge feed at 12 o'clock at night. They sure knew how to live it up. At the end of shearing, the contractor asked me if I would like to join his shearing team: first take up roustabouting then start up shearing. I kept his details for years bur never did contact him. One thing is for sure: I saved my back.

Dogs were hardly ever used on StonyHurst and I was to find why during one occasion that they were needed. Jim Alston told us to muster one paddock for ewes and lambs and we were supposed to head off at first light on horseback. He and his brother Pete would have a wing made up to guide the sheep into a gate way: a roll of hessian tied to steel posts. By the time we approached the wing, we had managed to muster the entire mob of ewes and lambs and had them quietly walking along a fence towards it. I could clearly see Jim and Pete standing there, but the next thing I knew, this bloody Border Collie bitch by the name of Snowy was running straight at the mob. Well, all hell broke loose. There were ewes running one way, lambs running the other and we were galloping across country, trying in vain to circle the mob. Everyone was yelling and swearing but it was all hopeless. There was no chance of getting them back. As I rode back towards Jim Alston, he was sort of kneeling down with his large 'Bluey' brand coat moving about. It was not until I reached him that I realized he had Snowy inside the front of his jacket and was belting the dog, telling her what he really thought of her. Snowy wasn't very popular for a long time.

Jim's yarn spinning was pretty interesting. I recall him telling me the story of how he was involved in mustering a large mob of sheep in the Riverina when he was Jackerooing. Out of this huge mob of thousands of white sheep, one little black lamb stood out from the rest. The overseer turned to the Aboriginal stockman and said, "Hey Tommy, did you play with that mob a few months ago, mate?" And the Aboriginal stockman replied, "Yeah, that's right boss, but you have a look at all the white ones."

Foot rot was a big fear on StonyHurst. The Alston's had invested in six thousand head of merinos and had brought them into a region with damper conditions than they were used to. Most believed that there would be problems and that the merinos would not suit the region. The Alston's proved them all wrong and with careful management the mob was free of all foot problems. Trimming the hooves of sheep was a large job and we would run the mobs through a formalin bath to kill any germ that might be on their feet. If we had been on another sheep property we would be required to walk through the foot bath ourselves. Once we were out mustering sheep that had come onto the property from a neighbouring area. They were running all over the place and I recall Pete Alston seriously threatening to sack both of us Jackeroos if we failed to bring the strays into line, so great was the fear of foot rot infecting their livestock.

It was a tradition in sheep country during lamb marking that the first year Jackeroos would use their teeth to remove the testicles from ram lambs. This was done by cutting the purse of the ram lamb, squeezing out the testicles and then removing them with your teeth with one swift movement. I was seeing a girl from Melbourne once who did not believe this practice was true until we both saw a documentary on the television showing the Jackeroos using their teeth. She would not even kiss me for a week after seeing the film.

Fencing was a major priority and we would head off to fence this very stony type of country, littered with rocks. The early settlers had made rock fences that went for miles but over the century they had become less stock proof. They made great habitat for the many tiger snakes that lived there. During mustering, your horse would be shying at the continuous encounters with the large reptiles.

Gelignite was used to blast holes for strainer posts when fencing. It was a dangerous job. We would dig down as far as we could go and to remove the 'yonnies' *rocks+ we tied a couple of sticks of gelignite together, placed holes in the gelignite and then inserted a detonator with a wick attached. Then we would place the gelly at the bottom of the hole, fill it up with dirt, top it up with "Antho" (a fertilizer product), light the wick and run for our lives. On one occasion, we had all thought we had it down to a 't'. So we placed the gelignite in about six different spots along the fence line, planning to have the wicks at different lengths, so the explosions would go off at intervals: one explosion after the other. We placed the explosives carefully and all headed up to the top of the hill next to the ute to watch our grand explosion. BANG! The first and farthest one went off and we watched all the rocks and dirt go right up in the air, way higher than any of us had predicted. The next thing we realized, the rocks were coming down on us. We all dived and hid under the ute or tractor, whichever was closest, and stayed there while the other five explosives went off, coming closer each time.

Another time we dug down into a wet area and protected the gelignite with a plastic wrap so the water would not affect the detonator. We waited and waited and there was no explosion. We all walked back to the hole and everyone knew that we had to remove the explosive. I said, "Don't look at me, I am just the Jackeroo." Chaz said, "Don't look at me, I am just another Jackeroo," and Jim Alston said,

"Don't look at me Pete, you wanted to buy the place!" The three of us took off back up the hill laughing as Pete Alston used all types of language on the three of us, calling us 'poxy Jackeroos', etc. As he cautiously lay in the hole removing the explosives, we all made comments to him from a distance, telling him how he could easily get on with only one arm. He removed it with no problems. Unfortunately, after time Chaz became allergic to the gelignite, which made his whole face just swell up.

The great thing I have found throughout the Australian bush is the humour most people have, especially in very dangerous situation's either horses bucking, busters (being thrown from a horse) or bulls charging. On one occasion, we were building a stock yard and using a petrol driven borer which required two men to hold it at each end as it drilled through the ground. Chaz and I were having all sorts of trouble as this thing would run all over the place. Pete Alston told us, "Get out of the way, one of you Jackeroos, and give me a go." So I did and away they went. The next thing I knew they were in all sorts of strife as this auger pawed through the ground. Then they lost control completely and it took off with them holding onto the handles of this contraption. As they spun around and around on the ground, neither one could let go. It was hard for me to turn the moving borer off while they were both circling around on the ground at top speed. Eventually I was able to get to the switch and turn the thing off, but not before they were bashed and bruised. We all laughed for weeks at the mention of this contraption.

In our spare time we would head off to town; drive the station vehicle to the start of the main road and head into the local pub at Beac and get on the 'turps' *beer+.Every few weeks I would catch the train from Colac to Melbourne where mates of mine would meet me at Spencer Street and we would do the city pub scene. When I turned 18, I went down to Colac and bought myself a Holden HJ sedan. It was metallic green and that car would eventually take me right around the country.

- In for a flogging -

The Melbourne Show was on during one of these weekend trips to the city. It was the first time I had been to the show without working there. Tony Digrande, Jeff Mullenger and I met up with past school mates and had a few lagers in the bars at the show grounds. As the whole show came to a close, we headed up a suburban street in Ascot Vale back towards my parents place. Tony Digrande grabbed the last bus to Footscray and three of us headed down the street when a group of twelve fellers walked past us in the middle of the road, yelling and swearing. They walked past but the next thing we heard was them running back towards us. It was all very quick; the next thing I knew, I had been knocked down and had six blokes kicking at me as I tried to get up. Jeff was also in trouble with another six bashing into him as he tried to defend himself while up against a wooden fence. The third person with us fled and hid on someone's front lawn. After this event Jeff and I believed that this person had said something to the gang as they had walked past yelling, and then ran and hid as Jeff and I tried to fight off the mob. I kept saying, "One at a time, come on, one at a time," as six hoons sunk their boots into me from all angles. I could even feel their laces from their runners as they continued kicking me. Not one punch, just repeated kicks. Every time I managed to try to get up, I would have my arms kicked away from under me. I recall a voice saying, "Give him some more, give him some more", as kick after kick was applied to my body. There was a car that drove right past my head when I was on the ground. It seemed they were trying to run me over and I just managed to roll my body a bit to avoid the tyre hitting me. Then a voice said, "Come on now let's see what you can do!" They stopped kicking me and I was able to get to my feet. At this stage my whole face felt like it was twice its size, probably because it was. I could hardly see, I was so covered in blood. I wiped one side of my face with my right hand and could just barely see a person so I threw a punch. It was hopeless; I felt completely uncoordinated from the bashing. I then moved next to Jeff so we both could fight them off, but the next thing I saw was some of them getting into a vehicle. I got my second wind and I went for them, dragging them out the car to fight. How stupid could I be? Both Jeff and I got a second flogging. After they all bolted, in car and on foot, the person who had been walking with us appeared from hiding behind a fence without a mark on him. We got back to my parents place where the police were called and the next day we were at Flemington police station giving statements. The detective interviewing us showed us a fence paling with blood over it. He told us a woman had been bashed over the head not far from where we were attacked and was in serious condition in hospital. They sent us to have forensic photos taken, as we both looked pretty bad. Jeff copped a bit of a damaged jaw, and I copped more like damaged pride but the scariest thing was that neither of us was able to recognize one of that mob due to the dark night. I suppose we were just fortunate they were not able to run over me. We believe that they had the car close by for a purpose: go out to bash then to quickly get away. It amazes me what some people would do for kicks. Out of that mob, you would think at least one would have had the balls to try and stop this attack on us. Maybe the saying: **'water finds its own level'** is true with people as well.

Back on StonyHurst, the main job I loved was the cattle work; mustering shiny, coated Black Angus cattle. In some cases, we walked the beasts through the shallow lakes that were scattered over the property but there was other yard work such as drafting of cattle and marking calves. This was done by running the calves up a race into a cradle, a device that holds the calves in place, then tipping the calves over in it. As the bull calves lay secure in this device on their sides, we proceeded to castrate them by a careful incision with a pen knife, to cut along the scrotum then remove the testicles. We ear marked the calves by cutting away a couple of notches out of the ear. This was to create a registered ear mark; every station has their individual ear mark pattern. Jim Alston would take us to South Australia, buying bulls at the basin sale at Keith and to the Riverina, buying rams at Uardry station. Jim Alston left a big impression on me in life: witnessing his millionaire mind set and the foresight and determination of two brothers building their own empire. During a B.B.Q that Jim Alston hosted, I was talking to a person who was asking me questions regarding my ambitions to eventually own my own property. He said, "How does anyone buy a property if they have not come from a well to do family?" Jim Alston overheard the comment and told him, "He will find the way". He later said to me **"Never let anybody tell you that you can't do it."** I then decided I would never allow the word 'can't' into my vocabulary.

- Strathbogie Ranges -

I had completed my first year Jackerooing, and now had to find a place to commence my second year.

I made a trip to Queensland with Jeff Mullenger, sailing on a yacht on the Whitsundays and having a look around the country. Then I returned and headed around the north east of Victoria by myself, 'cold calling' cattle properties, looking for work but having no luck. After nearly running out of savings, I thought I should just grab any work for the time being. I drove to the Dalgety wool stores at Tottenham in Melbourne, hoping to get a job lugging bales of wool as I heard it was good money to be made. I approached one of the wool agents and said, "I have finished my first year Jackerooing and have been looking for a place to do my second year." After a bit of a discussion, the agent said to me, "Well, what part of the world do you wish to go to?" So much for the visit to the wool store to get quick cash lugging wool bales around! I told him, "the Strathbogie Ranges", and he said, "Right o." He then got straight on the telephone and I had an interview the next day with Jack Newton of Mount. Alexina, in Avenel.

After nearly a full day interview with Jack and his son Tom, they offered me the position. At $145 a week, my pay was 350% more than I was on a year ago. Then Jack said to me, "The award states a deduction for keep - $45 - but we rarely look at the clock around here, so you shouldn't look at the clock either. There's a bit of overtime now and then so we won't deduct the $45." I quickly accepted the job and again I was fortunate to be working with a great family. I had my own quarters and ate, with the family, three meals a day. Jack's wife, Amy Newton, did all the cooking. The day I commenced, Tom said to me: "This is your home now, treat it that way." For the entire year, not once did I feel like only an employed hand but always part of the family.

Mount Alexina was a 3,000 acre property on the southern side of the Strathbogie Ranges, an area renowned as Ned Kelly country. The Newton's ran a 4,000 merino sheep wool growing operation as well as running 160 Poll Hereford cattle. In predominately hilly country, the property was well treed with stringybark, and apple and yellow box. The flats along the creek had red gums growing on them. Koalas were throughout the property and the views from the top of the Mount were spectacular. Jack Newton, then in his sixties, had first taken up a thousand acre hill block in his twenties. He had cleared the scrub, built a home for his wife Amy out of the red gum timber cut from the creek flats, and over thirty years with his son Tom, increased the size of the property by three times, improving the carrying capacity to remarkable levels. Jack would say to me: **"Look after your stock, and they will look after you"**. He undoubtedly practiced this, as I cannot recall ever experiencing cattle or sheep of his that were not quiet and kept in fair order. The Newton's cut their own hay on the property, as well as buying in Lucerne or red clover from another property. This feed was used for any stock that might need a little extra in a tough season. For instance, when a heifer had twin calves, Jack separated her and gave her the legume hay to keep her milk levels up to feed the both calves. Old Jack would also milk the house cow using the mechanical suction cups to do the job. One of the out buildings was brick and served as the butchering area, where you would hang up killers and also separate the milk, cream from whey. The latter would be feed to the house pigs. The place was self sufficient with a small orchard and large vegetable patch only for domestic purposes. I had given away the silly smoking by this stage and appreciated the fresh home grown cooked meals.

I loved the mornings on Mount Alexina; the sun streaming through the trees, kookaburras laughing, and the smell of bacon and eggs as I made my way down to the main house. All mustering was done on motor bikes, but dogs were used too. All up, there were 14 dogs on the place. I was given a Border Collie, Jess, to work the sheep. She was a very temperamental animal; if you raised your voice at her while mustering she would spit the dummy on you and go and lie down in the creek or a dam. Only after trying to speak to her for ages in a calmer way would she then proceed to work, but still only if she chose to. She had a litter of pups and I was given one. I named her Koby after the Kobyborne range that went through the property. She became a great working dog, quickly picking up traits of her mother's great working ways but not the temperamental nature. I would stop the bike on a hill and just whistle out to push a mob of sheep along or just point a left or a right with my arms to direct them.

Superphosphate was spread over the property by aeroplane. Old Jack asked me to go up to see the place from the air. At this stage I had only been on a plane once before: a Fokker Friendship to Tasmania with the school, but flying around a small aircraft was something quite different. As I jumped in and closed the door, I could not hear anything but the large propeller that was just in front of the two seats. The pilot had put on hearing protection as he throttled forward and away we went, over the paddock air strip and up into the air. Before I knew it, the pilot dropped the wing and we were virtually on one side. At one stage, I looked out of my side window and there was the small figure of Old Jack waving up to me. Then I noticed the door on my side wasn't shut properly, and was opening. I also realized I didn't have a seat belt on and as the plane was on this 90 degree angle, I was sure I was going to be back on the ground much sooner than the pilot. I grasped onto the seat until the pilot straightened up the plane and then leaned over and closed the door.

Jack's son Tom was an active member of the fire brigade and I joined the Country Fire Authority. Jack and I were up on the Mount when a fire started in the lower country at Nagambie. We quickly headed down to it and on the way found a car that had smashed into a tree as the driver couldn't see the road through the smoke. The occupants were all cut up a bit, but not seriously. We got to the fire and jumped onto fire trucks, putting out the flames. Apparently this old feller had been on his tractor pulling out stumps when sparks from the exhaust set fire to the grass. He then ran back to his house and tried to lever his fire unit onto his ute but took a heart attack and died. We were mopping up when the son of the deceased pulled up in his car and asked what was happening. Unfortunately, Tom had to tell him of his loss.

On another occasion, I headed off fishing in the afternoon. While I was gone, Tom got word a little girl had gone missing just down the road. He went down on his motor bike to search for her but unfortunately she was found drowned in the dam later. Sadly there are too many stories like that in the bush.

The Newton's would take me to all the sales, be it the wool sales in Melbourne where the Asians would bid for bales of wool, or cattle and sheep sales throughout the region; clearing sales and property sales. The Newton's were responsible for replanting thousands of native trees across their 3,000 acres, engaging bulldozers to batter down gullies and stop erosion. The protection of the catchment area was a priority, and Jack would always state, **"Put what you can back into the land"**.

The mindset of Jack Newton was that **healthy stock and healthy land made you wealthy** and he certainly was a man of wealth. Maybe not to the point of rolling with money, but certainly in the sheer pride in his accomplishments. Scrubbing out a bush block, building a merino flock of 4,000 head, cutting medium wool and increasing the yields every year, lifting the carrying capacity by introducing improved pasture, building improvements such as bush pole sheds, a black smith shop and hay and shearing sheds, to improving them by building new and more efficient steel buildings, and handling facilities for livestock. All the gates throughout the 3,000 acres were painted white by Jack. All fencing on the boundary was rabbit proof, and we were to spend a lot of time shooting at night knocking over the odd kangaroo to keep the numbers at bay, and literally destroying the rabbit population. Tom and I would walk the hill country with fourteen dogs, fumigating rabbit holes while the dogs brought down any that escaped. Once while fumigating I was gassed by the larvicide poison as it worked its way out of a burrow. I ran as far as I could, gasping for air with my eyes watering. I received a small taste of what my grandfather experienced at the western front, as the poison was the same substance as the mustard gas used at the battle of the Somme.

The dogs would often try their luck on Mount Alexina's echidna population. We would run to stop the attacks on these incredible animals but the dogs always came off second best. The echidnas would dig deep down into the ground to protect themselves and the dogs mouths were always left bleeding from being severely pronged by the echidna's sharp spikes. You would think the dogs would learn better...

During mustering once, I was sent to the northern side of the property to bring out a mob of merino wethers. The paddock had a bit of scrub on it with lots of large boulders and bordered a gorge so it was easy to miss a few, as I did. At this stage I would pride myself in not having to remuster. Having Tom come back with the stragglers I had missed was a knock to my pride, until Old Jack told me of the time he was up mustering the Mount. When he returned to the yards, he counted out the sheep and was over a dozen short. Disgusted with himself, he rode back to the Mount and rode throughout the paddock but there was not a sheep in sight. With that, he returned to the yards and recounted just in case he had miscounted, yet again he was under a dozen head. At this point he was panicking, thinking he had been robbed, so he rode out again, checking all paddocks adjoining this particular paddock. Not a sign of any sheep whatsoever. With that he got on the blower [telephone] and called the local sergeant of police. The police arrived the next day and both of them went up to the Mount to see if they could find any evidence of foul play. They were looking at gateway entrances when the Serge said to Jack, "Are they wethers?" Jack said, "They are", and lo and behold, there were a dozen wethers camped under a tree. Jack had missed them on a few occasions. I never felt guilty about missing the odd beast from then on.

When I was up on the Mount either mustering or digging out horehound, [a pest weed], I would sit and have smoko near this huge wedge tailed eagle's nest. The nest had been there as long as the Newton family could recall, and every year the eagles would have their young ones in it. They were absolutely superb birds with huge wing spans. I would sit on the steep side of the hill and look directly across a distance of only a few meters to where they were. The eagles sat in the fork of an old gum tree on their collection of timber, acquired over many years and probably handed down from another pair of eagles.

During crutching time, I was to work alongside two well known local shearers in the region. These fellers, Brian and Max, had over thirty years shearing experience and could push out sheep faster and easier than I could. Like most shearers, they were renowned for their yarn spinning and I remember the yarn about this particular shearer they knew that was pretty hot headed. Once they were shearing wethers and the grazier was having a go at this shearer as he was cutting into the pizzle [penis] area, because at one stage he had cut the pizzle off. The grazier dragged the sheep back into the shed and demanded the shearer sew the pizzle back, as it was literally hanging off. This hot headed shearer had obliged by sewing the pizzle on to the head of the wether.

During the shearing on Mount Alexina I was paid roustabout's wages to work in the shed, picking up fleeces from the boards once the shearer had removed it. I had to throw it on the table and skirt the fleece, then sweep all the locks away from where the shearer was working. The shearing was a fun time, as everyone played jokes on one another. The cook had made some lamingtons for smoko, and it wasn't until Old Jack was tried to eat one of these chocolate coated cakes that he realized he was chewing into a rubber dish wash sponge that had been camouflaged with chocolate and shredded coconut. It was all fun in the shed until Glen the gun shearer decided it was time for me to be 'initiated'. This consisted of being held down by the shearers, while one applied shearing gear oil to a particular area.

There was a huge thunderstorm one night, with claps of thunder everywhere and the night sky lit up with bolts of lighting. The next day we discovered twelve sheep dead under a yellow box tree, and the tree itself split in half by a lightening strike. Tom tried to open up a gate and found the chain on the gate had been welded together when lightening had stuck the fence.

I eventually had my dog Koby working extremely well, as she had picked up all the good traits from her mother, but not the bad ones. Unfortunately, the only horse on the place had got into the dog yard and Koby was found kicked to death. I then decided to only get dogs that I thought would stand up to a kick, as the cattle work is where my heart was.

I went out and bought a Blue Heeler, an Australian cattle dog, whom I named Clancy; he would be with me for many years.

Mount Alexina, although hilly, produced fat cattle. I remember sitting on the rails with the Newton's at the Euroa sale yards as their steer vealers received $1.45 a kilogram. That was in 1984. In twenty two years time, Tom Newton and I would talk about that price as the cattle crash hit us. By then I would own several hundred head of my own cattle and could only dream of receiving a price like that.

After a year on Mount Alexina, it was time for me to move on. Old Jack did his best to try and get me to stay but as much as I loved working there, my adventurous spirit was in overdrive and all I wanted to do was to see and experience this great big country. Again I looked around for work in different districts, but finally decided that I wanted to see the Kimberley's at the northern end of Australia; the place of big cattle stations, the frontier country. But I really needed more money behind me than what was in my bank accounts, and the only way to do that was to step away from the rural sector for a while and find work in a higher paid job.

CHAPTER THREE
1985 - 1986

I HAVE EVERYTHING IN LIFE I NEED, WHAT I WANT IS ONLY A BONUS.

- Sales Retail -

I went to Melbourne, bought the Herald Sun newspaper, opened up the employment section and jabbed a pen onto one of the pages. And there, where the ballpoint pen mark fell, was my new job: key cutter, shoe repairer, engraver and salesman. The salesman part I was confident about, and how hard could the rest be? I got a position as a trainee with a company that repaired shoes on the spot in shopping centres throughout the world. They also cut house and car keys, along with offering engraving on everything from wedding rings to putter mugs. I admit to being a man with the worst hand writing God ever put breath into, but I learned to write in cursive script and began to engrave people's valuable items. I started out at a large shopping centre in Doncaster East Melbourne. It was the typical sales approach: a customer would come up and ask for a key to be cut, you then would suggest they get two made while trying to find a reason: the key they presented might be cracked or worn. If it was a brand new key, we suggested an extra one being cut as a spare. Seventy percent of customers would agree, therefore increasing sales 70%. Shoe repairs were the same: if they wanted a heel repaired, we'd suggest they have a new sole to protect the shoe. When it came to engraving, suggesting the client add a bit more in writing increased sales all the time. I was paid an hourly rate, plus a commission on sales. I worked 9 to 5, Monday to Thursday; then 9 to 9 Friday, and 3 hours on the Saturday morning, totalling 47 hours a week minus lunch breaks. Wages came to around $290 per week with commission on top, sometimes adding up to $400 a week in total. I had never made money like that; indeed two years previously I was only making $40 a week plus my keep.

I felt a lot of fear about the process of engraving items. I remember doing my first engraving job on a bracelet. A woman asked me to engrave her niece's name and then left it with me. As I started, I realized I had engraved the first letter too small so the rest of the letters would have to be smaller again. When the women returned and I showed her the result, she said, "It's terrible, I can hardly read the writing!" I explained to her that with an expensive bracelet like hers, a person should admire the item first and the name on it secondly, hence the reason for my using the smaller writing. She agreed and gave me a tip.

I worked alongside others operating the stall. I recall returning shoes to a woman who had given them to us the previous day to be stretched as they were too tight for her. After she put them on she told me, "They are a much better fit now." She started to walk around in them, saying that she could not walk in them like this before and then she paid for the service and gave a tip. Assuring us that she had saved the cost of a new pair of shoes, she left very pleased with herself. I looked at where I had picked up the shoes from and realized that due to the number of shoes to be stretched, we had not even placed them on the stretcher. The power of wishful thinking.

Within a few months, I was given my own store to operate in Greensborough, north east Melbourne. The company would place two trainees with me to be trained in sales and I increased sales at the location considerably. While I was still at Doncaster (prior to Greensborough) during the Christmas period, the company sent a memo to all trainees that had not yet been qualified [earned the company certification]. It said that the company would pay full bonus on commissions during the Christmas period. This was a great incentive, as many people throughout the company would be maximizing their sales in the most important selling period. If those people qualified after the Christmas period, then they were to be back paid their commissions, such as was the case with me. I qualified and was given a store of my own and trained others in salesmanship. But after a couple of months, and after continued requests for my commission earned over the Christmas period, the Company reneged on their promise. I was taken out to lunch by the state manager at the time to discuss this situation. I told him that I was leaving the company and he tried to keep me on by offering me Doncaster or any store that I wanted within Victoria; telling me that, with earning commission from being the operator of a store, I would be able to make what was owed to me plus more. But to me, principle and integrity is everything. I declined his offer, and resigned from the company.

At this stage, I had enough money behind me to travel again and was keen to see the top end of Australia. Although I could sell in a retail environment, retail work was not for me and that adventurous spirit was pushing me on to travel further.

During this time I had been dating Carmel, a girl from Melbourne. She was a sales assistant and we had been seeing each other since I was working on Mount Alexina. She wanted to travel around Australia with me, and although I had huge reservations about this, in the end she accompanied me, along with my trusty Blue Heeler dog Clancy.

I had $10,000 in savings and the Holden sedan HJ that I had purchased in Colac during my first year of being a Jackeroo. I bought a 6 x 4 foot trailer, four 20 litre jerry cans for fuel, three 20 litre containers for water, a swag, a shot gun, a bag of clothes and an esky full of cooking equipment. I also bought a Nikon camera that I was to use for almost 20 years, plus spare tyres, repair gear and tools. Then away we went, destined for the Kimberley's, far north western Australia.

We headed first to the Grampians and camped at the Rockland reservoir with friends from Melbourne that had decided to meet up with us there for Easter. This was a common occurrence during any holiday time; camping in the bush, fishing and drinking. We then headed to South Australia, visiting the Murray River, Adelaide, Port Germain, Port Augusta and out to the Flinders Ranges.

- Desert country -

We headed east to a place called Chambers Gorge. It was one of the hottest places I had ever stayed, a rocky gorge with the sun bouncing off the rocks. We camped on a water hole where the water was very brackish, as is in most outback water points. The gorge sheltered some fantastic Aboriginal rock carvings that had been created thousands of years ago. I have a photo of me eating a freshly cooked tiger snake in the gorge. Over the years of living and travelling in Australia, I would often improvise on the food situation, finding bush tucker and cooking on an open fire became commonplace. This country was in grip of drought, and as we headed north into the heart of the continent, the drought became worse. We went to Marree, a small town on the edge of the Strzelecki desert, and the start of the Birdsville and Oodnadatta track. We headed up the Oodnadatta track, and camped one night at the Curdimurka ruins; an abandoned railway siding from the days of the Ghan railway. This is artesian bore country, where the only available water source is from a huge underground basin that covers three states. The water is extremely hot and in most cases is pumped out of the ground through a bore via a windmill, and left to run over the ground for a reasonable distance in order for the water to cool down for cattle to drink. These water points also attract all the wildlife from near and far.

During the night, I could hear all these black ducks coming in to land on the overflow. At first light, I was out there and shot a couple for breakfast. Roasted duck for breakfast, cooked with spuds and onions, in the middle of the desert. By the time you get a fire going, prepare your meal and cook it, the sun is up and blazing down. While Carmel and I were feasting on this meal and Clancy on a freshly shot rabbit, this old Land Rover 4x4 appeared, drove off the Oodnadatta track and pulled up next to us. The driver, an old feller with this huge old stock hat with a bash in the front of it, sat in the vehicle with it just rattling away, and said to us, "Good on youse" and then slowly drove away.

"Good on youse," and drove off like an old nomad, disappearing back into the desert. We headed up to William Creek and stayed the night at the back of the pub. Like a lot of these outback pubs, it's easy to stop for a drink and not to leave until the next day. We met up with a couple who wanted to travel along the dog fence to Coober Pedy. As they did not want to travel alone, we decided to travel with them; a trip of only 170 km to visit this famous opal mining town. It was pretty easy going in the HJ Holden and only had to plough through some sandy points in a couple of places on the track. When we arrived in Coober Pedy, the annual show was being set up and a lot of side show tents were being assembled. I quickly went around the showmen, looking to pick up some work. There I met up with a travelling showman Ken, who had been running side shows across the vast outback region for years. He had several trucks loaded with all the old tent shows: tin can gallery, shooting ducks, hoops over boxes, money machines, etc. I said that I had worked for old Ron Potton for four Melbourne shows and he knew of old Ron and put both of us on, paid by commission on our takings: 25%. I ran the tin can alley and Carmel worked the hoops over the boxes. It was a pretty entertaining place, Coober Pedy; full of men that were trying to make a fortune by digging into the earth, hoping to find an opal seam. It was renowned as a wild town, a place were people went missing. Just prior to our arrival, there had been a gun fight in the town, and the use of gelignite to settle disputes was legendary. There was a large Aboriginal population also, and a lot had come in from different areas of the desert for the show. It was not easy money, spruiking on the side shows, as a huge percent of the crowd were drunk and you had to keep your wits about you and dodge the odd punch. The other showies told me that at one of the shows in the Territory, a person had died during a brawl and that a court case was proceeding.

We pitched a tent at the back of the show tents. Clancy was chained up to protect our gear, and all the other showies also had dogs do to this. The Coober Pedy show lasted a few days and I was asked if we would join them to do a show at Indulkana Mission. The travelling show had obtained a permit from the Pitjantjatjara land council. I accepted the offer, and we arranged to meet up with them on the reserve in a couple of day's time.

- Aboriginal Land -

Indulkana Mission lies about 100 kilometres south of the Northern Territory border, west of the Stuart Highway. Back in 1986, the highway was dirt and near Marla bore, you could easily get bogged in the sand. I had to plough through the sandy road and in some places the bull dust covered the wind screen; the windscreen wipers would work hard, scraping off the dry dirt from the windscreen. We arrived at Indulkana right on dusk and as we drove into the Mission, there were camp fires flickering all over the settlement, housing a large population of hundreds of people in amongst sand dunes. I could not find the show group and had to go from camp to camp asking people where the travelling show was. Only a few could speak English. I would ask, "Do you know where the show is?

Side show, carnival?" They would go back into their humpy and bring someone out who could speak a little English. "CARNIVAL, CARNIVAL!" They would point in a direction and off we would go, until we eventually did find the show camp. The group had arrived only a short time before us and we all started to arrange the tents and gear with the assistance of the generator for lighting. Then a vehicle pulled up, containing two elderly men and a younger man as the translator. He started telling us that we were not able to stay where we were as the women in the next camp were in mourning over the death of a family member. We asked, 'Where shall we go?" and were told, "You go from there to there". The translator pointed to one spot to another, only a few meters from were we had started unpacking. So everything went back into the trucks and we drove just a few metres along to keep everyone happy.

The next day, we had the whole side show arranged with all types of amusements. The show was run by generator, decorated with coloured lights dangling from one tent to another. The music of Slim Dusty echoed out over the desert. Most of the settlement was over the other side of a sand dune and we were all impatient for the arrival of this several hundred strong Aboriginal tribe. It was looking pretty grim as no one turned up. Then all of a sudden, as the sun was going down literally hundreds of people were walking towards us on top of the dunes, the disappearing sun making them into silhouettes. There were women with babies on their shoulders and men with head bands, all bare footed and all speaking their tribal language. Some of the men wore large brimmed hats with the police band [a blue and white checkered strip] around it, and I was told they were the settlement authorities. At the tin can alley, the people would hand money to me for a couple of shots, and accurately knocked every can over. I really enjoyed the entire show, as there was not one drunk or any bad type of behaviour. There were dogs everywhere, and I would have to admit they were the worst kept animals I have ever come across; most in a starved condition. The next morning, I awoke to all this laughter as a lot of the Aboriginal children had taken a liking to my car and were on top of the roof, jumping up and down. One of these kids was named Wally, and he would ask me for cordial. He would sit with us laughing as he would drink down a cup. There was trouble with the children, as some had turned to petrol sniffing to get their kicks, and I could see that all were living in squalor. One night, a few of us were sitting around a fire and one of the fellers travelling with the show informed me that he had got himself into a bit of trouble back in Victoria. It was something to do with him owning items, but not really owning these items, being charged and released on bail to later attend court. He knew he would do a stint on behalf of Her Majesty so he decided to up and run, see Australia first, then give himself up when he returned a couple of years later. This story was typical of many that I met over the years and I found that a lot were known only by their first name or nickname.

I was asked by Ken if I would continue with him on his travelling show, but I was set on heading into the Northern Territory and picking up work on a cattle station to learn a bit about the desert country. As Ken was driving off, he stated, "Hey Al, you're the only white feller around here.

They may want all their money back tonight!" and drove off laughing.

The next morning, I awoke to all this moaning. I got out of the swag and walked towards where it was coming from, at first thinking that it might be one of the poor camp dogs. It was coming from behind a large bush, and as I walked up to the bush, I was shocked to find this naked Aboriginal woman with blood running down her face. She had some sort of sharp object in her hand and was inflicting wounds on herself. She was the person in mourning. I just let her be, quickly packed up, and headed for the Northern Territory.

- *The Centre of Australia* -

We travelled along the Northern Territory and South Australia border, following the Northern side of the Musgrave Ranges. One night I awoke in my swag to find a dingo staring at me, only inches from my face. There where a few of them and all had taken liberty with our gear, tearing at our food supply in the trailer. We travelled throughout central Australia; Ayres Rock the Olgas, and Kings Canyon. I got a position on a cattle station, trapping stock that came to the water points and Carmel got work in the property store. The station was over a million acres. It was in a four inch rainfall area, but they had not seen four inches for four years. I was amazed how cattle could survive, mainly by eating leaves from mulga trees. There was hardly any ground feed. I witnessed cattle eating the dried up skins of dead animals. I was sent out to man a set of stock yards that had the water points [troughs] in the middle. Another station hand would be sent out to trap at the next yards. There was some 50 km between water points. You would shut the gates into the yard for a day or so and the cattle would have to hang around the yards or walk to the next yard 50 kilometres away to drink. In the dark of night, you would wait until cattle came into the yards and before they walked out, you would close the gates, trapping them. After moving them into the holding yard, you would then reopen the gate and wait to trap the next mob. Most other stations had already made up 'spear gates', where the stock automatically went in and were trapped, eliminating the need for man power. During the trapping over a couple of nights, I had trapped a mob of brumbies [wild horses]. During the last night of trapping, there was a mob of camels that where too wary of my presence, so did not venture in. We made camp in the out station, a small hut in the desert; and after a few drinks, it was suggested we go back out to the yards, and charge in with vehicles and on foot to see what we could trap. Charging up to wild cattle in the dark was not the brightest idea, but in the mad rush we were able to trap 3 head with a handful of men. With two vehicles' headlights shining into the yards, we could see one was a large black horned bull - known as a mickey - which had never been yarded. We moved the other two beasts into the holding yard, but had trouble with the bull as he would charge all of us, smashing into the rails. The boss of the show said, "I think I will try and ring him", meaning to run behind the bull, grab his tail and throw him to the ground; again not the brightest idea I have heard, but it is amazing what a few beers can do. With that comment, he stepped into the yards and ran behind the bull. Well, this bull just lifted up his back leg and kicked the boss fair into the bread basket [stomach]. Then the bull turned around and rammed the boss as he was frantically getting to his feet. With a twist of his head and flick of his horns, the boss went up into the air and landed in the next yard. It was sheer luck that he was not killed. One of the others yelled out, **"I was just about to hop in and give you a hand but could see you had a handle on things."**

At the Station, the cook had the most important position: feeding people. He was a very temperamental feller and would go off abusing anyone who asked anything about the up coming meal. He told me he had learnt to cook while serving a prison sentence in South Australia. A lot of people that work in remote areas are mostly nomadic, staying only for a short time then moving on. We were out branding all the cattle that we had trapped and I was on the branding irons. When the beasts would move up the race to where I was, I would place the red hot iron on the rump of the near side of the animal. There were all these white faced cattle [Herefords] that I had trapped in my area and they were obviously from next door, as the station I worked on did not run Herefords. I said, "What do we do with these?"

The boss simply picked up the iron and started branding. Buyers from South Australia arrived, and all the cattle were sold, including the Herefords.

Cattle duffing [stealing] is a common occurrence throughout Australia. In areas, it was sometimes acceptable for a cattleman to steal a neighbour's beast as a "killer" *for food+ for his own consumption only. Poddy dodging was also common, where someone would knock off clean skinned [unbranded] calves and claim them to be his. Whatever the wrongs and rights of the situation, I was not too keen staying on at this property and so went back to the station, packed up and headed for greener pastures. Payment there was $150 per week and we had every second weekend off, but I was not there for money. I wanted to experience different operations and was content just to make enough to keep on travelling.

We spent time around Alice Springs exploring the gorge country then headed up north, meeting lots of station people on the way. One night, we were asked back to a station near Tennant Creek for a meal and to stay on. The manager of the station was arguing with his neighbour about the term "cattle duffing", compared to "poddy dodging". The neighbour, full of rum, would say, **"It's the done thing; you knock off theirs, they knock off yours."** The station manager with whom we where staying said, "Cattle duffing is cattle duffing, dodging poddys, for killers or not, it's all stealing." His neighbour in his drunken state said, "That pains me, old mate, as I only knock off a dozen of yours a year and I am sure you knock off a lot more of mine." The station manager looked at his neighbour and said, "That can't be right, I have never taken a beast in my life." His neighbour, who was quick to sober up, said, "I was only joking mate!" trying in vain to cover up his drunken honesty.

- The Kimberley's -

We travelled across the top of the Tanami desert, along the Buchannan and into Wave Hill. One night, lying outside in the swag, maybe a hundred or so wild donkeys came right through the camp. They took off galloping in all directions when they were startled by Clancy's barking and at one stage I thought they were going to run over the top of us. As we travelled over the Western Australian border, the country began to change. There was feed about and water in creeks, so the cattle were in good order. We stopped at Old Hall's Creek, some abandoned ruins from the gold mining days in the last century. As I was walking along the dry creek bed, an older Aboriginal man was walking, carrying his spears and trying to control all of his dogs. Behind him walked his woman carrying billy cans. We approached each other, and he extended his hand. As we shook hands, he said, "My name's big Georgie Johnstone, I'm Catholic." He was out hunting and his wife had been collecting bush onions. Georgie's spears were his pride and joy. He showed me how he had used kangaroo entrails to bind the sharp points to his spears. The Woomeras [throwing sticks] he carried were also works of art and he explained how he cut saplings down and created the shape by heating them over a fire. We later drove both of them back to their camp with all the spears strapped to the trailer and a dozen dogs running behind.

When we arrived in Hall's Creek, about 20 km west of the ruins, it was like paradise with sprinklers going on green lawns. We stopped at the pub and walked into the bar. There were a lot of Aboriginals in the bar; in fact they were all Aboriginals. They asked me where I was headed, and I told them I was looking for stock work. "I am a ringer too," they told me, as most of them were stockmen. I talked with them for a long time, getting information on where to get my next job. I kept walking to the bar for service, but the bar attendant would just give me acknowledgment from a distance. After a while, I said to the Aboriginals, "What do you have to do to get served?" We walked around to the next bar, and there was the bar attendant, ready to serve us. As I looked around, there were all white fellers. I had been in the black feller bar and I would not be served until I went to the white section. I could hardly believe it; a country made up of so many diverse cultures, and people still insisting on segregation< it was way beyond me. While in the bar, I met up with the station manager from Alice Downs Station, a 350,000 acre property north of Hall's Creek. I got work mustering, and Carmel got a position as the camp cook. The stock camp was out on Phantom Creek. A large tarp was placed up over a pole, and this is where all the food was prepared. Every stockman slept out in swags. We had our own tent and vehicle on the camps. There where fourteen stockmen, made up of New Zealanders, Englishmen, local Gidgewa and Jaru Aboriginals (that is how I pronounced the names of those tribes). The rest were white Australians. There were 12,000 head of cattle on the books, and all the mustering was done during the dry season. Traditionally, shorthorn cattle were used; then the Santa Gertrudis breed was introduced, as they were more suited to the tropical north. Then later Brahman were introduced across most of northern Australia. They were heat tolerant, tick resistant and were larger types, able to walk the distances needed to feed and drink. Horses were used in conjunction with helicopters for mustering. All men were given four horses each and would swap them after each days work. I loved the Kimberley and I loved the work: the large stations, the big mobs of cattle. Wild country, wild cattle and wild people. The horses, unfortunately, were also wild. I thought I could ride until I went to the Kimberley. Every morning, well before dawn, we would be out of the swags to eat and drink pannikans of billy tea. We ran all the horses through the yards, saddled up and were away, mustering. Saddling was a huge ordeal, as a lot of the horses would try and kick you as you were saddling; then when mounted, the horses would buck, sideways to reverse. I quickly learned to change my whole style of riding. I would approach a horse with my left hand on its near side shoulder and my saddle positioned up on my right hand shoulder. If the horse tried to strike me, I would be able to push myself away. Once the saddle was on, it was still an effort trying to strap it up as most horses would be trying to move about. To mount was an exercise in itself. If the horse decided to buck, I learned to have the leather reins run loosely through my hands. A bucking horses head would literally disappear, tucked under its belly, so you always let the reins slide through your hands, then leaned back as far as you could, feet forward in the stirrups, **and tried to stay on as this outlaw gave you a tour of the yards.** It was not always the yards where the horses would play up. Once when we were out and the cattle were breaking from the mob, a helicopter went over me. The shadow of the blades on the ground sent the horse into leaping bucking frenzy. Somehow I managed to stay on but felt the saddle come away, and then both saddle and I lay in the dust. My horse was caught and saddled again and back on I went. I picked this bob tail chestnut filly out of 60 horses in the plant [the camp outfit of horses and gear]. She dropped me once and somehow managed to come down on top of me, pushing every bit of air out of my lungs. It was ages before I could get my breath back. I've ridden plenty of unpredictable horses, but over the next two decades I would never come across horses as wild as from this plant. There was a ringer called Trigger on the station. We were all rugged up in the morning, and as the sun came up, he needed to shed the jacket he was wearing which turned into a huge ordeal. As I sat on my horse, I watched him carefully dismount and tie up his jacket but as he attempted to tie it to the saddle, his horse quickly spun around and kicked him in the chest with both back legs. I could hear his ribs breaking as he hit the ground. The manager arrived on the spot, and had a go at Trigger for being hurt. Although he was coughing up blood, the manager would not let him be driven back to camp in the station vehicle. I protested at the managers' uncaring attitude, but he said, "Come on Al, the vehicle's got a job to do." Trigger just walked back to the camp, went into town and was diagnosed with broken ribs, then packed his gear and left, along with a couple of others.

Mornings were a spectacular sight in the Kimberley. Parrots and kite hawks made a noisy chorus as the sky was lit up with every colour imaginable as the sun emerged from the east. In one muster, we brought in close to two thousand head of cattle, and any beasts we missed were shot from the helicopter. I could understand mickey bulls were being shot in order to stop that breeding line but on this place, everything that broke away got shot. We had some Santa Gertrudis bullocks yarded, and when they busted through the cable yards the manager and two of his station hands started shooting at random, destroying the animals as they ran. What a waste, what a bloody waste. Dale Zaddow, a fellow ringer, once stated that none of us stockmen could ever understand the cowboy mentality of that manager. On another occasion while out mustering, I was cantering along the side of a breakaway - a heifer that I was bringing back to the mob - when rifle shots from the helicopter above me dropped the beast in front of me. I could only imagine what the Alston or Newton families would have said about that senseless waste of money, and the sickening killing of stock. I realized then how fortunate I had been cutting my teeth as a Jackeroo with such great mentors.

Helicopters would head out to start up the mobs and bring them towards the horsemen who would wait on a hillside for the main mob to be brought in closer. On one of these mornings, I said to one of the Aboriginal stockmen, "Dave, what's your surname?" He said "Calwyn." I said, "Is that Aboriginal?" He said, "No, me grand father born Calwynyarda Station, Fitzroy Crossing." I then said to another Aboriginal stockman, Raymond, "What's your surname?" He said, "Yeeda." I said, "Well that's a black feller's name, isn't it?" He said, "No, my grandfather born on Yeeda Station, Derby."

Dave would have to be one of the best riders I have ever known. Over the years, I have ridden with literally hundreds of riders, but no one with as much balance as Dave Calwyn. He would try to bet anyone that he could roll a smoke while bucking out an outlaw, but none were game enough to take on his bet. He was only a few years older than me, bearing tribal markings on his chest and he would tell me of his Aboriginal traditions: of how boys were initiated by the elders, taken out in the bush, circumcised and had their chests cut with stones with their tribal identifications. They were shown how to hunt and learned bush skills before returning to the females of the tribe. Dave would show me different types of bush foods such as berries and how to watch the budgies land in order to find the fine kerosene grass, and how to strip the dry leaf for the very small black seeds. He would tell me how his people would make flour from this, and cook their bread on the coals. The Aboriginal stockmen would tell me of their hero, a man called Pigeon. He fought against the white invasion at the turn of the century and led a small army with military precision before being caught and killed.

Once Dave and I went mustering together after a new plant of fresh mustering horses. We climbed a ridge made up of rocks and stone and were cantering along with Dave tracking the horses. We pulled up to see over 200 head below us; both station horses and brumbies. Also amongst the mob were mules, a sign of when the odd donkey stallion had mingled at some stage. We rested our horses a bit, prepared ourselves by gripping our stock hats between our teeth then galloped down into the side of the mob, wheeling them towards the east. It was fantastic galloping with the brumbies, their nostrils flaring as you rode alongside them. We were yelling at the mob to turn them and causing huge clouds of dust to rise over many kilometres. We travelled with them until we had them up against a fence, where other ringers were to assist us. By the afternoon, we had all the horses yarded, ready to start choosing our new plant.

We would run the horses through the yards and select our choices one at a time; looking for four each in total: three broken and one colt [unbroken horse]. It was full on during breaking: fourteen men starting out horses all at the same time. You would rope a horse, then 'bag it down', a process of getting the horse used to a hessian bag by touching it all over with it. Then you'd start to gear up a horse with tack. We used 'monkey gear', tying up the front and back legs with hobbles made of chains; then girthed up the horse and 'mouthing' it, placing a bit in its mouth then tying up one side of the bridle, then the other. Within a couple of days, you were on the outlaw, being bucked sideways to reverse.

Shoeing was also a task in itself. You would have to collar rope the horse; placing a harness type rope over the shoulder, then using a rope connected to a hobbled hoof to tie the leg back and shoe it. Other difficult horses would be thrown on the ground and tied up to shoe them. Raymond had a wild horse that could hardly be handled. Raymond went to town and never came back, and I foolishly took the horse on. After a day handling him in the yards, I took him out to a dry creek bed and he let rip, bucking non stop. In all honesty, he was the only horse on whom I rode out the buck until he was exhausted due to the sandy creek bed. On all the horses I rode, I could ride out the bucking in small yards, but as soon as they would stretch out in the open country, I would come loose. I absolutely loved all the horse and cattle work.

If a mickey bull came through the race during marking, we would trip him over by tying ropes to his legs. Once castrated and branded, we would take it in turn to stand astride the animal and as the ropes were let loose and he stood up, we would ride the bull out into the yards.

Carmel's position as camp cook was by no means easy. She was given flour, potatoes, onions and we would knock over a beast every few days. She was also rationed a couple of cans of veggies and given two eggs. How she was expected to feed fourteen men with just that is hard to comprehend: the manager was miserably tight. Somehow she managed to feed the men, mostly by making stews. "Killer" night, when we would go and kill a beast then bring it back to camp, was traditionally the cooks night off. We would place the rib bones into the coals of the fire and I preferred this method of cooking beef than eating the freshly killed meat that had not had time to set. One afternoon, some of the local bush girls from a tribe north of the station came into camp. They hung around all afternoon, and became quite friendly with a couple of the men. The girls disappeared with these fellers and we didn't see those men until dawn. The next night, sitting around the camp fire, one of the Aboriginal stockmen who was also from the same tribe as the girls said, "No good, these two fellers gone off with those girls, those girls be at there home now, their fellers ask were you been? They get really mad, they come down here tonight, they have spears, they might kill everyone." With that, he rolled up his swag and slept well away from the camp. We all had a very worrying night, but thankfully there were no repercussions.

The weather came in and we were rained out of the bush camp; there was no more mustering so we went back to the station complex. Then we all decided to go to town, except for Carmel, who stayed at the station. She had her own cooking room within the station complex. We all rode in the back of Dale Zaddow's 4 x 4. Town was sixty kilometres away, and we all planned to be back within a few hours. During the events of the night, two of our group were arrested by the police. When we asked why they were arrested, they just said we could pick them up later. Within an hour two more from our group were arrested. And as the night went on, there were just three of us left. I was standing outside when the police pulled up in the prison van, stepped out and grabbed one of our group for absolutely nothing at all. They ordered me not to try anything, but after they had put him in the van with their batons, I was forced into the van as well. They drove us to the Hall's Creek lock up, and reversed up to the cells. They opened up the prison van and escorted us inside, where we were greeted by the rest of the men from the same station. Dale Zaddow was the only one to escape the false arrests. I was thrown into the cells. Never in my life had I seen anything like it. It was like something out of the movie "Papillion". The cells were full, mostly with Aboriginal people, twenty or so; all lying or sitting on the cold cement floor. Some were hiding under blankets. There was one toilet for all and one can only imagine the state of it. During the course of the night, this elderly feller started vomiting and nearly drowned in his own vomit until his head was moved away to a safer position. There was yelling from the Aboriginal girls in the adjoining cells; they would place their hands through the bars, offering all sorts of things. While we where back at the Hotel, one of the women had propositioned Dale, saying, "You can have me for one can of beer." He continually told her, "Don't you understand? I am not interested." She then said, "You can have my sister too. "

The next morning, the cell door opened and a police officer said, "Well, we have all the Alice Down boys." After a feed of stale Weetbix, a police officer asked, "How much money do you have on you?" I stated: "$20." "That will do," he said. I was disgusted but there was nothing I could do. I paid the money, as did all the others, and we left the lock up.

Back on the Station, we had to take all the horses to the next stock camp on Panton Creek. It was about 40 kilometres away, and there were 60 horses in the plant. Horses are much harder to drove than cattle. They seem to trot out and can keep going for a long period of time, so most of the time you are trotting to keep up with the mob. As we were riding along, it was a great day with the sun shining and the sweet smell of the bush after rain, I was in my element, and Dale Zaddow said to me, "Hey Al, you bloody love this, but the novelty will run out one day." Ironically, it would be twenty years later and Dale was to contact me, and find that, at the time it was during the drought and cattle crash, the novelty had indeed run out.

We all had what is called 'barcoo rot', a scurvy-like skin disease caused by the lack of vitamins. Eating limited meals and not being supplied with any decent vegetables or fruits had taken its toll on us all except the Aboriginals; they seemed to be resistant to the disease. The bush nurses even came out from Hall's Creek to check up on us. We went back to the Station from the stock camp and found, to our amazement, oranges and vegetables in the cool room. The manager had kept all these items for himself and two of the station hands. We were all furious, having been working long hours without weekends off for $150 a week, and given poor rations that caused us to come down with barcoo rot. Most had pulled the pin at that stage. That night the two Station hands returned from town and they were all pretty drunk, making bad remarks to all that had pulled the pin. In the Station mess hall, one Station hand started speaking to Carmel in an improper fashion. We all walked outside and an old saddler by the name of Gerry said, "I thought you were going to punch him in there, Al." "Not in there, Gerry," I said. As the Station hand walked out, we both went punch for punch. Dale was also punching on with the second Station hand. After the whole brawling ordeal was over, these two went back to their quarters. One had to be carried. Dale and I thought we better hide the rifle bolts in case these two woke up feeling a bit vengeful.

We hid the bolts in the flour tins. The next morning, Dale, Carmel and I asked for our pay, rolled our swags and headed off to explore more of the Kimberley. The three of us camped out near China Walls and we climbed up this spectacular range to view the eastern escarpment. Carmel and I decided to head to the coast then travel up the legendary Gibb River road. Dale decided to go to Darwin, but arranged to come back into the Kimberly and travel down the Gibb River track himself. We both agreed to leave a message at the Derby Post Office for whoever got there first, as it could be a month or so until we both travelled to Derby.

Carmel and I travelled to Fitzroy Crossing and towards Broome. We camped on the Fitzroy River where I become extremely ill, contracting food poisoning on top of the barcoo. It took a few days before I could eat anything. I lay in my swag for days with severe stomach pains. Once I came good, we travelled on to Broome. This was an old pearl diving town; an incredible place with old corrugated iron buildings that served as their shops, and an outdoor picture theatre. An aqua blue sea, filled with old pearl luggers in Roe Buck Bay. The population of this town was mixed: Aboriginal, Asian, Caucasian and others. We visited the local cemetery where many Asian divers who had died from the bends were buried. Their tomb stones made from local rock were pointing to Mecca, in keeping with their Muslim faith. We travelled up the coast for sixty kilometres and stayed for weeks; camping on the coast, watching the aqua blue Indian Ocean rise and fall with its incredibly massive tides. We lived on fish - bream and trevally - that I would catch in the inlets. This is where I recovered from my ordeal with barcoo and food poisoning. I spent my 21st birthday camped under a beach tree. Carmel had made me a cake in the camp oven and took a photo of me blowing out the candles. The photo clearly shows that I had lost an extreme amount of weight.

The ocean would wash up all sorts of things: large turtle shells and sea snakes. The snakes are some of the deadliest in the world and would come ashore to lay their eggs in the sand. After we had enough of the sea life, we travelled to Derby and went to the Post Office to see if Dale had come through. If he had not, I planned to leave a letter for him. As I walked inside, there was Dale coming out. The timing could not be any better. He had a friend with him and we all camped out in the bush together. Dale went on in life to own a very successful goat enterprise. He owned Windimurra and Anketell, two large stations out from Mount Magnet West Australia, covering 750,000 acres.

Carmel, Clancy and I then headed off up the Gibb River track, a 700 kilometre trip. The warning signs stated: "Four wheel drive only, no fuel until Wyndham". This was going to test the Holden HJ, being only a two wheel drive. What a trip it was; this, the heart of the Kimberly: the Leopold Ranges, Adcock Gorge, Calvin's Gorge, Barnett River. Mountain ranges with jagged cliffs, spinifex ridges, black soil plains with boab trees, fresh water in creeks and rivers. We would swim in these magnificent gorges, sometimes climbing up the rock cliffs and jumping into the pools below. The rivers were full of black bream. I would catch them with beetles caught around the fire, then would use the guts from that fish to catch others. At night, I would place the fish guts in a hole in the ground, only to find fresh water crocodile tracks and an empty hole the next day. We would swim with these crocs in the same water hole, as the fresh water crocs are known to be harmless. While I was laying my swag down at dusk, this huge King brown snake slithered nearby, too close for comfort. As I watched him disappear, shot gun in hand, I realized his back half was going away but his front half was coming at me. I was forced to shoot him; he was over six foot with a huge bull head. If you were bitten in this country, there would be no chance of getting treatment in time.

Aboriginal paintings were prolific throughout the Kimberley and I spent ages walking to different areas to look at them. The 6 x 4 foot trailer had taken a battering, so while camped on the Pentecost River, I did some repairs. They mostly consisted of a piece of number 8 wire and the Cobb and Co. twitch. At one stage, I had the doors tied up with ropes and the springs of the trailer held on with wire. When we got to Wyndham I got hold of a welder and repaired things properly. The Cambridge Gulf borders the town of Wyndham, and although their local meat works had closed 18 months ago, we went out to find this large salt water crocodile still frequenting the blood drain. Along the mud flats of the Gulf, Clancy went out amongst the mangroves and this large salt water croc - I would say at least fifteen feet long - stalked him. It was pretty hairy for a while, as he got up quite close to Clancy before I was able to call the dog back, away from danger. We travelled south in what is known as King River country, a huge dry river bed. We came to a fantastic freshwater hole and made camp. I went out and caught some fresh water fish known as 'long toms'. During the night, I pulled in a fish only to be spiked by its prong. As I lay back in the tent, feeling sorry for myself and in terrible pain from the cat fish prong, there was this huge splash and a loud noise like a cough. Then I realized that the catfish was a forktail, a saltwater fish and what I heard was a salt water croc. We were camping too close to the water hole for comfort. The Aboriginals would tell me never to get water from a well worn track leading to a water hole, as a croc would wait until animals have become used to it then pounce on their next meal when the time was right.

There were trees in the Kimberley that were used as burial places. When a person from a tribe died of unnatural circumstances, they would place the deceased up into the fork of the tree, and down below they would place rocks, with each rock representing individual members of the tribe. When the body of the deceased started to decompose, whichever rock received a dripping from the decomposing body would indicate the tribal member to be blamed for the death of that person. **You have to be tough to live in the bush.** We travelled to Ord River, Kununurra then back into the Northern Territory.

- Across The Top -

We travelled through Victoria River country to Katherine and then out towards Daly River. This country now was very tropical, with pandamas palms and large mobs of buffalo. The government had started the eradication of buffalo to control tuberculosis, which was hampering the cattle industry. At that stage, the buffalo were in plague proportions, damaging the country by wallowing and grazing in the wetlands and causing damage by over grazing. We visited Darwin then out towards Kakadu. One night, we made camp out in the bush near Humpty Doo. We thought this spot was isolated, but the next thing we knew, all these cars came in, one after another. They were bringing people to a camp only several hundred meters from where we where camping. We could see a large blaze from a fire and then there was humming noise from a didgeridoo, clapping of sticks and Aboriginal singing. That was all fine; in fact, it was pretty exciting having all this going on not far from where we were camped until this car came driving past us with Jimmy Barnes' "Working Class Man" blasting from the car. You could hear all this argument coming from the corroboree. It was as if a group of drunken young ones had disrupted a traditional party. The next thing that happened was the same vehicle came driving back towards us and pulled up. The people started abusing me, calling me a white maggot and all sorts of other names. There was one person with them that started trying to convince them to leave and stop causing problems. It was pretty hairy for a while, but in the end they sped off. We quickly threw everything into the trailer and car and drove off; the quickest packing up I have ever done.

We were now in the South Alligator River country; large river systems and plenty of crocs. We went into Kakadu, camped at Cahill's Crossing - the start of Arnhem Land. I fished the East Alligator River but the mosquitoes were terrible. I had to cover myself in mud to protect myself from the constant stings. I caught cat fish and it seemed that's what we lived on throughout our time travelling across the top of Australia. In the East Alligator, huge manta rays would come up the river. I would keep a distance from the edge as I never felt comfortable, always worrying about the crocs. The Aboriginal paintings in the area are second to none. Some would show the entire structure of the bones and the insides of fish, others showed a man with a pipe, which dated it back to the trading with northern neighbours. There was a painting dating back thousands of years of a Tasmanian Tiger, a creature that once inhabited the top of Australia.

While camping at a creek called Jim Jim, we had the tent set up for some degree of protection from the mozzies when all of a sudden Clancy started barking. Out from the smoke of the fire, an elderly Aboriginal feller appeared. Behind him was his wife. "My name Nipper Gumjarra, this is all my country," he said. He spent the whole night sitting at my fire chanting, as a light rain fell. As soon as the light of dawn came, he was gone.

There was a bit of rain that had caused the Jim Jim creek to rise slightly. We needed to cross it but as we had seen a salt water croc only a hundred meters from where we were crossing I was not eager to wade into the water to check if it was safe to cross the car. But, being an optimist, I drove in only to find it much deeper than I had hoped. We came to a stop as the water covered the bonnet and we were waist high in water. We both got out of the car and waded ashore. A person on the other side handed me a drag chain from his 4 x 4 vehicle, and so I waded back out and went underwater to tie up under the car and get pulled ashore. We would spend time exploring the whole region, travelling to UDP falls, down south to the Roper River country then out to the MacArthur River country at Borroloola. This is where I saw more salt water crocs than in any other place. I would shoot galah parrots and use their meat for fish bait. With twenty pound hand lines, I cast out into the river and caught plenty of bream. Now and then a salt croc would grab the bait and pull me towards the river before breaking the line. We would camp a distance from the river and have a large fire going. Further back from that Clancy would camp, then we would have the tent up and I made sure my female off sider was closer to the opening of the tent than me; as crocs prefer women. Then I would be next with my shot gun: four degrees of defence! (Only joking)

During our stay there, I wrote a letter to my grandmother Laurie Hamid and explained that we were camping on the MacArthur River with heaps of crocs, etc. It was two weeks before she received the letter and while reading it she heard a news flash on the radio about a man by the name of MacLeod, who was taken by a crocodile whilst camping with a companion on the MacArthur River Northern Territory. Apparently this person with the same name as me rolled his swag too close to the edge of the river one night. My grandmother was pretty concerned for a while.

We left the Northern Territory and travelled through Queensland, Cloncurry, Mount Isa and Normanton to Karumba, a fishing port on the Gulf of Carpentaria. Then we moved into the Atherton Tablelands and explored the rainforest country to Cape Tribulation and the Daintree forest. Then we continued onto Cooktown, where we camped on the beach at Quarantine Bay. It was a magical place, with white sandy beaches and the Pacific Ocean at our feet. There were two other couples camping along the beach, both from Victoria. We all socialized together and Chris and Jeff and I went off hunting, hopefully trying to get a wild pig. We had walked for miles with no luck until we came on a water hole. It was like natures own cathedral: a lagoon with water lilies and large paper bark trees. We watched a huge goanna go up a tree. Goannas were plentiful in that country, and I said, "I have never eaten goanna before." Both Chris and Jeff voted for the death sentence, and the goannas fate was sealed. We got a large fire going and cooked him in the coals, as it was, in his own skin. The three of us ate everything except the head and about four inches of the tail, as this was all that wasn't cooked. Back at our camps, we would fish off the rocks. One day Chris was stuck by the barb of a sting ray while wading with a net. After a few days, as we all were sitting around a fire we could smell something rotten. It was

Chris's foot; gangrene had set in. He was taken to Cairns hospital where he was treated.

Funds were becoming low, so Carmel and I headed south for work. The wet season was starting to come on us, so it was time to leave the far north. At Tully, Queensland, we got work on a banana plantation. We camped in the packing shed of the property on the banks of the Tully River. I worked alongside an Aboriginal feller named Andrew Henry. Carmel worked packing bananas in the shed. Andrew and I would do the farm work: spraying ginty grass, cutting down bunches of bananas, carrying them to the packing shed by tractor and burr chipping, which involved walking along the banana rows with a hoe and chipping out any weeds. Once while we were out with mattocks, chipping burrs in the new banana rows, Andrew rolled a smoke and said, **"There's a big bloody snake up in that tree there, Al."** Nearby was a patch of rain forest and up in the trees was a large staghorn fern, growing on the side of a tree. Andrew reckoned the way it was shaped meant that a large snake had made it his home. I walked around the tree and could see the huge coils of snake skin moving. It was immense.

Tully had a 200 inch rainfall and one afternoon a storm struck. Many inches of rain fell in a short space of time. The entire banana crop was washed out and the market crashed with it. We went out with cane knives, chopping up bunches of bananas as they lay on the ground and preparing the new suckers to come through. We were paid a couple of hundred dollars a week, better than stockmen wages. But I knew then that I would never be able to buy a property of my own while working for others on a wage basis as I would be only able to save a pittance. I then decided to find contract work where I would be able to save a reasonable amount of funds.

CHAPTER FOUR
1986 - 1989

SUCCESS IS A JOURNEY NOT A DESTINATION

- On The Wallaby -

We travelled south, back to Melbourne via the Snowy Mountains. I picked up the trusty Weekly Times paper and there was a notice: 'Fruit pickers wanted, Goulburn Valley, paid contract'. I started on a pear orchard near Mooroopna, which was owned by the Turnbull family from Victoria. Carmel stayed in Melbourne and got a bank job. The orchard was one of the largest in the district, and had the largest work force of pickers. There was a dormitory on the property where you could bunk in with others or stay at a caravan area. I chose to pitch my tent and have all my gear locked in the car. People were coming and going; a lot of travellers from all walks of life and a lot of undesirables. The pickers were given a large picking bag and travelled out on trailers in the back of bins towed by tractors to the orchards. You were given a ladder and a set of trees and you would pick the fruit, place the bagful into the bins and go back up the ladder to pick another bag. There is great skill required to do this work; a knack in how to turn the fruit so as not to bruise it, how to work your ladder so to pick every piece and to be able to work the sets of trees so the bag is filled as quickly as possible. After a stint on the pears we were sent into a plum orchard; much smaller fruit, grown on a trellis. I made $120 for a mornings work, and I had never made so much money for one day's work before. There were gun pickers: the people known to be the best, who would travel the fruit circuit, picking all types of produce and making huge money. Most people would hardly make enough to feed themselves as they could not get the technique or were just lazy. We usually worked a six day week and had the Saturday off. I found the beauty of picking was that I could work longer hours if I needed by asking the tractor drivers to leave bins for me to go on with when others would knock off. At Turnbull's, I met John McPhee, a New Zealander who was from a dairy farm. A lot of pickers were Kiwis and would come over to Australia do the fruit circuit during the milking dry season. While I was in a line at the office to get my fortnightly pay, a person came up to me. It was the feller I met in Coober Pedy who had absconded from the law. He said he was having the time of his life and decided not to give himself up after all. There were some pretty wild parties at this picking camp. Friday night was when it all happened and Saturday was the recovery day. I made a commitment to myself that I would only have the odd beer, only on a Friday night and only if there was no work the next day, or at 'cut out' when we finished a farm and moved on.

One Saturday, a rest day, a group of us were sitting about and this old beaten up car drove in. Two men, both wearing sunglasses and supporting heavily tattooed arms, got out and walked around the place. We were all very suspicious of what they were up to. They walked around checking the entire camp and word got around to watch these men as they must be up to no good. After an hour or so both of them walked over to where John and I were and asked, "What's the fruit like?" Then they said, "Geez mate, there are a lot of undesirables here, we think we will keep going." **You never judge a book by its cover.** After the pears had finished, John McPhee travelled with me to Tumbarumba and Batlow for the apple harvest.

It was great to get back into the mountains and we got work picking on an orchard owned by Mike Smart near Batlow. The orchard was very well kept, full of a lot of the new apple varieties. We camped on another orchard nearby, owned by the same family. I camped in my old two man tent, John camped in his dome tent and we ate in my large tent. It was a pretty good set up: we would be up before dawn, and have breakfast cooked on a fire outside, then start picking as the sun was coming up. After we had finished on the orchard, we travelled around Tumbarumba looking for work, and got started picking granny smith apples at Geoff Blair's orchard. Geoff was a Vietnam veteran who had obtained the block after he returned from the Vietnam War. He had established an extremely viable operation only to have the last few years turn for the worst, with hail damaged crops year after year and a fall in apple prices. John and I camped on the Blair's property down along the Three Mile Creek. It was a very enjoyable place to work, with fresh mountain air and the aroma of the apples. We would have our showers in a make-shift shower built in an old shed. The shed had a huge lean to it, and every year that I worked there, the lean became worse. There was always an older crew that worked there, ex-Second World War soldiers and Old Lou, a miner from Newcastle originally from Hungary. He would camp in the old hut, and once when coming out of the shower that we all shared, I noticed he had tattooed numbers on his arm. I asked the reason for the numbers and he told me about the concentration camp he was in. During the Nazi invasion of Europe, he was involved with a group that would smuggle Jewish people out to safer areas, and one night he was caught while crossing a railway line. He was sent to a concentration camp, survived the ordeal and then came to Australia. He was a very positive type of person; always had time for a yarn, and seemed to love life. I have found that the most positive types of people - those that love life - are those who at some time have suffered hardship. On our days off, John and I would head off trout fishing or rabbit shooting in the mountains. The novelty of camping out on the ground came to an end with the onset of winter. The wet weather came in, the daylight hours were getting shorter and we were having our meals around the fire in the dark. One night we had a roast cooking in the camp oven but when we had just dished it up and were sitting outside to eat, flakes of snow came down all over our meal. As for sleeping in the swag on the ground during winter: NO WAY. By the next afternoon, I had driven to Tumut and bought myself a 12 foot caravan. It was like owning the Taj Mahal. We finished up picking at Geoff Blair's and I decided to drive over to South Australia and pick the oranges. John headed back to New Zealand.

Off I went to South Australia with my home on wheels and my trusty Blue Heeler Clancy for company. On the way, I door knocked on orchards near Mildura and on the New South Wales side. I remember pulling into a property and asking if there was any picking work. The woman I asked about work turned her back on me and said in a foreign accent, "NO, NO WORK" and she walked away. I had never had that kind of reception before so I drove to the next property where I found two men standing outside a packing shed. I walked over to them and said "G'day." They did not respond. I said, "I am looking for work." They looked at each other. "We got work," one said. The other responded to his offsider, "Have we got work?" They just played this silly game, asking each other if they had work. I said, "Thanks for nothing," and walked away. I drove through Victoria and into South Australia, camped at Remark then set off looking for work. I drove to one property and parked my car, walked to the house and knocked on the door. The door opened and a woman said hello. I introduced myself and she was very friendly. I said, "I noticed your orchard from the road." She responded conversationally, and started having a chat with me and was very friendly and polite until I said I was looking for picking work. "OH NO," she said then shut the door in my face. I then went towards Loxton and pulled up to a packing shed. It was a hive of activity and so I asked someone again, "Is there any work going?" I was pointed to the boss, so I walked over and said, "I am looking for picking work." He just said, "NO, NO, NO" in a foreign accent and walked away. I could hardly believe what had happened in the last few days. I had never come up against such rude people, one after another. Most people I had met in rural Australia were friendly and hospitable. The next day, I was back at it and finally got a job at an orchard between Berri and Loxton. The orchard was on the Murray River and they grew mandarins and ling navel oranges. I was paid $40.50 for picking half a bin of mandarins. You had to snip the mandarins off with clippers, and the fruit was only a bit bigger than a marble. The most you could pick was two part bins per day due to the size of the fruit: $60 total. I continued clipping the mandarins while waiting for the oranges to be ready to pick. After a few weeks, a group of pickers were given a row of orange trees each and bins were placed between the rows. Large aluminium ladders were supplied. I had my own picking bag, a one and a half bushel canvas bag I had bought at Shepparton. Over the years, I would go through many a bag, wearing them out from a lot of work. The foreman of the orchard said to go for it. I asked, "How much are they paying?" He did not know. I stated, "I will wait to see how much before I commence. " He suggested that I start, and he would get back to me with a price. I decided to not waste time and started to pick. The ling navels have spikes, so you can easily cut your fingers picking. But besides the spikes, it was pretty good going and I had three bins picked in the afternoon. I would time myself for every bin. The foreman came back and still did not have a price; and then he went around checking the progress of all the pickers. We were not given a price until the next day, and then were told it was $11 a bin. I protested over the price and stated that I would not be working for only $11 a bin. Then I was told by the foreman, "The management timed everyone, and you picked the most fruit, so they will pay you equal to an hourly rate." That meant that everyone else was working for less than an hourly rate. I said I would not pick for under $16 a bin, as I had been making between $100 to $150 a day picking apples, pears and plums. The foreman said, "If we paid you $16 a bin, you would be making a ridiculous $100 a day!" On that note, I asked for what was owed to me then hooked up the caravan and drove to Victoria. I headed to the Mallee country and got work on Nangiloc Colignan farms. At the lowest price of $16 a bin, I was making up to $200 a day.

This grape farm was a large concern; they were fresh fruit growers [as opposed to vines for wine or sultanas dried] and it was a new farm, with both the vineyard and orange orchards under development. They had a large caravan park on the farm and there was a large work force. During the frosty mornings, I would be paid to pull out the old vines under contract. I was able to negotiate a price as with most of the contract work. When the sun had dried out the trees from the morning frosts, I was out picking oranges: lings, Washingtons and Valencias. I was given a tractor with a trailer that held four bins and once it was full I would drive it back to the shed and unload. I negotiated wiring up grape trellises under contract, and in all areas made much more than the average wage. Thirteen bins of Valencias was the highest number I picked, alongside a fellow picker named Andrew, whom I only just managed to beat. Andrew would do the circuit of Tumbarumba and back as well. On my days off, I would head down to the Murray River where I would have a camp in the Redgum Forest and catch yellow belly fish. At one stage, I had overworked and strained the muscles around my chest and the doctor advised me to rest up. He also advised me that I had a slight heart murmur. I headed up the Darling River, fishing at Pooncarie, where I caught carp after carp, [feral fish] and had dozens of them lying on the banks of the river. I also had a shrimp net, catching my bait using Velvet soap, which apparently has a high concentration of animal fat that attracts shrimp. There was a character there named Wild Jack who picked fruit throughout the Murray Darling country. I got along pretty well with Jack, who was indeed a wild sort of feller. He had once won a Tattersall's prize estimated at $100,000. He told me that back in the '70's, when he got notice of the win, he went straight to Melbourne to collect his winnings, only to be told they would send a cheque to him back at his home town of Wentworth on the Murray river. He hurried back to Wentworth and waited for days on the steps to the Post Office. He was worried as there was another Jack in the area that he feared might mistakenly get his cheque and that he would lose the 100k. After the cheque arrived, his worries were over and he went back to the orchard were he was working with a trailer full of grog and tucker. He invited all the pickers there to come for a bender and none of them worked for two weeks as it was fun for all on the banks of the Darling River. I believe Jack was banned, never to work on the orchard again, as not a piece of fruit was picked for a fortnight because of his party.

When I arrived back at Nangiloc, my mother got word to me that my father was ill. I packed up camp and went to Melbourne. Dad was diagnosed with cancer from his lungs up to his neck. He had smoked cigarettes most of his life and now was to pay a huge price for his habit. He tried the chemotherapy treatment and had a brief stint in hospital, but returned home to Archer Ave for his final days. He went from a reasonably fit sixty eight year old to a skeletal figure in only weeks. I was with him when he passed away. He had worked his whole life at the same place - forty five years - and only enjoyed his retirement for a short time. I decided then that I would never stay working at something I did not like doing and always be where I wanted to be. **Never allow the fear of change or failure to stop you from succeeding in what you wish to do.** As with everyone who had lost a loved one, it was a very emotional time but in my case I mourned with pride, knowing that I had a father who spent all his spare time he could with his son; and that I had grown up knowing that I was a priority in my father's life. He was cremated and I travelled with his ashes to a junction of two mountain streams, the Rose and Dandongadale River, which both flow into the Buffalo River. His ashes were scattered into the three mountains streams that he had fished and enjoyed for nearly fifty years of his life.

Carmel decided to join me again travelling around the fruit circuit. We went to the Goulburn Valley where I had been picking on and off in between returning to be with my father, as it was about three hours drive from Melbourne. The farm I was picking at was at Tatura, owned by the Simpsons, and after the season we headed for Tumbarumba. I had upgraded the caravan to accommodate both of us, going from 12 foot to 16 feet and adding an annex. We picked at the same farms, and camped at the Blair's orchard, where the granny smith picking took us up until June. I had heard of citrus picking in sunny Queensland, and so we travelled up north and got work at Eidsvold for Ray Lockes. It was ideal: mandarins, grapefruit, navels and then Valencias. The frost would melt earlier than down south due to sunnier days and less rain. Therefore there was more picking and more money. I held most of the gun positions on the properties I worked on. My biggest tallies were: 17 bins of apples at Blair's in Tumbarumba; 15 bins of pears at Simpson's in Tatura; and 14 bins of oranges at Nangiloc in Colignan. I loved the picking, the travelling and meeting all the different characters, the itinerant workers living a nomadic lifestyle. As the old bush saying goes: they were **"on the wallaby,"** meaning the itinerant life on the road, seeking work where you could. At Eidsvold in Queensland we camped on the farm, on the banks of the Burnett River. There was a great social life in all the camps throughout the circuit. We would fish on our days off as the Burnett was renowned for huge eels. They were like enormous serpents, coming from the deep water holes in the river. We would have trouble bringing them onto the banks and I would smoke them to eat. I camped and fished with a great group of people. Ray Farrell from Eidsvold showed me Aboriginal paintings that were on the property of Ray Lockes. Ray owned a lot of cattle country but the orchard was the main business. After several months picking citrus, we had our cut out and headed for Bundaberg to pick tomatoes. I had heard they grew on trellises so I thought it would be fine on the back. Over the years, I had stayed away from any work that involved bending, like potatoes and onions. After all the sheep crutching I had done, I knew back work was not for me. The tomato work was not what I had expected; you were picking for size and colour so it was too slow for me. I would quickly time myself to see if any contract work was viable or not; and I developed a policy to only accept strip picking [taking all fruit as opposed to selective picking]. After a stint at the tomatoes, we tried the beans at Gympie, a little farm at Kin Kin. You were paid by the weight; given a hessian bag, and worked your way down a hill. The owner of the farm had recently been released from Boga Road Goal in Brisbane after serving time for growing marijuana on his property. He and some others in the area had tried to grow a different type of farm produce and as a result served 12 months for having a bumper crop. On several occasions while I was camping there we had the police helicopter drop in for a bit of a closer look at his beans and the banana plantation. After the beans, we went back into N.S.W. and travelled to Griffith, a town in the Riverina, where I picked Valencia oranges, being paid by the ton. I towed a large trailer bin behind a tractor and spent the day picking citrus, filling the huge trailer bins. Then I weighed them at the packing sheds and was paid accordingly. I worked for several fruit growers in the region and Carmel worked in the packing sheds of the properties.

While waiting for the oranges to be ready to pick, I heard of a carrot factory where they paid an hourly rate. As I had time on my hands and was always keen to make a dollar, I drove down to the factory at dawn. I stood out the front with dozens of other people as the sun was rising, and the owner of the factory came out and stood on an upside down fruit bin and started to look over the crowd. He pointed to people: "YOU, YOU, YOU!" It was like something out of the Depression of 1920's. After he had enough, he told everyone else to go away. I have never been a shy type, so I walked up to him and said, "How about me?" He said, "YOU AS WELL, all the rest go." **You have to go the extra yard in life to achieve anything.** The people were given a position in the factory, either to sort carrots into their right sizes, or to wash and box them. This owner yelled at people while we were working, telling them: "NO TALK, NO TALK!" After non stop work, it was time to knock off; we had all worked for many hours with no break. I asked for my pay and left that sweatshop for good, and started at another property the next morning.

I had a wedding to attend in Geelong, Victoria. A mate of mine, Paul Duncan, was getting married and I was a groomsman. Paul and I had knocked around a fair bit as kids; in fact it was with Paul that I started the pub scene, being passed off as an eighteen year old when in fact I was much younger. Paul spent many years with the Union movement, first as a delegate shop steward, then later as a main organizer with the Construction Forestry Mining Energy Union (C.F.M.E.U.) I was starting to have a much better understanding of the importance of the union movement after working in places of pure exploitation.

During the trip to Geelong, I also travelled to Dargo, a small town in the high country of eastern Victoria. There was an advert in the Weekly Times reading: "490 ACRES, UNDULATING, SUIT CATTLE, $80,000." I rang the owner and was given all the details: frontage to two major rivers and creek flats as well. I had enough money for a decent deposit, and I had realized that every time I saved $10,000 within a year, a $100,000 property had gone up by 10%, making it worth another $10,000. So now was the time to make a start in buying a property. I needed to get my foot in the door. **The best time to buy is now.**

We left the caravan at my mother's new property in East Keilor on the Maribynong River which she had bought after selling the old home in Ascot Vale. After many hours travelling to Dargo, we arrived at this small property and the owner drove us into the mountains in the back of an old Landover 4 x 4. After the odd river crossing and driving through a steep cutting into the side of the hill, the owner said, "Here we are." I could not believe it; IT WAS A CLIFF. When I asked, "Where is the undulating country?" he then drove back to another property and took this goat track, winding up a steep ridge. It took forever, and then all of a sudden we drove out on a ridge where both sides of the mountain were sheer cliff drops. It was not even suited to goats, let alone cattle. NO SALE.

There was another property coming up on the market: a run down mountain cattle holding known as 'Sugarloaf Station' situated on the Buffalo River, south of Myrtleford in an isolated part of the mountains. I had spent time in this country with my father and over the years with mates, chasing the trout in the spectacular mountain streams. After inspecting the 600 acre property, I was keen to buy. I arranged financing with the State Bank of Victoria where I had an account since I was very young, and was given the go ahead to purchase the property for the value of about $100,000. The property went up for auction at a hotel in Myrtleford and I was there, ready to buy my first property. Unfortunately, there were also others that had the same idea, and the property was eventually sold for $130,000. Back to the wallaby trail and SAVE, SAVE, SAVE.

I criss-crossed the states over those years, and had a great system of work. Cherries at Wombat near Young, N.S.W.; then apricots at Cobram on the Murray River, oranges at Griffith, pears in the Goulburn Valley in Victoria and back to Tumbarumba for the apples, and then finally up to Eidsvold, Queensland. Meanwhile back in the mountains, there was a new subdivision in the Paddy's River area, a place where I had camped with my father on numerous occasions, where we had fished the Paddy's or Tumut rivers and explored the surrounding high country. The property was called 'Allawah' and I met the owner, Axile Neilson, an ex-seaman from Denmark. He showed me a 100 acre parcel: the road to the property did not exist, there were no improvements, and only part of the property was fenced. Yet a lot of the property was improved pasture, with great shade trees throughout; watered by three dams in a high rain fall belt and spectacular views towards the mountains.

It was perfect and after a week of negotiating I had arranged to buy my first property for $72,500. I planned to settle there in August, when I had returned from the fruit run in Queensland and after the vendor had part of the boundary fenced.

I had about $60,000 in savings in three banks that were all earning me reasonable interest at the time. I poured all the funds into the National Bank then went to the National Bank branch in Tumbarumba and met with the bank manager. I requested a $20,000 loan, in order to cover all expenses plus interest and always keep money behind me as padding. After lengthy discussions that went from one day to another, I still could not get a loan from the manager. In disgust, I stated, "This is ridiculous! I am only asking for $20,000. I have a history of saving and a history of continuous work, and at present I am making a $1,000 a week." I walked straight out of the bank and down the road to the Bank of New South Wales. There I met the bank manager and I stated my case. I explained what had happened at the National Bank and said, "I do not have an account with this bank, but I have $60,000 and I will deposit the funds into your bank on a term loan. In August, I plan to settle on a property of 100 acres for which I will require a loan of $20,000. I have always had continuous work and I NEED AN ANSWER NOW." The bank manager looked at me and said, "OK, you have the loan." I walked back to the National Bank, withdrew my funds and deposited it into the Bank of N.S.W.

After the apples finished and we spent two months in Queensland picking citrus, we returned to Tumbarumba, where I drove my car, towing the caravan, onto the property. Actually I had to get Axile, who lived on the neighbouring property, to tow my car with a tractor as the property was covered in snow. We made camp on the property and the next day I signed the mortgage papers, and settled on the 10th August, 1989. My first property; all the dreaming and travelling and all the hard work over the many years had earned me this: a 100 acre property in the Snowy Mountains. There is a photo taken with me sitting outside the caravan by the fire with Clancy by my side. There is snow covering everything and the bush shower is hanging on a sapling with only a tarp around for shelter. Anyone looking at the photo would think I must have had rocks in my head, living like that. But to me, I felt like a king looking over his whole domain; my own piece of Australia. At the time, Jim Alston, with whom I cut my teeth as a first year Jackeroo, had offered to assist me with stocking the property with cattle. He said to me that he reckoned he owed me for unpaid overtime and that I could pay him back when I got on my feet. It was a very generous offer but I did not accept it as I wished to buy my own line of cattle as starters, a high country breed. But to be offered assistance in finance from your previous boss was truly a great gesture of respect. **Integrity is everything.** I had a dream and a goal, and now with the ingredient of integrity, I was putting it all together.

CHAPTER FIVE
1989 – 1992

THE BIGGEST REGRETS IN LIFE ARE THE THINGS WE DON'T DO, NOT THE THINGS WE DO.

- 'Wangarra', my first property. -

The property was much smaller than I would require to run a viable beef operation, but it was a start. It had magnificent views towards the mountains; just under 900 meters above sea level with flat to undulating terrain. The property lay on the top of a mountain range, with the occasional large and oddly shaped boulder amongst ribbon gums, stringybarks and peppermint trees growing in the granite soils. From some points of the property you could have an 180 degree view and see as far as Victoria. The main view was east towards Mount Black Jack, a steep mountain standing over 1600 meters above sea level and dropping down a sheer cliff face of 1000 meters. It was like Mecca for me, as every morning I would look towards this magnificent mountain and pay homage. In the evening the views were at their best with the setting sun to the west shining its last rays on the western escarpment of the ranges. Beside Black Jack, there was Mount Manjar, Jugumba, the Dargals, China Walls, and the Maragle Range. Between the Maragle Range and Black

Jack was a gap called Wangara. It was where the morning sun rose up, and also contained the track into the higher area of the mountains. I named my property Wangara after this gap in the mountains. When my mother had a sign made up as a present to me she spelled it with two R's, becoming 'WANGARRA'. It bordered the Clarke's Hill State Forest and looked towards the Kosciusko National Park. There were a couple of large springs on the property, and it had a high rainfall of 40 inches.

The day after settlement, I started work at dawn to develop my 100 acre property. I would fell stringybark trees with a Stihl chainsaw, cut the timber into 6 foot lengths then rip the logs, making six or eight posts out of it. Then I measured up saplings that would suit yard rails; cutting and debarking the trees with the back of an axe. I used my Holden HJ to drag the freshly cut posts along the fence lines, and the rails to the area where the yards were to be. I dug hole after hole with crow bar and shovel, three feet down for strainer and yard posts and two feet for fence posts. I believe if I was to measure all the holes I have dug over the years, I could have reached China. I would sight the fence lines and pace out steel post after steel post, then ram them in with a post rammer. For the timber fence posts, I would bore holes through the post then run the wires.

I attended the district clearing sales, picking up bits and pieces for materials, always looking for a bargain. I built a small 20 x 10 foot shed to store my tools in, and also did a bit of roustabout work during shearing on a neighbour's property. There was a huge dead gum tree that stood about 100 feet tall on the spot where I was planning to build. I felled it and the firewood from that tree lasted for ages.

I looked around the district for female cattle and contacted a stock agent from Corryong to arrange an inspection of Hereford heifers at Mount Falcon Station. Mount Falcon was situated in hill country at Tooma, 20 kilometres from Wangarra. The owner and agent ran a small mob through the yards and I selected 11 unjoined [not in calf] heifers and negotiated a price: under $400 each. I had bought my first line of cattle and over the years it would eventually grow to be several hundred head. Once I had the females delivered, I bought a young Hereford bull from Ournie, in the Tumbarumba district. Once I had joined the bull to the females we packed up camp and headed out west to Colignan, a citrus farm in Victoria which was next door to the property I once worked on. There was a snow storm on the day we left but when we arrived in the Mallee country it was extremely hot. We started picking oranges before dawn and on some days had to knock off before midday due to the extreme heat. I would rest up in the heat of the day and start up again in the afternoon. I would pick up to 14 bins a day; at $16 and $18 a bin, it was good money. My bin tally had been increasing every year. After a couple of months, we returned to the mountains and there I continued developing the property that was now my home.

After spending Christmas 1990 in Melbourne, I started working back at Wangarra on yard building, internal fencing and pulling out St. John's wort. Then we packed up again and drove to the Goulburn Valley in Victoria for the pear season in January.

- *Fruit Picking Strike* -

The property we now worked at was bought by a new owner. There was a large work force and most stayed either in their own caravans on the property or in the bunk rooms at another area. After a couple of weeks, I was down in my tally by about a bin a day. The fruit was reasonable and I was frustrated that my tally was down. After visiting a mate of mine who was picking at Ardmona in East Shepparton, I was told that the bins I was using were bigger than other bins. Every year the Workers Union, along with some of the growers, set a price based on a bin of fruit by the bushel and in this case the bins I was using were 3cm larger. This meant I needed one bag more of fruit to fill a bin, therefore I was losing a dollar a bin. Over a nine bin day and a six day week, I was losing $50 to $60. A group of us got together and decided it was not on, believing we were being had. We called a stop work and I stood on an upside down bin and told the large crowd of pickers about the situation. I said that I was not going to pick any fruit until the owner agreed to pay me my rightful rate of $17.44 a bin. With that 30 pickers also agreed not to pick until we received our rightful rate. We then arranged a meeting at midday with the owner at the property camp. By this time, most of the other pickers had checked bins from other properties, and realised that the bins we were using were indeed 3cm larger. At the meeting, the owner denied that the bins were bigger and arranged a further meeting in the evening, in a few hours time. At the next meeting, he arrived with another grower in a tray vehicle with several bins on the back. He told all of us to measure them so we did and, lo and behold, these freshly made bins were all the right size. We then formed a group with the two growers to go and measure the bins currently piled in the orchard. We went to this area and every one that we measured was 3cm larger than average.

The owner then told the pickers - 30 strong at the camp - that he would pay us $17.44 a bin, but he would still not admit that his bins were larger. This sent a lot of pickers into a very angry state. The owner called me a stirrer as other pickers began to abuse him, claiming that he owed them back pay. It got out of hand when he hopped back into his car and tried to drive off, causing some of the crowd to start to shake his vehicle. I was pretty concerned as I had initiated the whole strike and had won the justified rate rise, but I was not sure if it was going to stop there. In the minds of a few of the pickers there was a need for revenge. The owner eventually was able to drive away and we all went back picking at the new rightful rate of $17.44 a bin. Within the next few weeks, we cut out on the pears, and went back to Tumbarumba for the apple season.

I picked at the same properties: Smart's at Batlow and Blair's at Willigobung where we camped on the property. I was also looking for full time work in the district as I knew I could continue developing my property while living there and so get an income during a wet day [when there would be no picking]. I went to the Tumbarumba timber mill known as Hardy's and asked for work. I met one of the management personnel and he gave me a position on the night shift, stripping timber. This was contract paid work preparing timber for the kilns. I placed battens in between recently sawn timber to let the air get around the pieces when they were placed in packs and put into the kilns for drying. Who would think that in the years to come I was to develop and own a timber mill; and would produce these dry mill battens for a mill that was to become one of the largest in the southern hemisphere?

I have always worked long hours and this was no exception. I would pick fruit for Geoff Blair during the day light hours, and then drive the seventy kilometre return trip to the timber mill and stack timber at night, paid per cubic meter on contract. On wet days, I would drive to Wangarra and work on the farm. I could never be accused of wasting day light hours. During this time, I also picked fruit on other properties when there was a break in the fruit at Blair's. I had bought another vehicle, a Holden HJ ute from my cousin, which was ideal for the farm. I would use that and a trailer to cart gear and do all other farm work. In May of 1990, I attended the Tumbarumba Annual cattle sale, as I would every year. I bought thirteen Hereford heifers from the Mannus area, booked up to the local stock agent [bid on their account and billed after the sale]. I now had 24 females on Wangarra, and had a 100% calving rate in most years, hardly losing a beast. I wish that was the case on every property I have owned, but unfortunately that was not to be. In June of 1990, we finished the apples at Blair's and headed back to the farm and I continued to drive to the local mill every night. During calving, I had to pull nearly every calf but all were saved. That job was usually done late at night when I returned home from the mill work, and sometimes with snow on the ground. The bull I had bought was a pest, jumping fence after fence until I showed him the features of electric fences. We needed to develop a better living area as now we lived there full time and did not plan to travel again. I went to the Westpac Bank and arranged a loan for $22,000 to build a 40 x 30 foot shed and deck it out for a living area. I had a gravel road built up to our living area by a local earth moving contractor.

At the timber mill I worked at either stripping timber or benching timber [cutting timber into different sizes, on a bench, with a circular saw]. To push lengths of timber through the saw and adjust a ram to cut different lengths is a very skilled job: knowing what size you can get from a piece of timber and cutting to allow only minimum wastage. I also worked with someone opposite who would tail out the timber by separating the good sawn piece from the cut off. During this time, there was a down turn in the building sector and Hardy's Mill - owned at the time by Petersville-Sleighwere forced to retrench people: last on, first off. At the time there was a work force of over 100 people at the mill. I survived the first few retrenchments, but unfortunately the foreman of the green mill was given notice by the company to inform me I was to finish up that night. Looking back at the mortgage I carried and recalling my extreme worry, it is hard to believe that my understanding of financial literacy in those days was so totally different to what it is today.

I did some contract fencing work on neighbouring properties and after that got a job as bench man on a bush timber mill in the upper Paddy's River country. This mill was owned and run by Bill Waters from Jingelic and Rob Cox from Tooma, both livestock producers who had diversified into timber milling. Bill had successfully milled the old dead red gums from the Hume weir when the water had receded, tapping into the slab market. Then with Rob Cox, he had bought approximately 1800 acres of high altitude [1100 meter] forest country that had fantastic stands of ribbon gum and peppermint trees. The mill was built in an isolated part of the mountains and only accessible to trucks during the summer and autumn months. He employed timber contractors and others to fell and snag timber and then to mill it. It suited me as it was only a 30 minute drive from my property.

The mill was built under a large corrugated roof. There was a head rig, also known as 'the Canadian' that received the logs sent to it. After being cut into their correct lengths, the logs would be placed by a loader onto moving chains, where the Canadian, made up of two circular saws, would slice the logs into slab sizes from the top and bottom. Then the slab would be moved along on chains until it came to me and I would physically move these huge slabs of hardwood timber onto my bench. Then I cut 8 x 2 or 10 x 2 lengths or whatever was ordered for the finished cut. It would be stacked in its correct sizes and strapped up, ready to be trucked out. The whole operation was powered by a huge generator. The work force was only small and the operation fairly primitive when I compared it to the large timber mill I had come from. But I enjoyed working there in the bush, and working for two fellers who where not afraid to have a go. It was pioneering stuff, although in hindsight it was extremely dangerous. I recall using an old Stihl chainsaw with a bar and chain that felt as long as my whole body and that had no safety chain brake. Once it kicked back and nearly took my head off. I believe a splinter cut my eyebrow area; blood poured out and I was relieved to find I still had both my eyes. When you cut mountain ash - the Rolls Royce of mountain timbers - it can 'pinch' and there was the odd time where whole slabs would fly back as I attempted to put them through the saws. I was often knocked backwards, lucky not to be injured. Over the years I knew of many a man who would lose a finger or suffer a serious injury. The worst injury I knew of happened at Hardy's Mill. This feller I worked with for years had got too close to a Canadian saw and lost his arm just below the shoulder. Incredibly, he resumed work at the mill only a short time after losing his arm.

At the Paddy's River bush mill, there was a hut built where some would camp over and where we would have our lunch. Bill had a stick of salami hanging from a rafter which had been there for months and had the odd fly hanging around it, and those flies would be guaranteed to have flown from the pit dunny nearby. A truck driver was having lunch with us and commented about the stick of salami hanging up. Bill got it down and said to the truckie, "Its good stuff, have a go, bite it!" The driver looked at it and was just about to have a bite when he said, "Why have you not eaten it?" Bill said, "I wouldn't be game." There were two younger fellers who came there working and in the mornings we would all have a cuppa before starting up. They seemed a bit nervous during their first days there and one of the logging contractors said, "Come on, you two young blokes; come with me." He handed them several pieces of newspaper and they obeyed him, following in tow. Bill called out to him, "Where are you going?" The logger kept walking with these two young fellers following behind him. As he opened the dunny door, he yelled back: "FOR A SHIT!" These two young fellers did not know what to do as we all burst out laughing.

- *Horse Injury* -

Tony Digrande floated some new horses up to Wangarra. He had bought an irrigation property at Kerang in Victoria and was doing a bit of bush racing and had horses to train. One morning before dawn, we headed off to chase some bucks [brumbieswild horses] from Wangarra and rode through Clarke's Hill and up to the Maragle Range. We rested the horses on a beautiful small high plain with its own large spring coming out from the sphagnum moss bed. There were fresh signs of brumbies and we were following their tracks, and closing in on them, when the horse I was on - Tipsy, a speckled gelding - jumped a creek but did not reach the other side. We came to a complete stop and I looked down to see the water turning red with blood. I jumped from the horse to see I had 'staked' him: that there was a large stick in his chest. When I pulled the stick out, Tony and I were shocked at how far it had penetrated into Tipsy's chest. Blood just poured out and I placed my hand into the wound to stop the bleeding. We cooled down the horse by pouring water over him, and walked him home, fourteen kilometres. We treated the wound with antibiotics and he recovered well. Remarkably I was to eventually own nearly the entire valley within the next 15 years, including that high plain where we stopped as well as the other grazing properties we had walked through with the horses that day.

One morning I went to a horse sale in Young, a town a couple of hundred kilometres away and selected four horses that I thought would suit me. One I bought was a well broken grey mare called Salt. I had met the owner prior to the sale. There were two large type blood [thoroughbred] horses that were to be sold as a pair. I did not know their background, but I bid for them against Metro Meats. The auctioneer said, "$185 each, okay, you buy the pair at $185; knock 'em down to<?" I called out my name and they were mine. I also bought an unbroken dark bay filly that I named Nipper, after Nipper Gujarat, the Aboriginal feller I met near Arnhem Land in the Northern Territory. Once they were trucked home, I was able to ride them out and see just what kind of trouble I had bought myself. The grey mare, Salt, was a gem. She could spin on a pin and had a great nature. Nipper I could not handle and she would try and jump the yards, prancing at every moment. When I roped her and put some gear on her, it was obvious she had not been handled much. I would spend hours with tackle gear on her, lunging her around the yards then paddock, getting her used to the bit and gear. I had her mouthed and rode her within a week but I had to ride out the buck a bit. She and I spent a lot of time together and she was to give me a fair bit of excitement over the next few years. The two big blood horses, well, they were a different story. The one with a white blaze down his face I named Metro. He was fine to saddle but once you rode him out into the paddock, it was on: either hunching his back and bucking or rearing up until he would topple back with you on him. It took a lot of work with Metro as he had no trust in anyone. One day when out in the bush, he started his silly behaviour and we both ended up in a blackberry infested gully. I was tangled up in berry vines and so was Metro. He tried for ages to get out but could not free himself

of the tangled vine and was cut up from the prickles. After a while I managed to free myself with my pocket knife by cutting the vines away. Metro was exhausted and lay still while I slowly cut the vines and freed him too. The process took ages but from then onwards, I never had any trouble with him. In fact, over the years he became my best trekking horse who looked after many a rider, not to mention his second job as a pack horse in the high country. The other blood horse, Big Feller, was an impossible challenge. He had scars on his side of the neck near the shoulder that I believed were spur marks, probably from time as a rodeo horse. It did not matter what I did, I could never get the buck out of him. I was trimming his hoofs back one day when all of a sudden he toppled over on to me. I awoke in the corner in the yards with blood covering my face and aching all over. He had somehow knocked me out when he decided to jump over me. I quickly sold him and I daresay he made lots of meals for a number of pet dogs. I spent a great deal of my spare time riding in the mountains with my horses, exploring everything the high country had to offer.

The bush mill I was working at temporarily closed when it lost its market, so I went off fruit picking at Batlow. We camped near the orchards that had amenities. On the wet days I would head back to my property where I was building a large shed and partly decking it out for a living area, bathroom and lounge. I had also had a dam built on the property with a D4 bulldozer. I had a Honda pump and pumped water up to tank that gravity fed water to service the home area. Once there was a day's wait in the picking and so I headed home to work on the shed. Late in the afternoon, I went for a shoot and came across a large sow pig with a few piglets by her side at the spring dam at the back of my property. I crawled on my belly until I got close enough and when she up and went for me, I shot her point blank at two feet. I walked back to get my vehicle and butchered her by the lights of the car. Unfortunately the battery of the vehicle went dead so I had to walk to the only neighbour's house several kilometres away. Once assisted by the neighbour's vehicle I was away and headed back to pick fruit at dawn. By this stage, it was very late at night and I knew that I was not going to get much sleep when I returned to camp as I had to get started at dawn. I also knew that the fruit the next morning would be the choice of the crop: young trees with large apples, and that I would make terrific money picking. On my return through the hills in the fog, a wombat appeared and BANG, I hit him. Somehow the force of the impact pushed the fan of the motor through the radiator. It now was in the early hours of the morning and I was sure I would just have to go straight to work. But when I tried to start the vehicle, the battery was flat again and there was not another car in sight. I spent a very cold night sleeping in the front seat of the car but at dawn, my old Chinaman mate Hong drove by on his way to the timber mill at Tumbarumba. I got a lift with him back to the picking camp. I missed out on the cream of the fruit, but the pig feed and entire camp having a pig roast night at cut out nearly made up for it. While at the timber mill, Hong asked me what food you could eat in the bush.

"Al, can you eat fox?" I would say, "Don't be silly Hong, I would not eat anything like that". He asked, "What about kangaroo?" so I brought him a whole 'roo, all butchered. For a long time afterwards he would give me vegetables from his garden and other gifts in gratitude as the meat fed him and his large family for ages.

Tumbarumba held its annual cattle sale late every autumn and a lot of producers would send their weaner cattle to it. I sold my first lot of weaners through the yards. In June 1990, Tumbarumba was declared drought stricken and in the same month 40% of N.S.W. was also declared a drought region. I have kept diaries over the years, ever since I bought my first property, and I jog my memory by reading them and looking at my huge photo collection. It is generally believed that there will be droughts every seven years, but noone was ready for what was going to happen in the next seventeen years; an ongoing drought and the threat of climate change were in no-one's thoughts back then.

I got a job with the Rankin family who owned a pine nursery and sheep property in the Mannus Valley, south of Tumbarumba where I was put on as nursery foreman. It was an incredible farm where the pine seedlings were run on the same principle as a cattle stud farm. All the trees and their progeny were recorded. You would take cuttings from the partly established areas and record all subsequent plantings. Once at a particular size and age, the saplings would be pulled up and transported to a new pine plantation. The work was fairly easy but the conditions were terrible as the work was done in the wettest and coldest weather that winter has to offer. At some stages, I was working in deep mud dressed in water proofs to keep the rain and cold away. I would also buy round bales from the owner and cart them back home on my ute to feed during the winter drought. I had to travel an 80 km return trip from home and the work was not consistent as you were knocked off at midday if there were no orders. I worked there for several months until I was contacted by Hardy's Mill to return.

- *Hardy's Mill* -

I was approached by the management of Hardy's Mill who wanted me back stripping timber under contract, guaranteeing me ongoing work. We negotiated a price per cubic meter of timber to be de-stripped [removing the timber from the battens that had been dried and strapping packs of timber for sale]. I was also promised the operation job of stripping the timber to prepare it for the kilns with the automated machine that was installed when the mill was re-developed. I started work back at the mill after I gave a week's notice to the Rankin's. The money I made destripping was terrific; working my own hours in a large dry shed. Some days I would make over $200 a day. Dunlop Pacific had bought out Petersville-Sleigh and along the way had acquired the timber division consisting of Hardy's Mill. The timber mill went through a huge re-development and had become totally automated. There was a work force of approximately 200 people on the site with two shifts going. I was given a position operating the automatic stacker on the afternoon shift from 3 p.m. to midnight. It was a monstrous automatic machine that collected freshly cut timber from the green mill and passed pieces of timber individually over many rollers and chains. The wood was sent to an area where mechanical forks placed the timber into layers, with dry battens [stickers] automatically being placed in between. From there it was sent out automatically on rollers to await another forklift to place large steel weights on the top of the packs and then be moved into kilns to dry. This whole process required several people working on various areas, from fork lift drivers to panel operators and kiln attendants. Geoff Blair, who I used to pick fruit for, came to work with me on the stacker after leaving the apple farm. This shift suited me down to the ground as I was able to work and develop my property during the day: digging trenches, laying poly water pipe for the home and stock, spraying thistles and blackberries, fencing, building numerous out buildings, and developing the living area in the shed, etc. Then I headed off to work at night, earning consistent money. This working both day and night lasted for seven years, right up until I developed my own timber mill. Wangarra was starting to become a real home with chooks and a veggie garden, and electricity supplied by a 5 ka generator. At this point I had nearly fifty head of cattle and three horses.

In December 1991, Carmel and I went our separate ways. Carmel had been working a couple of days a week in the local bank in town and with my long work hours, we had drifted apart. I was pretty upset at the time of our split and initially thought we would get back together after a break apart as it had been a fairly good relationship over most of the seven years. Maybe it was "the seven year itch". I went to Melbourne for Christmas and New Years Eve and returned to 'Wangarra', deciding to head off into my beloved high country on a pack horse trek.

- Pack Horse Trek -

I shod both Nipper and Metro and packed Metro using an old used stock saddle I had picked up at a clearing sale. It was terrible to ride in due to the pads low on the sides but I rigged it with a breast plate and crupper and strapped a large canvas bag to one side and my swag the other. In both my swag and canvas bag, (which I referred to as my dilly bag), were shoeing gear, a set of spare clothes, cooking gear and food for many days, consisting of my mother's Christmas pudding, packet foods and fruits, and dog biscuits for Clancy. I rode Nipper in an old poley saddle [a type of stock saddle], using only a breast plate as she would continually play up with a crupper. I put saddle bags on the side of Nipper for my camera and away we went: horses and faithful Clancy in tow. Leading Metro, I headed up through the stringybark and apple box country until we reached the 1000 meter mark where the timber changes to peppermint and ribbon gum. The air in this county is clearer due to the higher altitude and the distinctive smell of peppermint trees is everywhere. I camped one night at Richardson Creek on the eastern side of Mount Pilot reef, tethering my horses to the trees. The Maragle Range is a magnificent place, covering tens of thousands of acres of open forest, fern gullies and numerous logging tracks. There are mountain peaks such as Pilot Reef; 1400 meters above sea level and dropping down 1000 meters into the Tumut River gorge with spectacular views, bordering 1.5 million acres of Kosciusko National Park. I led Metro behind Nipper, heading further up into the mountains. At Back Creek, I had a black brumby stallion creating some havoc, trying to fight Metro. I was yelling at the brumby, trying to scare him off while Clancy barked at him and we eventually got the brumby stallion away. Over the years I would have many encounters with brumbies trying to fight my horse plant. When I climbed up to the 1500 meter mark, I could see to Cabrumurra, the highest town in Australia. Here the vegetation becomes stunted snowgums with gnarled and twisted trunks that have withstood years of long cold winters. I rode to Mount Black Jack, 1600 meters above sea level, and then down the south side of Mount Manjar where I decided to camp for the night on a little high plain. I stepped off my horse and as I went to clip Metro to his tether rope, Nipper pulled away and both horses slowly started to walk off. As I moved quickly towards them they moved more quickly away until all of a sudden away they went, cantering back down the track the way we came. There I was, standing there with my faithful mate Clancy with the sun going down and not even a box of matches in my pocket. I imagined the horses not stopping for a couple of days until they reached their paddocks at home. After I had cursed and sworn, Clancy and I tracked them for a couple of kilometres until we found them grazing on a sweet patch of grass. The pack saddle was hanging to one side and both Nipper and Metro looked at me, probably wondering what all the fuss was about. I rode back to where I planned to camp and tethered them both securely for the night.

The next morning I saddled up and explored the Emu Plains area, a unique high plain with the Tumut River running northerly through a huge gorge on the eastern side. On the western side, it drops away to an area appropriately named "Worlds End." It is here that the legendary plane, THE SOUTHERN CLOUD, crashed in 1931 and was not found until 1958. Charles Kingston Smith owned the plane, but was not on board. Two pilots and six passengers lost their lives in the crash. When I visited the site, the frame of the old plane was still there. I rode up on to Fifteen Mile Spur, up the ridge from Bradley's hut, where there was a 360 degree view as far as the main range. I rode down to the Tumut River and near Farm Ridge. The wet weather came in on this particular trip and I sheltered for the night at Round Mountain hut, with three bush walkers who camped the night with me. There was a huge storm with lightning and heavy rain. My horses were tethered amongst tea trees to protect them as much as I could from the storm. The next morning, Mount Jagungal had a light cover of snow at 2,000 meters. The weather had turned for the worse and I only had my Drizabone coat for protection and at least a two day trip ahead of me, riding back out of the mountains in terrible weather. The heavy rain had started up again and I was very low on food so I had no choice but to ride out in the terrible conditions. On my return I found that Emu Plains had become a large area of water covering the entire plain. I had difficulty negotiating a way over it as there were streams of water running everywhere. All the small creeks had become large torrents of water. Once I had ridden over Mount Manjar and down into the Maragle Range, I camped the night near Wangara Gap amongst a stand of alpine ash trees. It was a pretty wet night but I managed to build a large fire and all my gear in the swag was dry. I got into dry clothes and ate the rest of my food supply. That particular area is full of lyrebirds and the numbers seem to increase after rain. The next morning I rode the 30 km trip home, enduring another thunderstorm near McPherson Plains. That was to be the start of many years of riding into the western side of the mountains with dozens of different horses; covering an estimated 6,000 kilometres over the next decade.

- Defacto relationship claim -

Back at home, life was pretty good until I received a notice from a sheriff to appear in the local magistrate's court. Carmel had started proceedings against me, claiming she was my defacto wife and was demanding money. I was not sure what a defacto was; I thought she was just my girlfriend. Although we had been seeing each other for years, we had only spent a short time living together at Wangarra. All the other times we were travelling and she had also spent a year in Melbourne. At all times we kept separate bank accounts. When it came to financial ownership, what was mine was mine and what was hers was hers. The car she was driving was the one I had bought at 18 years of age, the fuel she was using and the car's registration were paid by me. She lived on the property I had bought with my own money, with no financial contribution from her whatsoever. In fact, when I calculated her income from her part time work it was obvious no one could live on what she had made. I was the one who had subsidized her living expenses, so what was she claiming? Now she was saying that she was not a girlfriend but a defacto wife and deserved some sort of financial payment after our breakup. Up until that point I had thought we might get back together. But as soon as she started demanding money from me after I had been the one who had supported her shortfall in living expenses for years, there was no chance of any reconciliation. I had no idea then that this was to be the start of many legal proceedings that I would deal with throughout my life. In fact, it was only a small legal incident compared to what fate would deliver me later in life.

I was very naive about how the whole legal system worked back then and I found it very unjust that I had to prove that my former girlfriend did not contribute towards creating my assets. At the time Carmel was making a claim against me she was still driving around in my car so I quickly got my vehicle back. Several months after we had broken up, she had also taken the liberty of returning to the property when I was not there and taking my entire photograph collection. I was very disappointed to say the least. The only thing I still had of hers was a small freezer and some clothing. In fact, these are the only things I can ever remember her buying. I arranged to collect my car and the photo collection from her at her work place which was at the bank in Tumbarumba. I was to exchange the freezer for the car at this spot. I could hardly believe what was going on; this girlfriend whom I had spent so many great years with was doing exactly what she had said she would never do. "I would never claim anything against you," she told me on numerous occasions. I was so angered by what was happening - being dragged through the courts for something I believed to be morally wrong - that I backed my ute up to the bank and emptied the contents onto the footpath: the freezer and countless heaps of her endless clothing. I do not apologise to anyone for my actions. I would never do anything like that today, but at the time, gee it felt good. I employed a lawyer from Wagga Wagga and then engaged another female lawyer who specialized in family law. I found her to be extremely biased as she believed that just because Carmel lived with me, she deserved something. I then engaged another female lawyer, also from Wagga Wagga, who had a great sense of humour and I felt comfortable with her representing me. It was over twelve months since we had parted and the whole legal action lasted nearly eighteen months. I recall the sheriff coming to the property with a summons for me to appear in court and warning me in a friendly way of how the legal system could destroy a person simply through a claim from a former girlfriend. Every time there was a hearing, the case would be adjourned. I lost count of the number of court cases that were held, only to be adjourned for one reason or another. In the end I gave my so called defacto wife a small token payment of $5,000 to finalize everything. The crazy thing about the whole ordeal was that I was arranging to buy her a car from my cousin just prior to us going our own way. Unfortunately I didn't learn anything from that experience and I was to really drop my guard in the relationship area the next time around.

- Knocking around the mountains -

In 1992 and for many years afterwards, I was to spend a great deal of time riding into the mountains on horse back trips, a lot of them with a variety of different people. During the winter period I took up cross country snow skiing; again either by myself or with others. Mick Obendorf, a mate of mine from Melbourne, would accompany me on most of the longest snow trips and also came bush walking with me, sometimes for days on end. On one of our early day trips, we arranged to ski around the Four Mile Hut area, east of Mount Selwyn Ski resort. A mate of mine from Tumbarumba - Brandon Bliss - accompanied us out for the day. Blissy had never skied at all and found it pretty hard going. I was just learning at the time too, so I was also very ordinary. We arrived at Four Mile Hut, a little old timber hut built by a former gold prospector. It was very small, made up of one room and a fire place with air blowing through the many cracks in the walls. Blissy, who at this stage was exhausted, said, "Gee, Al, what would you do if you were caught here at night by yourself mate?" I said, "It would be OK once you got the fire going." Blissy said, **"I reckon I would bite me tongue off with me chattering teeth and bleed to death."** Brandon would have to have the driest sense of humour I have ever come across. He bought a couple of acres north of town and was told by the locals how silly he was for the price he had paid. The land had a huge spring and it was considered nothing but a boggy useless block. "You're mad!" they told him, full of negativity.

He showed me this block of ground while talking positively about that boggy spring on it. In a few year's time Blissy's spring bottled water business was born.

On another ski trip to Mount Kosciusko. Mick and a woman I was seeing *whom I will refer to her as 'Mish'+ and I skied in terrible weather from the top of Thredbo Ski Village at the North Ramshead towards Seamen's hut, travelling on the far eastern side of Lake Cootapatamba. We were relying on the pole markers to show us the way to the hut as visibility was poor. Eventually we arrived with Mish being a little worse for wear. After we had a fire going and were all dried out and had eaten a big lunch, Mick and I decided to make the trip up to the highest point of Australia and back to the hut. There was a break in the weather so we thought we could comfortably do the return trip. But as we were skiing up towards the Mount, the weather came back in and before we knew it we were in a white out. It was my first white out experience; the scariest situation anyone can find themselves in snow country. You can't see your hand even if you put it in front of your face. As you ski along, there are times when you even lose your sense of balance. We quickly decided to turn around and head back to the comfort of the hut but it was extremely difficult to know where we were headed. Then all of a sudden I felt myself falling and all I knew was that I was tumbling down and down through snow. I did not know what was above or below me until I came to a slow stop and I lay there for a while. There was a break in the weather and I looked up, and there was Mick looking down at me. I had fallen over a twenty meter ledge and luckily not injured myself. I struggled back up the hill and then we headed to the hut. After a rest we were off again, skiing towards the village of Thredbo and the comfort of the chair lift ride. When we arrived at the chairlift we found to our shock that we had just missed the last ride back. There we were, the three of us, looking down this steep chairlift track towards the village and knew the only way we were going to get down there was hike the two kilometre trip back down. So we did it, part of it in the dark.

On one adventure in the summer months, four of us took a three day trek into the mountains. We were all galloping towards Pilot Reef, a spectacular mountain top at 1400 meters above sea level, and I pulled up my horse at the summit. Mish pulled up her horse. Jodie [a friend from Sydney] pulled up her horse. Then Mick galloped up and Metro came to a halt< but Mick didn't, and over the neck of the horse he went. He had a slight bit of claret on his face and he was groaning with pain. "Don't be a big girl," I said. He replied, "It's not the cut on my face I am worried about, it's my leg." I persuaded him to get back on and told him he would be all right after a few beers in order to impress the women. Silly macho stuff.

We rode off and camped the night at Back Creek, which is on the south eastern side of Pilot Reef. The next morning while having breakfast, we found that Mick's knee was now huge. He had obviously broken his knee cap. I felt very guilty as I had talked him into riding to camp. I said, "I will ride back and get a vehicle." He would not have it, saying, "I am riding for another two days to Mount Black Jack. I am not having Al Macleod thinking I am a big girl." It did not make any difference what I said to him. He was determined to ride for two days, all the way to Black Jack and back, with a broken knee.

CHAPTER SIX
1993 – 1994

WHAT WOULD LIFE BE LIKE IF WE DID NOT HAVE THE COURAGE TO ATTEMPT ANYTHING?

- Exploring New Zealand -

I had commenced a relationship with Mish, and was now living with me at Wangarra along with her two daughters. I had refinanced and turned the shed into a three bedroom house with a study, lounge room, bull nosed veranda and the main power connected. I had been able to get all of the timber for the framing from the mill at a greatly discounted price. I carted it back at night when I knocked off work and built the 'shouse' during the day. I referred to my home as the 'Shouse' as it was a shed turned into a house. A year ago Mick and I had planned to make a trip to New Zealand and after I had completed the home we arranged passports and away we went. Landing in Christchurch, we hired a camping van and travelled throughout the south island. We went to Mount Cook National Park and hired a plane at Lake Tekapo to give us a look at the New Zealand high country from the air. It was the most spectacular flight you could imagine; a small Cessna plane flying around ten mountain peaks, all over 10,000 feet. The spectacular glaciers of the Hooker

Valley lead up to Mount Cook itself and so we decided to walk up onto the Hooker Valley glacier.

We left our vehicle at the Mount Cook car park, and with our back packs walked up the valley, planning to camp the night at the hut above the glacier. On the way there were many cliffs with swinging bridges that criss-crossed up the valley. The river had huge boulders in it with icy water running past and signs of avalanches were common. At one point there was a sign that read: "Avalanche Zone: route ahead can be dangerous -- rest only at sign posted safe zones". Once we walked up into the valley and were at a higher level, the track and rocks were iced over. Prior to the walk we had seen a memorial to climbers who were overwhelmed by an avalanche and while we were walking in this dangerous territory, I had an uneasy feeling that I had never before experienced in the mountains of Australia. We arrived at a point where an avalanche had previously swept away the very narrow track so we had to climb around another area. Dark was upon us so we decided to retreat to an area that seemed a safer spot to camp the night in case of an avalanche. We put up the dome tent and dived into our sleeping bags as it was freezing. Then we heard a voice and found a woman, Catherine, who had also been trying to get to the hut and had been caught out by the dark due to the track delay. She camped the night with us but the ice on the ground made sleeping impossible as I had to keep turning over every now and then to get warm. The next morning we made the attempt to continue, but it was for crampons and ice picks only, in order to go the rest of the distance. Mick and I were just two Aussie fellers out on a bush walk and this climbing up over unstable ground was not for us. Catherine told us that she had been in an accident years before when she was injured in a fall and had to be air lifted out. When the sun lifted its head from the eastern escarpment, the heat on the western mountain peaks caused small avalanches. We were forced to retreat back along the track and at one point were able to walk along the frozen icy river.

We had come prepared with our telescopic fishing rods and had been catching trout in most places we tried. We drove down to Fiordland and took a boat out exploring the Sound, which was a huge sea-filled valley, full of sea life: seals, birds and fish. We met a feller at Milford Sound who was a keen deer hunter and fishermen who made a living fishing at sea and during other months would trap deer in the bush. He advised us to walk into the Hollyford and Peke River country as we were guaranteed to catch trout. It was amazing country; wet, lush rainforest full of tree ferns with a narrow track scattered with exposed tree roots. There were snow capped mountain peaks and a huge crystal clear river, in some places opening out to a lake. We met a couple of fellers who were living in the bush hunting possums. They were after the Australian possum that had been introduced to New Zealand and had caused environmental havoc there. They were laying strychnine poison around the trees and then skinning the corpses and selling the pelts to Canada. Along the way there were some fantastic waterfalls and there were huts for all kinds of different bush users: deer hunters, fishermen, walkers, etc. We had our 'Tassie devil' lures and it was not long before we were catching some fine sized trout. I was gutting a large rainbow on the bank of the river when all the pebbles started moving. I stood up and started feeling very uneasy on my feet. Then I noticed everything else was shaking, including the trees. It was an earthquake and we were later to find out it registered 6.5 on the Richter scale. If it had occurred in a city, it would have brought every building down. After three days of walking and catching trout, we returned to the van and explored the west coast. We met up with a deer farmer who was making a good living on his 150 acre deer and cattle property. He also prospected for gold along the beach, separating the gold from the black sand. I was considering going into deer at the time and while I was in New Zealand I studied the pros and cons of the industry. Later, Mick bought a deer farm near Colac in Victoria. Whilst buying supplies from a local store in New Zealand, I picked up a poster with an environmental statement written by Chief Seattle, a Native American, in 1864. It described the conditions of the sale of land and is now known as the greatest environmental statement ever written. I have put the poster on my wall in every office I have had from that time until now and in it I have found an understanding of all properties I have occupied over time. Chief Seattle stated: "**How can you buy or sell the sky, the warmth of the land? The idea is strange to us. If we do not own the freshness of the air and the sparkle of the water, how can you buy them.**" His statements demonstrate a deep understanding of the land with many insights about protecting it. He states: "**contaminate your bed and you will one night suffocate in your own waste.**" There is always a consequence to everything we do in life.

- Wangarra High Country Retreat -

When we returned home, I was keen to start a horse trekking adventure business. Tourism in New Zealand was huge and travelling there gave me many ideas. Since riding with Herb Hain over in the eastern side of the Snowy Mountains as a kid, I had always wanted to own an adventure trekking business so now was the time to put everything into action. I was offered a job as a stockman on Rippling Waters station by the manager. The job came with a house supplied and a few months previously I probably would have taken it, but I had built my own home and loved living at Wangarra and I was now keen to get this tourist business off the ground. I still worked nights at the local timber mill and went about developing the trekking business. I arranged public liability, registering a business name: 'Wangarra High Country Retreat.' I submitted the development application to the local council and applied for permits with the State Forest and National Parks. I designed fliers and put up advertising everywhere I could think of, from tourist centres around Australia to placements in magazines, newspapers and the Yellow Pages. I made up a large poster with people riding along on horses and the mountains in the background. Then I developed a logo with two riders and three mountain peaks, with 'Wangarra High Country Retreat' written around it. I put together the flier with a short story about riding from the foothills of the Snowy Mountains up into the alpine ranges and created riding packages from half day treks to full one, two and three day trips on request. I would spend the days working out the different treks and camping spots and arranged with the new owners of McPherson Plains Resort to accommodate my riders and to put on a feed at night with breakfast in the morning. Later on I was to build my own accommodation and do all camp-outs as well. I got the go ahead from the State Forest to operate in the Maragle and Clarke Hill State Forests provided that I had $2.5 million worth of liability insurance. The National Parks were not so obliging; they gave me documentation that seemed as thick as a legal brief filled with conditions that were totally unacceptable. For instance, I needed to have approval from them regarding advertisements, they needed me to contact them prior to any trek, and they could refuse to back me for any reason they felt fit. There were so many unreasonable conditions that I decided not to operate in the Park. Considering I had so much country to operate in, I really did not need to cross their boundary. Although over the years I would receive the odd letter from them, telling me they believed I was operating in their Park, I never did. The council gave me the go ahead, indicating that the technical officer of the council wanted me to have a horse crossing near McPherson Plain Resort. That particular spot is isolated but has 2,000 head of cattle running in the mountains - not to mention the numerous wild horses – that frequently cross at this spot; and this technical officer wanted me to have a designated horse crossing with signs up! To get things going, I submitted to this ridiculous request and showed where I would cross the road in this remote region. The technical officer (I cannot remember his name nor want to remember it) knocked the application back on the grounds that he thought the crossing site was not appropriate. We arranged a meeting at this isolated spot; 40 kilometres from town and with only very light traffic; the kind of place where you could wait hours before anyone might drive along if your car broke down. This man, who I would describe as an educated idiot, stood on his car and said, "If I was a rider on a horse, how tall would I be?" and went on saying that we would probably need four signs in total: one prior to the crossing and one at the crossing, announcing: "Horses are about to cross" and "Horses cross here". I could not believe it. This whole crossing event would take place only a few times a year with no more than eight riders at once. I eventually persuaded him to do away with any permanent sign and that I would only place a sign up if it was needed.

Common sense is not all that common

Finding suitable horses for the adventure treks was an effort in itself. Over the years I owned dozens of horses and eventually developed a plant of trekking horses that were totally reliable; all of whom you could trust with novices on their backs. Nipper was just too flighty to be a trekking horse as she would stir up other horses; so I needed another couple of good lead horses for the business. Chris Wilson was a well known horse dealer from Wagga Wagga, and he would organize horses for me to go over in his yards so I could select the right ones after putting them through a few tests. When they arrived at home, I would spend ages working them; getting them used to all types of situations from making sure they were calm with coats and all sorts of things hanging from them to training them to trot out at a consistent pace. Now and then, after I had a horse at home, I would have to decide to cull it if I still believed it was not safe enough to put a rider on. My rule was to ask myself: would I place my elderly mother on this horse? So after a while I had horses that I would trust with anyone. Out of one lot in Chris Wilson's yards, I selected a palomino mare with a solid build of about 15 hands or so. She was a very excitable type and would step out for long distances through the mountains. She would not stir up other horses but became the matriarch of the mob and all other horses showed her respect. She soon became my lead horse; I named her Redgum due to the colour of her coat, and over the years I was to ride her an estimated 5,000 kilometres throughout the high country. I bought horses at sales and privately, always on the look out for a suitable mount. I also bought saddlery, again at auctions or privately. Most of the saddles were brand new, and I always bought wholesale, not retail; quickly learning the power of buying in numbers for huge savings over time.

In Easter of '94 we were taking in bookings and had a few treks organized. My cousin Stuart Hamid had lined up people from Melbourne for a two day trek and they were booked in for the Easter weekend. Stuart had recently been in an accident on the Murray River where he had been sucked under a house boat and carved up by the propellers. He was lucky not to have been killed and he had been told he would lose 90% of the use of his arm. He proved the medical world wrong and was able to get back the full use of his arm, subsequently winning the 'best and fairest' at his football club. The first customers from Melbourne arrived for a two day trek and away we went: the start of a five year adventure horse trekking business. The first trip was a ride from the foothills up into the alpine ranges. We were tracking brumbies throughout the trip, and Mish met up with us at the designated lunch spots. I had large saddle bags that contained a billy, tea, sugar and pannikins as well as fruit cake and we had billy tea breaks on the way with a cozy fire to warm up. Then we headed on to McPherson Plains Resort, where I yarded the horses and had the meals supplied. The evening was spent yarning about the great day and the plans for the ride back tomorrow. My riders stayed in the cabins and I camped out in my swag with the horses as brumbies were a common problem, coming in to attack the geldings. The next morning we were up at dawn, all saddled and away. We went back down the mountains towards home, arriving late in the afternoon. Everyone packed away gear, hosed down the horses and turned them out after a large feed. We said our goodbyes to our riders and they left for Melbourne. It was a great feeling to have finally gotten the business up and going and to make a dollar at something I loved to do. The whole trip was a success, and by 9 p.m. we were in bed, exhausted from the two days trekking but totally content and extremely happy with life; filled with the excitement of the business and what lay ahead. Never in my wildest dreams could I have imagined what was about to happen to me; that my whole world was about to be torn apart.

- *The Shooting* –

It was April the 3rd, 1994, only hours after our first horse trek, and Mish and I had just gone to bed. Mish's two girls were with their father for the weekend. Everything was in complete darkness when we were awoken by the yelling of people and the revving of a car. Startled, I quickly jumped from the bed, put on my bathrobe and walked to the window of the lounge room. From there I could see the headlights of a car shining all over the place. It seemed they were doing 360 degree turns, spinning the wheels in the front paddock and driveway to the house. There were people yelling and my horses were galloping in fright through the back paddock. Then the car drove to the crest of the hill at a flying speed, went back and then up to the crest again. All of a sudden the car came down into our fenced-off home area and was driving all over the garden with screams of what seemed like male voices. Wheels were spinning on the gravel road then the car drove straight towards us, only coming to a stop at the garden at the front of the house. By this stage I was extremely frightened. I did not know who these people were or what they wanted, but I quickly put together a 12 gauge shot gun for protection, loading it with a couple of shells. We 'played possum' for a while, not knowing what was going to happen, then I walked towards the entrance to the house. I turned on the outside light and looked through the window at the veranda but could not see anyone. It had now become totally quiet. I have never been so frightened in my life; I did not know if they were just hoons looking to scare someone or mad people who could have guns and open fire on the house. I thought that I would quickly open the door to see who or what was going on. To my fright as soon as I opened the door I saw two men standing there. The closest one to me I had never seen in my life, but the other person was a man called Robert Jovanavic; he lived in the district and was known to be an undesirable with a history of crime. They were obviously affected by drugs or alcohol. I could certainly smell the alcohol on them and they were both in a crazed state. I said to them, "What are you doing here? Why are you terrorizing us?" But all I got from them was threats and abuse. I asked, "Why are you here and why are you terrorizing us?" but they just continued making threats of violence. I kept asking them, "Why are you terrorizing us? Go away, there's no reason for this." I could not reason with them and every time I tried, all I got was threats towards me, and fists clenched at me. I even told them that I had a five and six year old inside, 'though I didn't at the time. I tried everything to get these people to go away. The whole stand off lasted about five minutes and I believe it was the longest five minutes of my life.

There was a call from the car, and a woman's voice screaming at them to leave but these two fellers would not go and continued their threats of violence. In a crazed state, they raised their clenched fists and threatened me, saying, "We're gonna fix you, you're gonna go, we'll get you, we're gonna fix you now!" All kinds of language came with it:

"You're f—ing dead, you're history." Then the person closest to the door, the person making the most threats, said, "We're going to get you, we're coming back for you," and his clenched fist became a pointed finger. I thought: great, they are finally going. A great feeling of relief come over me; after five minutes of threats they seemed to be finally going and I tried to close the door. Then all of a sudden this manwho I had never seen in my life, who had been threatening me for five minutes - charged me through the doorway. With his clenched fists up, he entered my house, attacking me. At this stage, I had the gun up and I was walking backwards to avoid his attack. I was unable to shut the door as they both lunged at me through the doorway, the person who I now know as Christopher Godfrey leading the attack. I told them, "Get back, get back, I am telling you, get back!" I lowered the gun slightly for an instant as I did not want to shoot him in the chest and I did certainly not want to kill anybody. But I was in fear of my life, and the fear for the safety of Mish. I retreated as far as I could go and then I shot my attacker in the leg, at the knee cap.

He quickly changed his tune. His accomplice also stopped in his tracks and said "You've shot him!" instantly retreating to his car. It was a nightmare: this person's leg was literally blown off, only hanging on by a bit of flesh. I quickly tried to put pressure on the leg to stop him bleeding to death. Mish appeared and we both worked to put the two pieces of the leg back together. At one point, Robert Jovanavic went into his car, an unregistered Land rover. I thought he was reaching for something under the dashboard of the passenger side and at the time I believed it could be a gun. With my firearm in my hand I told him, "Don't think about it!" He was very hesitant then and stepped away from the passenger side. The woman who had been yelling at them from the car appeared and stayed for this whole ordeal. She said, "They're getting the cops, Rob."

"Not the cops, man, not the cops!" Jovanavic replied, then jumped into his vehicle and drove away, still yelling out threats: "I'm coming back to torch the place!" I quickly contacted the police and asked for an ambulance, explaining what had happened. A neighbour appeared some time later and it was discovered that he and his son had socialized with these people who had attacked my home previously that evening. Forty minutes later, the police arrived and Constable Gary Lewis said, "What has happened?" He seemed to go into shock himself as he saw the man lying there with blood everywhere. I said, "I shot him." With that I was hand cuffed and placed into the police van. The nightmare was becoming worse.

I sat hand cuffed in the back of the police car until the ambulance arrived, one hour after the event. The constable who had arrested me removed the handcuffs and told me the person I had shot was Christopher Johnston, who only recently had dealt with the law for an assault against a police officer and had been released on bail. Then there were police everywhere: detectives, ballistic squad, etc. I watched this ordeal from the back of the police van as Jovanavic the person that had made the attack on my home was given cups of coffee from my house and was comfortably seated on my veranda. I was still covered in blood and only wearing a bathrobe with no other clothes. I was extremely cold and in the van for a long time. I was later transported to the Tumbarumba police station, where I was photographed and asked if I would make a recorded interview. I was given warm clothes and allowed to finally wash the blood off me. The record of interview commenced at 1 a.m., so it had been a period of nearly four hours that I had endured being covered in blood while only wearing a bath robe, freezing cold in the back of the police van. A detective by the name of Tony Vincent conducted the interview with Constable Gary Lewis present. The detective told me that it was up to me whether I answered questions or not. I thought to myself: I have nothing to hide, so I agreed to have the interview. I was not allowed to wash the blood off me until I had the photos taken and by now I had lost all track of time. During the interview which lasted until 2.35 a.m., I was asked questions such as, "I put this to you Mr. MacLeod: I know you were in fear of your life, but did you consciously pull the trigger?" I said, "I was the only one with the gun and my finger was the only finger on the trigger." The detective would say again, "But I put it to you again; did you consciously pull the trigger?" Again I explained what had happened. Again and again the detective tried to get me to say if it was my action or the action of something else causing the gun to discharge. I said again, "It was a result from these people attacking me in my own home!" Again I was continually asked to state if my actions caused the gun to discharge. To this day, I am not sure whether the detective was trying to 'verbal' me or help me or was just doing what he was trained to do. 'Verballing' is to have loaded questions put to a detainee; it is known as a corrupt way of having someone charged with intent to cause harm as the police can show within a statement that the suspect did intend to commit harm. The detective also said, "Our hearts are in your best interests." I was charged with several serious offences: 1. maliciously inflicting grievous bodily harm with intent to inflict grievous bodily harm; 2. maliciously discharging a firearm with intent to inflict grievously bodily harm; and 3. maliciously inflicting grievous bodily harm.

It was dawn when I arrived home, driven in the front of the police car this time. The scene there was horrendous, with pools of blood, fragments of bone and medical debris everywhere. The next morning I was assisted in cleaning up the mess by a member of the fire brigade with a fire hose. Peter and Ruth Blackman, close friends from town, came out to give their support. Before I knew it, there were telephone calls coming from all over the place expressing support for my actions. Journalists asked if I would give an interview. I agreed and had our photo on front pages of some newspapers. It was reported throughout the entire media, from newspapers to television. The headlines read: "Shooting was self defence." It was at this time that I also learned the person I had shot was not Christopher Johnston but Chris Godfrey, living under an alias while out on bail on charges of violence against a police officer. It took two days before the police interviewed Robert Jovanivic, and eight days before Christopher Godfrey was interviewed at his hospital bed.

- *Court Proceedings* -

I appeared at the Local Magistrates court at Tumbarumba on the 26th April, 1994. The charges against me had been increased to five charges in total. The extra two were: 1. use of firearm with disregard to safety; and an assault charge: 2. occasioning actual bodily harm. The whole nightmare was becoming worse week by week. The Magistrate on the day, Clive Weary, adjourned the case and granted me bail, ordering me to appear in the local court at Holbrook on 1st June. He also stated it would be a paper committal and there was no reason for me or my solicitor to attend. On the same day as these proceedings, Robert Jovanavic and Christopher Godfrey were to appear in relation to the assault against a police officer. Jovanivic pleaded guilty and was fined. Godfrey did not appear as he was still in hospital. I was advised to place restraining orders on Jovanavic and Godfrey, which I did by attending the Magistrate's court at Tumut.

On the 29th of April, Mish told me she was pregnant. It was something that put everything in perspective. Although there were terrible times ahead, not knowing what my future held, the thought of becoming a father gave me the huge strength to go through the whole legal process. I had a lot of support, especially from the local community of Tumbarumba. The old saying, **'It's pointless having friends in the good times if they are not there in the bad times'** definitely came to my thoughts throughout the year. I had always been worried about what people thought of me, but during this time, my ideas changed about people in general. **There is no point worrying what people think of you; if you only realize how little time they spend thinking about you.** Although many people supported me at this time, one mate stood out more than the rest; he really assisted me by creating the right mind set to cope with my unknown future and an understanding of the legal system: this was Peter Blackman. I met Pete while he worked at Telstra. He laid the telephone cables to my home and I had also worked with his wife Ruth out at the pine nursery. Pete had lived an incredible life: a merchant seamen, traveller and bikie figure. He had even worked in movies on films such as Mad Max. He spent thirty years at Telstra and was a good family man. During Pete's bikie days, he lived what can only be described as a wild life. The bikie culture in itself could be described as a notorious way of life and Pete lived this type of life to the full. Fortunately he met Ruth, became a proud father and worked for thirty years honourably, later becoming a psychologist. By virtue of his past, he had an incredible insight into the legal system. Despite his brief period of life in the so-called bikie world, he would have to be one of the highest principled people I have known. In recent years he has been invited to speak on criminology at the Police Academy of N.S.W. His understanding of psychology is equal to none. Once when Pete was at my home during my birthday he said to me, "Do you think life is about kangaroos jumping your back fence? That's not life. Life is about a pizza at five o'clock in the morning and someone in the gutter with a knife in his back; that's life." When he first told me that I thought he was a nut, but I began to realize over the years that life is about hardship. **It's not about good things; it's about dealing with whatever life throws at you.** During the twelve month ordeal of being dragged through the legal system, Pete would keep at me: **"You have to think like a solicitor; it's all a game, mate."** I studied other cases and learned the legal process, picking up meanings and terminology, court procedure, and what the letters next to peoples names meant. Somehow I managed to understand what Pete meant, and over time I became able to detach myself from the emotion and concentrate on winning my case.

I had a local solicitor who called me into his office to discuss the case. He started reading out the charges, and after telling me each charge, would state the full term of the custodial sentence. After he had finished, I felt that I was facing the rest of my life behind bars. I left his office feeling like walking under the first truck that came by. Needless to say, I quickly decided his services were not required. A friend's brother was a detective in Sydney and he told me that I must employ the right legal representation. He recommended his friend Joan Lock; a well known barrister from Sydney who knew of my case. Joan contacted me and said that she would represent me if I wished. She also recommended a solicitor, so there was my legal counsel. We discussed the cost of fighting the charges at the local court at Holbrook; considering that it could run for 5 days, bringing the total legal bill to over $20,000. It was to be presided by a Magistrate, and if I was convicted then appealed, I would then stand trial again for another $20,000. It was not in my best interests to allow one person to decide my fate so a jury had to be the only way to go. That meant going to trial at the District Court. There was hope for a 'paper committal', whereby the Magistrate could find that there was no evidence for a conviction and dismiss the charges. Everything seemed to be about the almighty dollar. The more money you were able to pay, the more chance you had of getting off the charge. There seemed to be no mention of how unjust it all was. The two people -known criminals - who attacked me in my home were never charged. I rang Detective Anthony Vincent and asked him, "Why are they not charged?" He told me that he had nothing to charge them with except possession of the drugs that the police found in the vehicle that Godfrey had confessed to owning. Detective Vincent said, "All I know is that there is a bloke in a hospital bed with his leg hanging off." Unfortunately for Godfrey, his leg was eventually amputated.

On the 1st of June 1994, I appeared at the local court in Holbrook. There was a television crew outside filming my case and the interviewer and camera people all shook my hand. Other people came up to me and told me how wrong the system was. One particular person, who I had never seen in my life before, came up to me and said, "You were obviously protecting your woman. Tell me: who now is protecting you? The system is only for the criminal." It really hit me. Who *was* protecting me? I sold my cattle through the local sale yards to raise money for my legal defence, and on this particular day, I was representing myself as I could not afford a full legal representation for all the pre-court cases preceding my full committal trial. I only had enough funds for one shot at a trial with a jury. When I stood before Magistrate Clive Weary, he said to me in a very friendly and respectful way, "What do you want me to do, Mr. MacLeod?" I said to him, "This is all a new world to me." I requested that he go over the police brief to determine whether there was enough evidence to warrant me to stand trial. He adjourned to his chambers for a couple of hours and returned after reading the brief, ordering me to stand trial at a date to be fixed. He also told me that we could have had a committal hearing if I had legal representation and was prepared. Yet at the Tumbarumba court, he had stated that there was no need for the solicitor to be there on the day at Holbrook, as it would be a paper committal only.

Besides selling half of my breeding herd, I extended my loan over a twenty five year period to reduce the monthly payments. I was operating the adventure horse treks, working at a timber mill at night and during any spare time would head into the mountains to get away from it all. It was an incredible feeling, heading up into the higher altitudes. Once I reached 1100 meters above sea level all my fears disappeared. It did not matter whether it was on horse back, skiing or bush walking, the mountains were my escape, and when I was literally on top of Australia, everything else seemed to be insignificant. Mick and I bought two sets of cross country skis and were to cover a lot of snow country over the winter. I received notice to attend a court meeting to arrange for a trial date. The meeting was in Wagga and I attended in person. We all sat down: the register presiding over the matter and the prosecution. It was stated by the prosecution that the victim, Christopher Godfrey, had sustained serious injury to the point of losing a leg, still had infection in the leg requiring further medical assistance and was in a serious state. "The Crown is waiting for an outcome. If he dies then these charges will be upgraded." I could not believe what was happening, When you don't think things can become worse, they do. I now faced the prospect of Godfrey dying and facing a manslaughter charge or worse.

My relationship with Mish was deteriorating. I felt like she was not supporting me at all, and it was decided she would go away. She had received a settlement from her previous marriage and went to the Northern Territory for a few months with her two daughters. I spent this time escaping into the mountains and operating the horse riding treks.

- Snow Country -

I have to admit that at some stages I was not at all confident I would beat the charges. I had to prepare myself for the small possibility that I might go to prison, and it would be a maximum security goal for the seriousness of my charges. I studied many books from different people who had served time, as well as asking first hand knowledge from a mate who had done time. It was pretty scary, the thought of being incarcerated. I spent every opportunity doing the things I enjoyed. Mick and I skied the main range to Mount Kosciusko, this time on a clear day. We also packed supplies into the Black Jack hut and hid food and some beverages into the ceiling of the hut. We cut firewood and stored it under the hut. When there was a good covering of snow we drove through the Maragle Range as far as we could, usually 1300 meters above sea level, then skied with back packs on further into the mountains for three days. On one trip to Mount Black Jack, we were shocked to find that someone had stolen the pot belly stove prior to the big snow fall. Thank God we had the casket of port. We were in our sleeping bags before sunset. There were huge icicles - up to two meters in length - hanging from the buildings. We would make the hut our base then ski out to Emu Plains, and the natural ski runs. Brumbies would push their way out of the mountains during this period and we found them moving down to lower altitudes. I was skiing down the northern side of Black Jack when I came to grief in a gully and managed to dislocate my shoulder. It was a serious ordeal in the cold, trying to get the shoulder back in. I have dislocated it about fifteen times over the years. On these trips I would have a 'trangie' stove: a metholayted spirit device that was a life saver in the snow country. Whether skiing or horse trekking into the mountains, when the going got tough we would say: **the best place to be is here, and the best time to be here is now.** If anything, saying this gave us the push to keep going.

I also headed off skiing by myself, usually just day trips. I once drove to the Mount Selwyn car park and skied out to Broken Dam hut. On the way out, dark clouds were coming in from the west, but I knew the country fairly well and was confident that if the weather turned for the worse I would have enough time to get back well before dark. This particular afternoon I was making good progress and knew that I could get to the hut, have lunch and return just in time. The weather was coming in but I was more determined to get to my goal of the hut than to worry about a bit of snow. I arrived at the hut and put on my warm clothes and had a feed with hot tea I carried in a thermos. When I was ready to go after a thirty minute break, I geared up again and started to ski off when a blizzard hit. I panicked and went back to the hut. I was not equipped for an overnight camp but time was running out. If the blizzard did not lift I would be forced to spend the night there. There was a break in the weather and I took the opportunity and headed back towards home, but as soon as I was about a kilometre from the hut the blizzard hit again and there I was in a white out. I managed to find some ski tracks and followed them, and then a hut appeared. It was the Broken Dam hut; I had been travelling in a circle. I went back into the hut and a huge wave of fear came over me. I had lost my bearings, and so realized how easy it would be to die out in the blizzard. Again there was a break in the weather. I looked at my watch and realized I still had time to get to Four Mile hut, half way between the car and where I was. I headed off on my third attempt and again only got a kilometre away before the storm came in once more I was again in a white out. I was now helpless. I cursed myself: why the hell had I left the hut? It might have been a cold night in the hut, but there would have been no chance of dying. Now I was out in a blizzard and unsure of how to find the hut as the new snow had covered up my tracks. When I tried to ski back, I was lucky to see my hand in front of my face. I knew where north was from my compass, so I thought I had no choice but to try to get to Four Mile hut. I skied on, finding myself in a steep valley. I was starting to get very worried, not sure if I had veered off to the north-west and would end up in the upper reaches of the Tumut River country, or if I had veered to the north-east I would eventually get to the Four Mile hut or the Eucumbene River side. I decided to keep to the eastern side. If I missed the hut then I would at least be closer towards Kiandra. Dark was on me and the weather was terrible. I was about to dig in and make myself a snow cave when there was a break in the weather and the stars shone through. I skied out into open country that I was familiar with and, now with a moon lighting the night, skied back to my vehicle. I returned exhausted, disgusted with myself for having pushed my luck more than once in leaving the safety of a hut to get back to the car.

Back in the low country, the whole legal proceedings made life very stressful. I wanted the trial to be over and done with but everything was a slow procedure. Mish had returned from Alice Springs where she had lived with her girls for a couple of months. During this time I decided to place the farm in three names: my mothers, Mish's and mine all having equal shares. I thought this was a fair way of keeping ownership in equal percentages so there would be no confusion about ownership. I was not to know **that morally right and legally right are two different things.** In six years time this action would come back to haunt me

Wangarra high country retreat accommodation hut 1996

Alistair holding King Brown Snake Gibb river track Kimberley's W.A 1986

Alistair & Clancy, Pentecost range Kimberley's W.A 1986

Crossing Jim Jim Creek
Northern Territory 1986

Humble beginnings "Wangarra" Snowy
Mountains Tumbarumba 1989

First mob of cattle Herefords at "Wangarra" 1989

Metro & Alistair "Wangarra Yards" 1990

Metro pack horse, Alistair riding Nipper &
Clancy near Round Mountain 1992

Hollyford river New
Zealand 1993

Happys hut Snow trip 1997 This hut may have saved our lives.

Alistair skiing the main range near Mount Kosciusko 1997

Alistair & Brumby catch, "Wangarra" 1996

Alistair riding Redgum along with Wangarra high country retreats horse plant "Wangarra" 1996. Mount Black Jack in the back ground covered in snow

Alistair & Brandon strapped for comfort with
a stirrup leather, Bago range 1996

Trade cattle Alistair & Brandon at Reid's
yards Tumbarumba 1998

'Wangarra" accommodation hut

Pilot reef Maragle range Alistair on left with customers three day winter trek 1995

Bush camp Milpirinka NSW Brandon & Alistair 2004

Back in the black Brandon after a property deal 2003

The Mighty Tumut Gorge, I would ride throughout this country countless times.

Alistair guiding riders up into the mountain ranges on an adventure trek. Snowy Mountains 1996

News paper articles about the shooting 1994 & 1995

Alistair & Brandon mustering the belted gallloway cattle "MacLeod's Run" Snowy mountains Ned & Kelly pushing the mob along 2005

Father & Son mustering the belties MacLeod's Run 2005

Boiling the billy, MacLeod's Run 2005

Broken dam hut, a safe haven in a snow storm

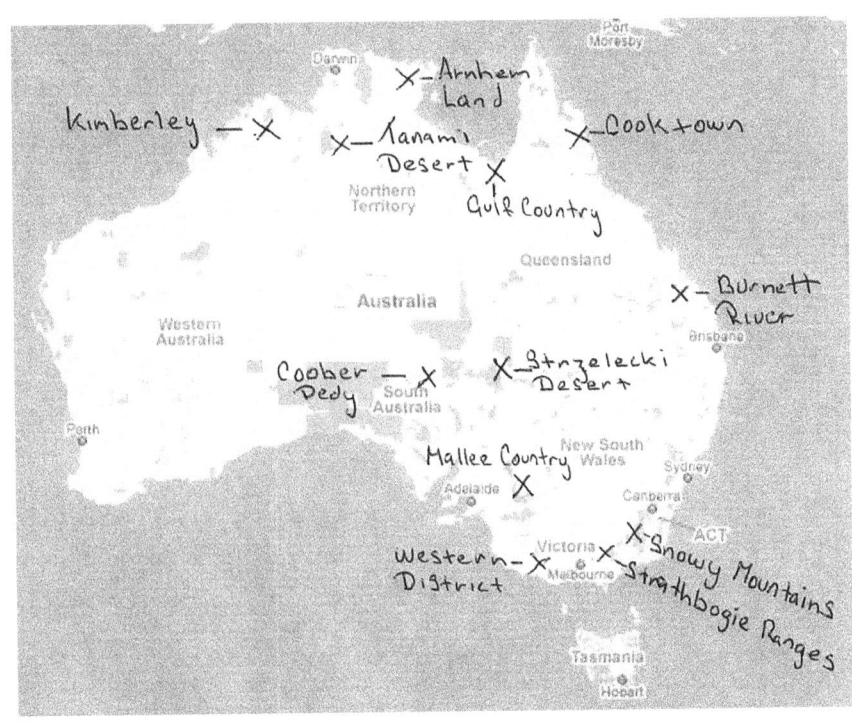

CHAPTER SEVEN
1995

SUCCESSFUL PEOPLE MAKE QUICK DECISIONS AND RARELY CHANGE THEIR MINDS. UNSUCCESSFUL PEOPLE DELAY MAKING DECISIONS AND ALWAYS CHANGE THEIR MINDS.

- Injustice of the legal system -

I contacted my local State member, Ian Glachan, the member for Albury. He had heard all about the incident and did everything possible in his position as the local member to have the charges against me dropped. Letter after letter was sent to the Hon. John Hannaford MLC, Minister of Justice and Attorney General at the time. The situation was, given the philosophy of the legislation in regard to the Director of Public Prosecutions Act of 1986, the prosecution process must be made independently by a person free of political interference. So in other words, I had fat chance of anyone besides the Crown being able to withdraw the charges against me. I met up with my legal counsel in Sydney. I had planned to be there for the day but my barrister Joan Lock was delayed in court, so I had to wait a couple of days before we could have our meeting. It seemed when anything legal was arranged, it could never actually be held on the day arranged. As with court cases: you would have to stay around the courts for days until your case was heard and sometimes the hearing would then be adjourned or called over to a different date.

As with all legal representatives I have known over the years, I got the feeling they were only worried about what they could make out of me. I had to sell most of my cattle in a depressed market to fund the retainer fees and briefing payments being asked by my legal counsel. I was advised by them that legal aid was not available for committal hearings, and I was told to concentrate on my finance for a trial. This was why I had represented myself at the hearing in Holbrook. One of my biggest fears was due to the so called victim stating that he was shot on the veranda, and not inside my house. But six months after the shooting the Crown finally gave notice that the shooting did occur inside the home. Although it was obvious that he had been shot inside with the blood splattering the wall and floors, it was very unnerving, to say the least, to wait this period of time for the prosecution to agree on where the shooting took place. At this stage I was hoping that the Crown would dismiss the charges but that was only wishful thinking on my behalf.

The banks had told me that it was ridiculous for them to fund my court case when I was morally in the right, and I was not sure where the rest of the money would come from. My solicitor said to me, "You will just have to go and get yourself another job." At that stage, I was working night shift at the mill and running the horse treks on the weekends. On the 5th December 1994, I was to stand trial at the District Court at Wagga Wagga, NSW. I should have stood trial earlier but my legal counsel suggested the Judge who would preside over the case at that time would not be suitable for me, and my barrister was engaged elsewhere.

Meanwhile, my barrister was charging me $1,500 a day and my solicitor was charging me $1,000 a day. At the time I was lucky to be making $100 a day at the timber mill, working at night. I had to pay for their travel fares along with their accommodation in the finest establishment that Wagga had to offer. As I picked up my legal counsel from the airport and dropped them off at their four star accommodation, I thought about my family staying at the local caravan park. I kept saying to myself, "You only get what you pay for." I had to think this way to justify the cost. One main thing I learnt over the years is that when you are paying others huge amounts of money: it is only huge money when one only has a job as a mere worker for someone else. In my case, that J.O.B meant 'just on broke'.

I knew then that I was to have to change my whole income stream, although it would take several years before it would eventuate.

When we arrived at the court, Christopher Godfrey was there, sitting on the steps of the court house. He was trying to eye ball all the people that I had with me. Joan Lock stood her ground and just stared at him in a disgusted way. I accidently dropped a pen when I was walking up the stairs near Godfrey and bent down to pick it up right next to him. He looked at me, visibly shaking, and said, "Don't f— with me." I smiled and walked into court. Godfrey had been living in Port Augusta, South Australia, and now had a prosthetic leg. The Crown had paid for him to be flown over as a witness and paid for his accommodation, as well as $160 a day. His mate, Jovanovich, was also paid as a witness. To my dismay, the case was adjourned again and another case was given priority. I would now have to wait until April before I could stand trial. This would make it a full year of living without knowing what my future held. All of the fees I had paid to my counsel had been wasted. Nevertheless, I drove them out to my property to give them a feel for the event and then returned them to the motel on the same day.

It was on this same day as the trial should have been held that Chris Godfrey appeared at the Magistrates court, in the same building as the District court, and was convicted of four charges. Three of the charges were from an incident prior to the shooting. He and Jovanovich had abused a police officer at Tooma. They were convicted for violent disorder, throwing stones so as to endanger people and property, a motor vehicle offence and also drug possession, as Godfrey had admitted to owning drugs in the car he was in when they attacked my place.

- Birth of a son -

On the 26th December 1994, Mish gave birth to a baby boy in the Wagga Wagga Base Hospital. It was the most incredible thing I had ever experienced, assisting in the delivery of my own son into the world. We named him Brandon Alistair MacLeod and all my concerns over the court case and my future seemed to disappear. All of a sudden I had a different purpose in life; or I should say now I had one main purpose, and that was to be a father. I made a commitment to myself and to my newborn baby at that time: that my son would be the number one priority in my life.

- Across the Alps -

I had arranged with Mick Obendorf to do a bush walk across the mountains from Cabrumurra to Khancoban. After I had taken some riders into the mountains for two days, I packed my back pack and Mick and I were dropped at the Round Mountain car park near Cabrumurra. The week of weather had been fantastic while on my adventure horse trek, and so we had planned to walk across the mountains and climb down to the township of Khancoban within three days. The first day we walked to Dershkos Hut, which is on the western side of Mount Jagungal. That night the weather changed for the worse, and the next morning we awoke to wet conditions and thick cloud. We headed off towards the Grey Mare Hut, but by mid afternoon the light rain had turned to snow and visibility was very poor. Neither of us had ever been to the Grey Mare before so we were relying on maps. The whole track was now covered in snow and we were both extremely cold. I had lost the feeling in my feet and we decided to put up a tarp to get out of the blasts of freezing wind. We tied the tarp to some saplings, making a type of lean-to and we both huddled out of the gale. We got the trangie metho stove going and poured some hot soup into us. With the compass out, we knew that the hut should be somewhere in front of us but it was very difficult to find, as we could only see a few meters in any direction. At this point, we were both soaked to the bone and the cold was really playing havoc with us. It was a long walk back to Dershkos Hut, so we kept on looking around the area for the Grey Mare Hut. As it was, my hands had now lost feeling and it was an effort to keep the stove going. Everything was looking grim and we knew if we did not find the hut soon we would have no option but to make the return trip in the dark. All of a sudden we stumbled onto an old tin hut. This dilapidated cold little hut was a great sight as we staggered through the door, and we had a roaring fire going in no time. We dried ourselves and our clothes out, had a big feed and a few ports. Thank God for those mountain huts. Over the many years I was to use many of them to escape the weather, but sadly most of the huts I knew were lost in the 2002 fires. The Grey Mare was originally an old mine and the relics of that bygone era were still visible around the hut itself. Its name came from an old legend about a grey brumby mare that once roamed the area. Later the book "The Silver Brumby" and the movie were named after this area. The next morning we awoke to a clear day and decided to start walking. We climbed up the Strumbo Range, 1800 meters above sea level, and then the weather came back in to test us. The visibility was very poor again and we were once more caught in another snow storm. We headed to another hut called Pretty Plain which we had both used in recent years. As the snow turned to rain and soaked us both again, we arrived at the large log hut. We dried out and listened to the huge storm that lashed the mountains all night. The next morning the snow had covered everything. We walked on, as we had arranged to be picked up at a spot in the foothills of the mountains up from Khancoban township: a 1000 meter descent out of the covered snow mountains. The snow continued down to 1100 meters level, so I used plastic bags over my socks to keep my feet dry and warm, as I always did in bad situations. We arrived from the higher altitude to our pick up spot, exhausted but content. Of the many walks I have done in the mountains over the years, this was the most trying, but at that time I needed something like it to get my mind off the trial that I was about to undergo.

- Standing Trial -

Ian Glachan, my local member for Parliament, contacted me and asked if I would allow him to bring up my plight with Premiere John Fahey and to speak to Parliament at the next sitting. I had just been contacted by my solicitor who told me that my barrister had been appointed to the bench as a judge and would no longer be able to represent me. I asked about the money that I had already paid towards her briefing and was told that it was all gone. I was furious; she had contacted me in December and had told me that everyone she knew was on my side. She had said that it was ridiculous that I had to go through this whole ordeal, and not to worry as I was in good hands. That was the last time I heard from her. I had correspondence from the Attorney General via Ian Glachan regarding the Legal Aid process and what was available to me. I contacted legal aid and was told that I could have a barrister paid by the legal aid commission.

At the pre-trial on the 10th of April, I appeared before Judge Twigg. My solicitor in Sydney had arranged for a local solicitor to be there with me as my legal representation. The Judge and the Department of Public Prosecution talked about the length of my record of interview, and the Judge went to great lengths explaining to me about the upcoming event. On the pre-trial day, the local solicitor, my assigned legal representative for that day only, stated that my original solicitor would prefer to have the case postponed until September. Judge Twigg stated, "Mr. MacLeod is here and waiting and the trial date will be set on the 18th April." My impression of Judge Twigg was a good one and I felt comfortable that he would preside over the case.

I contacted my solicitor in Sydney the following day and asked him about the offer of legal aid assistance. Trying to keep me feeling afraid, he asked, "Do you want to go to gaol?" He said he wanted a second mortgage put on my property as security for his payment. I refused, as I had already paid thousands of dollars for nothing. I found it disgusting to be left out on a limb by a barrister who was briefed and paid to represent me. I said, "I will represent myself." He said, "You have a piss poor attitude." He told me that he had already engaged another barrister and that he would not brief a barrister paid for by legal aid. He refused to appear himself without the new barrister he had chosen, whose main qualification was apparently representing some of the bikie figures during the Milpeera gun fight trials. He said, "He is working on the case now, and if you do not allow him to represent you or you pull out, there will be funds owed to me." I was caught between a rock and a hard place. I reluctantly borrowed some money that my Aunt Pat McLean insisted on lending me.

- In the prison dock -

On the 18th April, I arrived at the Wagga Wagga District Court with my family and friends for support. My new counsel, trying to persuade me to have the case called over to September as he knew the other Judge personally, said, "Judge Twigg will send you to gaol if you're found guilty." In his arrogant way he kept telling me, "Your world is black and white; well, this is my world and it is all grey." After talking to my new barrister for a while, I realized he had not even been briefed and did not know anything about the case. Again I was disgusted with my solicitor, but I believed the evidence would speak for itself. I said, "We're going ahead with it today", and with that I walked into the court room. Within five minutes, we had priority over other cases and the Jury was sworn in. The process of swearing in twelve people for a Jury involves calling them to the stand and asking them several questions to see if they knew of the case and if they would swear on the Bible. We selected mostly women to be our jurors. After this I was ordered to stand in the prison dock flanked by officers. One turned to me and told me, "When the Jury comes in, stand and look at them in the eye so they will give you support." I remember reading that the great boxer Jack Dempsey said the loneliest place in the world is when you get into the boxing ring. Well, Jack Dempsey obviously had never been in a prison dock, **where twelve people you have never met are deciding your fate; it is the loneliest place in the world. Now I know how Ned Kelly must have felt.** My legal counsel requested that I sit with them at the defence table, but the request was denied by Judge Twigg. In the opening statement, the Crown admitted the victim was shot within the house. I was called from the prison dock to acknowledge if the person they were referring to had sustained an injury. I stated that he did and the Judge told the Jury, "Although Mr. MacLeod admits the person received an injury, at no stage is he admitting to any of the charges." I sat there listening to the Crowns' statements of events and by the end of the day I believed it had gone all my way, as the truth of the facts was finally coming out. My release on bail continued and I was allowed to spend the night with my family at the motel.

On the second day of the trial, Christopher Godfrey gave evidence, hobbling into the witness box on his prosthetic leg. He could not really give a reason why he was at my premises during the events of the night. Then Robert Jovanovic gave his evidence and said that he couldn't remember what had happened. If standing trial was not so serious, I would have found it comical, listening to the explanations that these people tried to come up with. Their previous convictions were called out: burglary, break and enters, possession of explosives, assault with weapons, numerous drug convictions and firearm offences; the list went on. I was looking at the faces of some of the Jury and saw that two of them would not even look at Godfrey or Jovanavic when they gave evidence. At the end of the second day of the trial, I was confident that everything was going the right way, and this was while we were still hearing the prosecution and had not even started the defence evidence.

On the third day of trial, the police evidence was called. Forensic and ballistic reports described the gun I used and the workings of that particular firearm. Then the police were called to the stand and Constable Gary Lewis had strips torn off him over his conduct and the length of time I had been placed in the prison van. But that was minor compared to what happened to Detective Tony Vincent. The judge accused him of verballing me and demanding that he sit in the witness box for one hour and forty seven minutes and listen to the entire record of interview. He also told the Crown that other, higher authorities would learn about this treatment. He then directed the Jury to come to a verdict and emphasized a 'not guilty'. The Jury stood and was escorted out to the Jury room. At this stage I was allowed to walk to the court hall way to be with my family while the media were all frantically writing things down. The Judge had directed the Jury to reach a verdict having only listened to the prosecution evidence, and nothing from the defence. In just seventeen minutes the Jury had reached a decision. I was escorted back to the prison dock and the judge asked the woman foreperson, "Have you reached a verdict?" The woman replied, "We have your honour," and with tears in her eyes said, "Not guilty to all charges". It was one of the most emotional experiences of my life. I called out to the entire Jury, thanking them for their common sense. Even my solicitor was teary, and I started thinking I might have had him worked out wrongly. My barrister requested my firearm be returned and the Crown had no objection. The Judge directed me to pick it up at the Tumut police station. The Crown Prosecutor told the Judge that he disagreed with the Judge's comments about Detective Vincent and went on to describe him as a police officer of good character. Judge Twigg repeated, "The authorities will know about this," and warned about repercussions. After the entire twelve month ordeal, I had lost faith in the whole legal system from the police to the Department of Public Prosecution; including Magistrates, solicitors and barristers; but one man managed to restore that faith: Judge Twigg.

That night all the television stations were broadcasting my acquittal. It was all too surreal. We were all still staying at the motel so I had a few beers but I could not sleep. I was up before dawn and went out walking. While walking along the banks of the Murrumbidgee River as the dawn came, everything in the past year went through my head and it took a long time to realise it was finally over. When I arrived home, the answering machine was full of messages and I spent the next week taking calls of congratulations.

Later in the next month at a sitting of the N.S.W. Parliament, Ian Glachan raised my case saying that I had been wrongly arrested and compensation should be paid to me. Unfortunately nothing came out of it, although I tried many angles to seek some recognition of the wrong doing. I met with the Deputy Prime Minister Tim Fisher some time after the event; he knew of my case, and later he sent a letter to me from the NSW Parliament with the Hansard Extract, which stated that I was wrongly and unfairly arrested and asked for consideration to be given to compensation. During that year I often wondered about why this had happened. **I used to think: Why me? Then I realized: Why not me?**

The adventure horse trekking business was taking off. We were taking half day rides through the foothills of Clarkes Hill State Forest, stopping to boil the billy and have a feed of cake at an old bread making oven built during the gold rush days on the Maragle Creek. Then we would ride up a trail I had cut through the bush back to 'Wangarra'. On the full day treks, I would take the riders up to the ruins of Hannam's homestead and the start of the alpine ranges and then return. The two day and three day treks were consistent with a full adventure trekking experience: riding up into the Alpine ranges and camping out. The following is from a flyer I used to market the business and describes the treks:

> *What better way to experience the high country than to spend a couple of days' horse trekking into the Mountain Ranges? The MacLeod's own and operate 'Wangarra High Country Retreat', a family business that takes riders into the Snowy Mountains on horseback. [A minimum of two to a maximum of eight people gives that personal touch].*
>
> *Starting off from their grazing property 'Wangarra', you head through the foothills with Alistair, crossing crystal clear creeks and slowly make your way up into the Alpine ranges, passing abandoned ruins from a bygone era and mining areas where past inhabitants separated gold from clay. At 1,000 meters above sea level, Mish is waiting with the 4x4 back up vehicle and camp ovens on the hot coals of the fire ready for lunch to be, enjoyed by all.*
>
> *After a feed and a rest, you climb up another 400 meters through huge mountain gums with the scent of peppermint in the air. Encountering brumbies is a common occurrence and you will feel your horse tense as the wild horses run by.*
>
> *At 1400 meters, you look onto the roof top of Australia; in some months covered in snow. Lyrebirds are frequently seen in the cool damp gullies and kangaroos and emus are*

often sighted. After 'boiling the billy' and fresh afternoon tea, you'll head towards one of the numerous camp sites where your horses are hobbled for the night and dome tents are erected to make camp. A B.B.Q. din-

ner is appreciated by all and then it's around the open fire to yarn about the days events and pass stories around, at times accompanied by the timeless sounds of the didgeridoo. At night you might hear the howl of a dingo close by. After a good nights sleep and a hearty breakfast, it's time to 'saddle up again' in the crisp mountain air and Alistair will guide you back through the mountains on different trails along the Kosciusko National Park boundary looking into spectacular gorge country to conclude your three day trek ride.

During the winter months the treks still operated, but with only the most adventurous of adventurers. On one of the winter treks we had the heaviest rainfall recorded in the year with seventy inches received in the mountain region and the Maragle Creek was in full flood.

I had a three day trek organized with some riders from Wagga Wagga. They were all confident riders who had been out with me before, and despite the terrible conditions I had booked them into the Macpherson Plains Resort, for the full three days. All of them had the sense of adventure which is a must when taking riders into the mountains during winter. The rain had eased in the early hours of the morning and we rode down into the Maragle Creek gorge. To my shock the creek was flooded more than I had ever seen before. I was tempted to cancel the whole trek and go back, but this group was keen to keep going. I got them all to dismount and crawl across a log that was over the flooded creek in order to get to the other side. Once they were there,

I entered the flooded creek upstream of the crossing on my horse Red Gum, leading one of their mounts. As I entered the water, the other horse followed me, swimming towards the bank and climbing up the other side. I was soaked from the waist down. Then I went back to the other side across a log over the creek and rode Salt, my small grey mare, across leading one of the other horses. Being smaller, Salt could not get to the opposite bank in time and we ended up drifting downstream. I let go of the other horse and it managed to climb up the bank, but Salt and I continued downstream where both of us got caught under a tea tree bush. It was pretty scary for a while as I went under the cold rushing water. I lost my breath and somehow managed to dislocate my shoulder. Salt, the little marvel, scrambled up the bank with me clutching onto her. I managed to put my shoulder back in place. (This seems to have happened to me on lots of occasions over the years.) I quickly put on the dry clothes from the saddle bags that the riders had taken over with them when they crossed the fallen log, and we rode on towards our lunch stop at Hannam's abandoned homestead. The great thing about riding at a fast pace is that you warm up very quickly. When we arrived at the old dirt bridge just before the ruined homestead, we found that the creek had cut its way through a different part of the bridge and that the large concrete pipes at the centre of the creek were now not visible. I asked my riders to walk their horses over by leading them one at a time. To our shock, as the last horse went over there was a ripple in the road then the whole earth bridge collapsed with an enormous sound. We had taken photos of the bridge prior to walking over it, and certainly afterwards. After a hot lunch, we climbed up into the mountains and met the back up vehicle where we hobbled the horses. I stayed the night with the mounts and the riders were taken to McPherson's Plains Resort, twenty kilometres away. It was one of the wettest nights I had spent in the mountains.

Besides having the hobble chains on the horses, I placed them in a temporary yard with an electric fence. I got a huge fire going, had a few ports and slept in my swag in the comfort of the tent as the rain poured down all night.

Over the years I was to take literally hundreds of people from all over the world into the mountains on adventure treks. In January of 1996 I completed building an authentic bush hut on 'Wangarra' to accommodate the riders. I built the whole hut myself by cutting down stringy bark trees for the poles and used rough sawn timber from the mill for lining the outside and inside. I built a high pitched gabled roof with an exposed ceiling and eight bunks out of rough sawn timber, with a pot belly stove for warmth. There was a veranda at the front and a kitchen, a toilet and a bathroom with a bath tub. I pumped water from a spring dam to a large concrete tank on a hill above the hut and it gravity fed the hut. There was an instant gas hot water service, and all the lightening was by kero lanterns giving it a very authentic feel. Inside I hung up stock whips, old hats and rabbit traps. There was a wall where I put up photos of the riders and our different treks, as well as many old maps and other nostalgia of the high country and its history.

A lot of riders would stay at the 'Wangarra' hut prior to the rides and after. We would have a fire outside where many a beverage was consumed and many a story told. On a couple of occasions, magazine writers came to do a story on the business. One such magazine used the title: "ENCOUNTERS OF THE WILD KIND" and did a great article on the operation. I recall signing a book for a couple of Dutch push bike riders who were riding around the world. Years later they sent me their photo, up on the top of the world standing with their bikes in the Himalayas. I trekked with people all over Australia from cattlemen to horse men to solicitors, barristers and a Magistrate, even the economic advisor to the then Prime minister. I refused to take young children on the treks and insisted older children were of a mature nature. In all, no one was seriously hurt over the five year period we ran the trekking business. There was the odd spill but I had a great line of horses that looked after them all. I cannot recall ever having an undesirable type of person on the treks and this restored my faith in people. I had a 55% return rate of clientele, and the business was going from strength to strength. Some groups returned throughout the years and covered most of the trekking country. On one occasion Tumbarumba experienced a tornado that swept havoc through some parts of the district, but it was not until I was on the treks that I saw the devastation. There were huge gums twisted clean out of the ground and a tangled wall of trees left many a kilometre of trail impassable. If we had been in its path during a trek, I believe it was impossible that we could have survived.

I also built some large timber stables on Wangarra where I would house the horses on those icy cold winter nights, and made a barn where we would prepare feed mix of oats and molasses. Hay for the horses was cut on the property by a local contractor.

In April 1996 Mish and I were married at Wangarra in a horse back wedding, since we lived and breathed the high country.

Led by Geoff Blair playing the bag pipes, we rode to the highest point of the property, with the Macleod's tartan draped over the horses. One hundred people from all over Australia attended.

I once arranged for horses to be carted over the mountains by Ron Wilesmith, a local truck operator who had carted everything from cattle, horses and timber for me over the years. He dropped the horses off at Kiandra on the east side of the mountains. My mother came up from Melbourne to mind Brandon, and Mish and I rode south near Lake Eucumbene with Metro my pack horse and two other horses. Then we headed over to the high plains visiting old cattlemen huts, camping out or staying in the huts. We rode down to the upper reaches of the Tumut River, then up over the fifteen mile spur to Emu Plains then home to Wangarra. It was not enough running adventure treks for business; our spare time was spent in the mountains as well.

- *On A Crusade* -

In 1996 I went on a bit of a crusade in life. I was still angry over how I had been treated during the whole legal process of my court case. I saw so many things around me that I could describe as unjust. Large areas of our beloved mountains were being locked up by the National Parks for what was being called a 'wilderness area'. As a result of this new gazetting of the area, horse riding was banned. I wrote letters in protest to this policy and the disregard of other bush users wishes, and encouraged all other riders to also write in protest of these bans, trying in vain to preserve what I felt was a way of life. There was also heavy gun controls being introduced across Australia, and I found myself at the rallies in Sydney with my mate Gaven Willis. We joined over 100,000 people protesting on rights of gun ownership, and I gave interviews to newspapers and had my photo and views printed. If that was not enough I was encouraged by my fellow timber mill workers to stand as a Union delegate and represent their rights in the work place. The timber mill had around 200 people employed and I was voted in as a union delegate with the Construction, Forestry, Mining and Energy Union, known as the C.F.M.E.U. This involved going through the process of Union training, learning the process of industrial relations, enterprise bargaining and health and safety issues. During the process of enterprise bargaining, a new site manager was employed. He asked if I could give a presentation to the accountants and new general manager of the company to explain how the work force had implemented structures in conjunction with management to improve the efficiency of the timber mill. I put together diagrams showing different areas of the mill and how we all implemented Key Performance Indicators (KPI) as a guide to improve the efficiency of the overall operation. At one of the meetings, I met a person who had managed the operation of Alco America, and now was employed to manage many timber mills for Boral throughout Australia. After a meeting he told me, "I don't know anything about timber." I was rather shocked at this comment: how the hell can someone who knows nothing about the product possibly run a huge timber company with a largework force with any success? He said, 'It's the same as aluminium, isn't it?" He went to great length to describe to me that with aluminium production, there are three areas: First, the purchasing cost of buying the bauxite. Then, the production cost to make it into rolls in the factory and finally the selling cost –to sell the product to the consumer. Timber is the same. Firstly, the purchase cost of buying logs. Secondly, the production cost of milling the timber into sizes. Lastly, the selling cost: to wrap the wood in plastic and sell the finished article. It quickly dawned on me why this person had been employed to run the timber division of Boral: **a simple attitude to business is a successful attitude to business.**

CHAPTER EIGHT
1997 – 1998

A GREAT SAILOR DOES NOT BECOME GREAT BY SAILING ON CALM WATERS

-New Year 1997 -

The start of the new year was spent at the annual Tumbarumba rodeo. This event was the town's biggest day and most of the district's population would turn out for a get together and watch the buck jumping and bull riding. It would usually turn into a long day and night for me, as I would catch up with people and a long drinking session would start. While at the back of the chutes [where the riders would prepare their rigging before mounting a beast] I was introduced to Ken Connelly, a mountain cattleman from the Victorian side by my mate Gaven Willis, who was also a local cattleman from Mannus. Ken was a renowned horseman who had been a stunt rider in films such as "The Man from Snowy River" and "The Light Horsemen". He had also won several Cattleman's Cups and other bush races. These races were not for the faint hearted as both rider and horse would risk life and limb in dangerous situations on a bush circuit, galloping downhill and through creek crossings at breakneck speeds. After a long drinking session, I found myself riding with Ken through the hills around my property at dawn. This riding adventure lasted a week as we headed into Victoria with both our families and horse floats and rode around the Rams Head, a well known rocky outcrop south of the Indi River in Victoria's mountain country. Ken claimed to have caught over 1,000 wild horses with a rope. He would track horses down then chase them with his tracking dogs, mostly in snowy conditions then riding up beside them. Getting a rope over the neck of a buck [another name for wild horse] he would then tie them up, blindfold them by covering their heads with hessian and load them into a horse float to break them in and sell. He would carry an old revolver in his belt to shoot the stallions that would always cause grief. This method was used by most of the old horsemen I knew, and they would then introduce better stallions to the mobs; usually a blood horse [thoroughbred line] and breed a better horse as a result.

Over the years I have knocked around with a lot of bushmen throughout the country and most of them always loved to compete to prove their bush skills, but never have I spent time with someone like Ken. He would compete with me in everything we did, from the time it took to catch and saddle a horse to who could catch the first trout, or the most trout. He competed over who could drink the most, who could recite the most bush poems, identify the most mountain names and tell the tallest stories. He seemed to know a lot of people throughout Australia that I knew and I was starting to become suspicious. I mentioned a truck driver from NSW who had carted stock for me on several occasions and when I said his name, he said, "I know him too, and I haven't heard his name for twenty years." I questioned him on this, as it was getting to a stage where it seemed Ken knew or had met nearly every person in Australia. I said, "Describe him to me", and he said, "He is the only person I know that has a boxer's nose and doesn't fight." This certainly was the description of my truck driver who did have a distinctly crooked nose.

Later in the autumn, Ken invited me to come to one of his properties and ride through the mountains with a pack horse to the Cattleman's Cup, the Victorian high country cattleman's get together. I agreed and spent a few days at the event which was held on the Gibbo River, just one of the many spots I had spent fishing with my father in bygone years. Ken entered the pack horse race, where I would hold Ken's riding horse and a pack horse, and he would have to roll a swag and billy and pack them with a dozen eggs into saddle bags and lead a horse along a circuit and back. Whoever arrived first without breaking the eggs won. Prior to the event, Ken looked at me and said, **"No-one mentioned anything about boiling the eggs prior to packing them, did they?"** At the back of Ken's bush property was a collection of dog tails, nailed to the door. Ken had cut the tails off his dogs when they became 'snow balled' *snow setting on their tails] after chasing bucks through the snow in winter. He then would collect them as souvenirs and nail them to the back door as a display. He also had a stuffed dog inside his house. It had been his close mate and Ken had decided to have him preserved as a mark of respect to him after he died. One can only imagine Ken Connelly walking down Collins Street in Melbourne during peak hour traffic on his way to the taxidermist with this dog in a state of rigor mortis on his shoulder.

- *Old Clancy* -

My faithful old mate Clancy had lost an eye from a kick from one of my horses whilst he was bringing them into the yards for one of my adventure treks. He had become very slow due to age and arthritis, and although he would walk out with me when I was riding off into the mountains, he would turn back for home before crossing the property boundary. Once, on my return from a trip, Clancy was not to be seen. I searched for days and rode back up along the tracks, thinking that he had followed me, but after a week I was convinced he had walked off to die. Then Phil Cussons, who owned a property east of Wangarra appeared with Clancy in the back of his ute. He had found him miles away from home on one of my horse trails. The nearly blind dog had obviously followed my scent and then sat there, waiting for me to return, only to miss me when I rode back. I presume I went past while he was drinking at the creek. It's easy to understand the old saying: a dog is a man's best friend. Where else could you get loyalty like that?

- *Near Drowning* -

I looked after my son during the day as Mish worked part time at a local vineyard. So Brandon would be alongside me during all my farm activities during the day. There was a large spring dam where I would pump water to a tank that gravity fed the troughs and the accommodation hut. One day, when Brandon was only three years old, I told him to stand next to me and not to go near the dam. He stood there next to me obediently and so I leaned over into the small pump shed, fuelled the motor then started the pump. As I looked up again, my little boy was not in sight. I panicked. It seemed to have only been seconds that I had taken my eyes off him while I started the pump. I looked straight into the water but could not see him, and then ran frantically along the edge of the dam looking for him or any disturbed water. I had really never experienced anxiety of that level until that moment. I thought my heart would stop beating. I searched the water and could just make out my little boys face looking at me as it disappeared into some deep water. I dived in and grabbed him and quickly got him out while he coughed up water. He said, "You saved me daddy, you saved me daddy." I felt sick for nearly a week merely at the thought of what could have been. I had only taken my eyes off him for a second.

- Rogue Brum Stallion -

During that year I bought some Aberdeen Angus cattle in calf. It was a change from Herefords as I wanted a beast with no horns and I was enjoying operating the adventure trekking business. I also was chasing bucks in my spare time. Besides the odd arthritic brumby I would ride up and throw a rope over, my success rate in catching brumbies was nothing to brag about, but I could not get enough of the mountains. I would float a horse, either Red Gum or Manjar, up into the high country early in the morning and then ride down into the little high plains where the brumbies would feed after their morning drink. I was hopeful to meet them full of feed and water. When I approached, one would snort then off they would go and I would gallop after them, jumping over logs and dodging trees through the bush. It is the most adrenalin pumping sport you can imagine. Once I was after two black yearling types; identical with a small white star on their foreheads. I had first seen them as newborn foals in the country I called Brumby's Run, a saddle in the mountains with the Tumut Gorge next to it, dropping into a fall of 1,000 meters. I was riding along a track when all of a sudden I rode into a large mob of brumbies, and amongst the mob were the two yearlings. They all galloped off straight down the track but I was able to make up ground quickly and before I knew it I was alongside one of the yearlings. I tried in vain to get a rope over the neck of the horse but either she was too quick or I was not quick enough. She cut out from the rest of the mob and we both raced through the bush. When I tried to drop the rope over her again, she darted off to my off side [right hand] All of a sudden, there was the Tumut Gorge with that thousand meter drop and she leapt right over the edge. I pulled my horse up and could hear the crashing sounds of the buck below me. I was not sure if she was still on her feet or rolling down the steep gorge. There is an old saying in the mountains that opposes brum running: **Why ruin a good horse trying to get a bad horse?** I was worried for a few weeks about the yearling, wondering if I had caused her to be injured or killed. Then during one of my adventure treks a couple of weeks after the event, I came across both yearlings again in the same spot, healthy as they were before the chase.

I was on a three day adventure horse trek with eight people from Sydney, all of Italian origin. We were camped at Native Dog Creek, a very appropriate name as the dingoes would howl on most occasions that I camped there. (Once I had some riders who had brought their trumpets and were playing the "Bananas in Pyjamas" tune. The dingoes were joining in, howling back at the trumpet players.) On this particular trek with the group from Sydney, we were all asleep in our swags only to be awakened by a rogue brumby stallion fighting my geldings. The geldings where all hobbled and this brum was up on their backs, stamping on them with his hooves. I ran him off but he had damaged one of my bay geldings, a horse I called Eucumbene. As the dawn was breaking, he came back again. Showing no shame he walked through the camp, past everyone, and started attacking the geldings again. My group of riders held him off with sticks while I saddled a horse and with a heavy lead rope, chased him off, giving him curry. I am not into flogging animals but this was the only way to get him away from my horses and I chased him off for a few kilometres.

- Union Strike Action -

I became heavily involved with the Union movement as a delegate at the Tumbarumba timber mill. We had an enterprise bargaining agreement whereby the employer, Boral Timber, agreed not to enter into any personal individual contract agreements. They had offered the 160 timber workers a pay rise of $8 per week; that is 20 cents an hour before tax, over a two year period. The consumer price index was $10. There were also trade offs with their proposals. During the whole negotiating process, we discovered that Boral had broken the enterprise agreement and had entered into personal contracts with the 'saw doctors' *the tradespeople who sharpen saws]. We called a union meeting and a motion was put forward for strike action. What followed was a lengthy strike that was to continue for weeks, including a picket line at the front of the site. During this time I addressed the crowd of workers from the top of a large sawn log, telling them about the process of negotiation and also the process of vote counting if we returned to work or stayed out on strike. There was another union delegate with me at the mill, and a shop steward who was sent to Sydney with other union officials to negotiate. Here is an extract from the Tumbarumba Times, dated 20th August 1997

BORAL IMPASSE MAY BE BROKEN

> *As this issue went to press there were promising signs that the industrial unrest at Tumbarumba's Boral timber plant, which has seen the workers going on strike on a number occasions over recent weeks, could be coming to an end.*

It appears the breakthrough came following a meeting held at 3 pm yesterday [Tuesday]. The dispute has raged for a number of weeks with claims and counter claims from Boral and the timber workers. The unrest began when workers claimed Boral broke the enterprise agreement by illegally entering into personal agreements with some saw doctors and fitters at all Boral sites, who were signed up for $10,000 to $16,000 a year increase in individual contracts. This offer was withdrawn after action was taken, and replaced by a change in grade structure to new levels that currently don't exist and a guaranteed overtime of 11 hours per week regardless.

The workers claimed the company offered them $8 a week [before tax], $2 below the CPI, which is the equivalent to about 13 cents per hour. They said this was totally unacceptable, as recent price rises in petrol, bread and milk would not be covered by the 13 cents and asked for a pay rise of $1 an hour to keep up with the national average.

The workers said with the latest offer Boral continually included other issues that were not relevant at this time and there were many hidden trade offs.

Then workers at Boral claimed employees from other companies, doing the same job, were receiving at least $2.50 an hour more and were now on their fourth agreement.

To give the general public an insight into their grievances, the timber workers issued the following statement to the "Times" on Tuesday morning:

"We the employees are disappointed by Boral breaking the Enterprise Bargaining Agreement and the new EBA

Process by introducing personal contracts. We have no gripe with specialist workers receiving a higher rate, as they may deserve it. However, Boral used the personal contracts to attract workers into their employment, which the workers would normally not consider because of the low pay package.

"We were insulted with the new EBA pay rise of $8 per week that we are offered, as this is only 20 cents an hour before tax. The CPI increase was set at $10 and Boral has the audacity to suggest this was to be their final offer and in good faith, over two years, but the personal contracts were to be given between $10,000 and $16,000 per annum.

"Their next offer was to be filled with promises of unguaranteed bonuses and $15 at the signing of the agreement rather than from July 1. This could be in October and maybe another $18 twelve months after that.

"We have done as Boral suggested. We went back to work and lifted overtime bans so they would sit down and negotiate, but to no avail. Boral broke off talks time and time again.

"We then gave them 72 hours notice to come up with a reasonable offer and extended that an extra two days, but the result was the same. Boral has not come up with a fair and reasonable offer under the new Enterprise Bargaining. The redundancy package was atrocious and still does not show appreciation for the workers and their long service. Boral says they are committed to the Enterprise Bargaining Process yet they still seem to have trouble with negotiations, which they claimed were going well. They broke that same agreement and are now taking us before the Industrial Relations Commission.

> "Lastly, and most importantly, we do not like having to take industrial action. Unfortunately, it is the only option left open to us that to receive the acknowledgment and action we require on behalf of the majority of the various hardwood and softwood workers employed by Boral."

During the strike action with the front gate picket line, I was approached by a few electricians who were not part of our union but were part of an electrician union. They had also been out for a period of time in support of us but now they wanted to return to work. They were under a different pay system and the Enterprise Agreement that affected the timber workers did not affect them. They wanted to return to work but were afraid of the consequences. As with any large group of people, there are a lot of factions and in the union movement there are militant types who will resort to violence, as so often has been seen. My public speaking to the workers had been very constructive. I would state, "As your delegate I have been voted to represent you and your wishes." I told them I would not vote either way, as I did not want to influence people with my beliefs but allow people to openly express their views, either for or against the issues. It had worked well; there were no bully boy tactics as there had been in the past with union officials who had come from afar to stir the pot. I also told the crowd that this was an issue between ourselves and the higher management of Boral, and we should at no stage be resentful towards any person who formed part of the management at Tumbarumba. This also worked well, as the site manager and others could visit union members at the picket line without an "us against them" attitude. This kept harmony within our community of 2,000 people. I thought it a fair request from the electricians to be able to return to work, but how was I going to tell a crowd of 160 people to vote to let them in? I imagined all kinds of situations in which the crowd would not understand their situation and not let them return, thinking they were scabs instead of considering the support they had given to us. I stood on the log and addressed the crowd, explaining the situation about the different unions and the electrician's request to return to work. I told them that as the EBA did not affect them, the electricians should be thanked for their support, as they had not returned to work for a length of time in order to support us. I stood on the log and thanked them and when I started to clap, the whole crowd applauded in a gesture of gratitude and nearly all voted to let them back to work. Common sense and respect had prevailed. Over the entire strike period and picket line occupation, nearly all the workers showed respect for one another when they were in discussion, whether in disagreement or agreement about action, and we had a consensus attitude towards the issues. Our motto was: **United we stand, divided we fall.**

However, not long after we had made an agreement for a more realistic pay increase and conditions through enterprise bargaining and had returned to work, a union official visited the site and held a stop work meeting. He was on the soap box, ranting and raving over an instance at another mill. Then he conveniently took a telephone call and told us, "They have gone out on strike, we must back them." He called for a show of hands, and to my amazement, most voted to go out on strike in support of another mill with no discussion amongst the members. These were just bully boy tactics and I believe nearly all who had voted were not sure of the true reasons that they had voted to go out over. I had had enough of the union movement at that stage and, more to the point, I had had enough of working for others. It would not be long before I was to build my own timber mill and employ my own work force, running the operation with simple common sense. One of the main lessons I learned was that there is always master-servant relationship. That is the way it has been in all employment situations since day dot. A master pays you for serving him. I then made a decision to concentrate on my own business and not be a servant at all.

- *Three Days In The Snow* -

During the industrial action at Tumbarumba, I had planned to do a three day ski trip with Mick, from Mt Selwyn ski resort to the Happy Jack Plain, then to the upper reaches to the Tumut River and back. We had a good fall of snow and left the Mt Selwyn area late in the afternoon. On these trips with overnight stays provisions for three days were carried, so both our packs were fairly loaded. We planned to camp at the old cattleman huts. The first one was "Happy's" which is on the northern section of Happy Jack's Plain. I had been there on horseback in the summer months on a three day trek from Kiandra towards Wangarra. We skied past "Yan's slip rails": these were a post and rail gate made of snow gum trees, adzed by hand by a well known bullock driver named Tom Yan many years ago and, remarkably, still there. We skied past the Broken Dam Hut area and Nine Mile Diggings. From there, we headed south, down what is called Arsenic Ridge and would come onto Happy's Hut from the north west side. Night comes quickly in the mountains during winter but we were blessed with a full moon so we could see while skiing at night. As we skied south over the snow covered high plains the snow became iced over, and the wind during the day had made the skiing difficult. We were skiing over literally corrugated snow. By the time we arrived at Arsenic Ridge we were exhausted. Due to the heavily timbered ridge, we then had to remove our skis and descend. It had now become very dark, due to the cover of snow gums shading the full moon that had previously been giving us light. Our feet broke through the snow and we fell into it up to our waists. With our packs on our backs and carrying our skis over our shoulders, the whole night skiing adventure became a concern. Mick lost his balance and fell, breaking a stock [ski pole] in his attempt to save himself. By the time we arrived below Arsenic Ridge we were both completely exhausted. Mick said he did not know if he could keep going, and at every place on the plain that I thought I could see the hut turned out to be just shadows in the night. I was starting to become worried as we both were now extremely cold. Then all of a sudden it appeared: Happy's Hut. It was one of the more worse-forwear huts in the area, but to us it was better than the Hilton.

In a few minutes we had a roaring fire going and cooked up a feed and dried off, with the assistance of a bit of carefully carried port.

The next day we explored Happy Jack Plains. We skied over to the next hut, "Brookes". In my opinion it was the best of the mountain huts, with large boulders for the doorway, a great fireplace and nearly draft free. Built entirely of corrugated iron, it also had a spring close by for water. Obtaining water in the snow would be sometimes an event in itself, as one would have to lower a pot through the snow down to the spring outlet. With our packs stored in the hut, we would ski out for the day and find some great ski runs scattered over an endless snow plain. After spending a couple of days in the area we headed back via a different route on the western side of Brooke's Hut, then went straight north to the Nine Mile Diggings. This was the site of extensive gold mining in the 1860's and even in the snow, 100 years later, you can still see the scarred earth. Of all the ski trips I did over the years I believe that these three days in the snow were the best, as in the snowy conditions all of our bush skills were put to the test.

- My Second Property -

At the beginning of 1998, I was keen to acquire my second property. McPherson Plains, a high country block of 500 acres with the old original homestead, came on the market. I spent several weeks negotiating to buy this property, planning to run cattle there in the summer months as well as incorporate it into my adventure trekking business. I put pen to paper and worked out a way I could buy it on a vendor term agreement. Expressing interest about purchasing on vendor terms, I arranged to utilise equity from Wangarra to pay for the initial deposit. I would pay the vendor over a three year period and receive the total of three titles one at a time, as a set value was placed on the titles on a per acre basis. After a long period of negotiations, we came to an agreement via a third party, a local stock agent whom the vendor insisted represent him. All of a sudden he pulled out of the deal. What's meant to be is meant to be. That was the attitude I developed and still have in regard to property purchasing. I always try to create a win-win situation, but sometimes situations arise when you are forced to walk away from a deal even if you had your heart set on it. Remove the emotions from property negotiating.

At this time Darren Hartnett, the general manager of Tumbarumba shire, had bought some country close to the Murray River and subdivided the block. He had also moved to Albury and so asked me if I would show potential buyers around his property. He emphasized, "Al, you have the gift of the gab when it comes to property; it's what you know best." I did show people around once or twice, but my work commitment did not allow me to be able to make a sale on his behalf. Although the Macpherson Plains deal and selling Hartnett's property were not successful, the year of 1998 would be the turning point for my business ventures.

Malcolm Reid, a mate of mine and owner of 'Maragle Park' (a property of nearly 5,000 acres east of my home) had confided in me regarding a situation he and his wife Karen were in. They, like most people in rural Australia, had experienced hard times on the land with poor cattle prices and a small timber mill that unfortunately had became a liability. They were hit with high interest rates and, as a means to cover the interest payments, entered into a lease agreement with a person who literally walked up and knocked at the door. With several hundred head of cattle and horses, this person and his family had moved onto the 5,000 acre property, home to the Reid family since the 1880's, and then decided not to pay his agreed price. In fact he decided not to pay at all. Why? one would ask. Well you see, this joker had a history of doing this kind of thing. He would literally squat on someone else's property under some dodgy lease agreement, which was all under a trust structure and therefore making him unaccountable. In vain the Reid family tried every means to get this person off their property but it was to no avail. The mortgagee then issued court proceedings against the Reid's as they had defaulted due to the squatter refusing to pay the lease as well as refusing to leave. Mal was looking to lose his entire property. They tried appealing to various government bodies to assist them, but due to the large number of livestock and the bush lawyer's way of ripping off others under the trust structure, it was a legal nightmare.

Mal had told me that he needed to sell a couple of his titles quickly. I had available equity on an open line of credit from my property 'Wangarra' at the time due to the McPherson Plains deal falling through. Now there was an urgent situation. Mal stated a price and I accepted. The terms were discussed over a cup of tea and the deal sealed with the shake of a hand. Mal, like anyone whom I consider as a mate, had the **two ingredients that make for friendship: integrity and**

loyalty. Nothing matters after that. Over the next few years, Mal and I would make several business deals, all on the shake of a hand. **It is better to deal with an honest man with the shake of a hand than to sign a contract with a crook.** Part of the agreement was that I would take possession of the property. Then we discovered that the squatter had placed a caveat on the property, making it impossible for us to settle. I contacted the mortgagee who was the owner and director of his own finance company and tried to discuss the purchase of part of the property. He did not want to assist, saying "You cannot purchase a property from the Reid's. I am having them evicted from their property and there are now court proceedings to have them evicted." After a week of lengthy telephone conversations, I explained to the mortgagee that the vendor and I had an agreement and I had taken possession of the property, and that there was no reason why he should not allow this settlement to take place as it was in the best interest of all, including himself. After several telephone conferences, it was agreed by the mortgagee to allow this transaction to go through but there was still one hurdle: the squatter who had the caveat.

The squatter confronted me one day in the Maragle Valley and stated many things concerning his arrangement with the Reid family that I knew were not true. As I had been shown all the signed documentation concerning the lease, I quickly replied that Malcolm Reid was a mate of mine and that I had now purchased the property from him. I said, "The caveat you have on the entire property now involves me,' and in particular words told him that I was not happy about it.

With Mal Reid's blessings, I mustered the property with my horse and dog and yarded all the squatter's cattle and then, for some unknown reason, the squatter removed the caveat. Court action by the mortgagee was withdrawn against the

Reid's. We then were able to settle on the 456 acres and the Reid's refinanced. All this happened over a six month period.

- Trade Cattle -

1998 was the worst drought in fifteen years so I decided to have a punt on the cattle market. I contacted my local stock agent and asked him to source some cattle. The plan was to pick up cheap Angus cow and calf units, walk them up to the mountains on the forest property and hope the hell to get rains prior to the onset of the winter weather. Then if all went to plan, the cattle would be worth 200% more than what I paid for them and I would have a nice breeding herd. If we didn't get the break in the weather, I would then muster the cattle before the first frost of winter and draft off the calves, keeping all the weaners; as it is easier for a young animal to carry through the winter in a drought than to try to keep alive a cow that was in calf again. So plan B was to off load the cows if the drought did not break. He who fails to plan plans to fail. That means keep to the plan unless a better alternative comes along. I was about to learn this the hard way.

I thought we could pick up cow and calf units for under $300 but my agent believed it was impossible. At the Wodonga yards in the coming week, there were several pens out of the Riverina for offer that were drought affected. I attended the sale with him and found that the condition of the cows and the calves at foot was good. The bidding started and I would nudge my agent in the ribs when I wanted him to bid. I bought the first few pens of top cows and calves, 120 in total, all well under the $300 per head. The next day they arrived by 'B-Double', a truck made up of two decks and trailer. I had arranged for a drop down side on the truck so I could off load them on the road *Elliot Way+ then walk them up Allawah Road to 'Wangarra'. But the whole cattle trade turned into a disaster as soon as the truck arrived. It arrived a day late and did not have a drop down side, so the driver had to back up onto an embankment of the Tooma and Elliot Way. Some of the cows were down inside the truck when it arrived. I was there on my horse Red Gum, and the first beast out went down between the back of the truck and embankment. Then one of the other cows that had been down stood up and charged out of the truck. She was very cranky and charged me on my horse, ramming Red Gum under her belly. In vain, I tried to ride out Red Gum's bucks, at the same time cracking my whip to get the mad cow away. Finally they all calmed down but I lost the mad cow due to 'transit tetney', a condition caused by the stress of travelling.

The next day, I walked the mob up into the mountains, taking them through Moody's Hill, a bit of stringy bark hill country. At one stage they broke away and I had to crash through the bush after them as they headed down a wallaby trail. It is always difficult buying cattle from station country and bringing them to a new area. Once I was below the hill, I started counting and discovered I was one cow and calf short. I found the cow at a later date, after she had spent weeks in the bush, unfortunately coming out in much worse condition than when she went in.

I went through two horses, having to exchange one for the other as they were exhausted from all the work. What should have been a quick droving trip into the mountains turned into a huge ordeal but that is the price you pay buying trade cattle from far away that were probably very rarely handled. It was March when I took them up, and then I waited for a break in the weather that never came.

The first winter frosts arrived early and were more fierce than expected. As soon as the frost hit mountain grasses, the cattle might as well be eating bark, as the frost burns out all the nutrition from the bush feed. It now was time to put plan B into action: to muster and off load most of the females. As it had been many weeks since I brought them into the mountains. I had arranged for my agent to meet me at Reid's yards about 5 km from the property that we referred to as "Macleod's Run". I had started the cattle on a urea/molasses preparation that they licked from a drum full of the watered down mix. This was a way of supplementing protein when there was insufficient protein in the available grasses.

I had lost a couple of cows in the bogs up on the run and when I had gathered them all into one area and bought them along the track to Reid's yards, another cow went into the bog. So there I was, in the bog with her, trying to drag her to her feet. She never got out and I lost her too. I kept calcium packs to inject cows in the side of the neck, a treatment that gives them the extra energy to get them back on their feet. But again to no avail. Once I had the mob drafted my agent was in my ear, saying the cow market had collapsed and that I would be better offloading the weaners and keeping the cows. At this stage being stressed over losing a few cows I did not keep to my plan and foolishly took the advice of the agent. This was my fault entirely, and the next day at the Wagga Wagga sale yard, I received between $68 to $142 for the weaners and they all went to 'back grounders' *cattlemen who grow out weaners to a heavy weight] in S.A.. All the weaners were in reasonable condition, it was just a terrible market. I returned to the females, having to shoot a couple more cows that had gone down and feed the rest through the winter.

I had arranged for a semi trailer of hay from out west that I bought sight unseen and the driver was two days late arriving. Then the rains came with the snow but they were too late, as the ground was now too cold to grow any feed whatsoever. The semi driver got bogged trying to drive up the road so with the help of neighbours, we carted the large square bales in the backs of our utes to my property where we covered them with tarps. The next day, when I headed up to feed the stock with the hay, I discovered I had been had as it had been damaged by water in the past and was mouldy. There was nothing I could do but to make do with what I had and continue the long feeding program through winter.

- Buster on Brum Run -

The run had a mob of brumbies on it, and they where getting into the cattle feed, and also the urea/molasses mix. However urea is only good for ruminants as a one stomached animal like a horse will die from eating it.

I arranged an old style 'brum run' where several of us on horseback would chase the horses out of the range and into the small valley of the Run and into an open paddock. Mal Reid would be there with his motor bike and tail [ride behind] by then the exhausted horses while we rested up our mounts and ourselves. Then we would run the wild horses into the yards. Well, that was the plan and it was more for a bit of fun than anything else. Jeff Mullenger was up from Melbourne and Barry Patton my neighbour and his mate Clint. Jacqueline Dawson stayed with Brandon and the kids at the camp. There was a bit of snow about on the higher areas and so we quickly tracked them down and off they took. We had two gate openings about 2 kilometres apart that we hoped to drive them through. They galloped along the fence at the top of the range and just ran past the first gate and down the hill towards the second gate. However the mob of brumbies would not go through that gate; they stood and snorted then took off in the opposite direction. The rest of the riders stayed put but my adrenalin was taking over again and as I was on one of my new blood horses,

High Plains, I took off in pursuit. They were heading through a heavily forested part and I was able to make up ground, galloping along the track and cracking my stock whip in an attempt to wheel them to the right and circle them back to the gateway where the others were. As I got to the leader of the mob, I tried to fit between a couple of peppermint trees and all of a sudden High Plains collected himself against the side of a dead tree. The off side of him hit the tree with my leg in between. I heard a 'POP' as my femur literally snapped in two, the smashed leg lifting up and coming over to the right hand side of my body. At this stage I was lying on the ground with High Plains stumbling back to his feet. There was not a hope in hell I would get back on mine. Jacqueline Dawson had heard the crash at the camp and thought the worst, but stayed with my son Brandon while the rest of the riders gathered around me. It was a clean break but the bone needed to be placed back in position. The only way this could be done was if someone grabbed hold of my leg and pulled it straight back into line. The cramps and pain were setting in but I told Barry **"grab hold of the leg, and bloody straighten the thing."** I was looking at Mal Reid's face while Barry pulled on the leg while I leaned back to assist in straightening it. Mal gave a horrified look and turned his face away while the leg was placed back into some sort of shape.

I was carted out of the mountains on an old door that was used on the feed vehicle to keep loose hay together. Then they carried me in the back of the vehicle and drove for several kilometres to where the ambulance was waiting. It was a painful ride and I recited poetry to try and keep the thought of the pain away. There was no morphine in the ambulance and I only received pain relief when I got to the Tumbarumba hospital, where Dr. Vetanayagan pumped pain killer into me. Then I was off to the Wagga Wagga Base Hospital where they operated, placing a plate on my femur and attaching it by drilling several bolts through the bone. That was the end of my gung ho attitude. In fact, I was lucky that I had not experienced worse accidents over the years. I now had a son to think about so taking risks like that came to an end. Over the years I experienced lots of busters and injured my ribs, collar bone, femur, knee, ankles, wrist, fingers and knuckles. I also dislocated my shoulder more times than I can remember. **I was immune to fear, blind to failure.**

CHAPTER NINE
1998 – 2000

A PESSIMIST SEES DIFFICULTY IN EVERY OPPORTUNITY; AN OPTIMIST SEES OPPORTUNITY IN EVERY DIFFICULTY

- Development of a Timber Mill -

Once I was discharged from the hospital and was sitting at home with a broken leg, I realized that it would be a considerable period of time before I was well enough to work. I contacted my health insurance and discovered that I was not covered for a broken leg. When I re-financed to buy the second property with Westpac bank (with whom I was also mortgaged) they requested I update my insurance policy. I did and although the previous insurance policy had covered a broken leg, the new policy did not. Things were looking grim. It was the biggest snow fall in nine years and at one stage there was snow from the mountains to the Hume Highway. Feeding the cattle had become an extremely difficult task and the continued loss of cattle in the winter drought was taking a heavy toll on me. I was not sure how I would survive this situation financially. To make things worse, my old faithful mate Clancy was run over by a visitor who was reversing his car in the front garden, which injured him badly. Due to being deaf and full of arthritis he just had no way of seeing the car. I knew I had to put my old mate down. It was the hardest thing I have ever done in my life. He had been with me for fourteen years and travelled all over the continent with me. I never drink alcohol while using a firearm, but I downed a bottle of whisky as I sat with him on the veranda in the cold dark of night, building up the courage to put my old mate down. With an enormous amount of hesitation, I did it; and Brandon and I buried him under a tree on a hill overlooking the mountains at 'Wangarra'.

During my recovery from the operation, I was visited by many people. My mother came up from Melbourne and assisted in running of the place. Roy Blake, a well known stockman, visited me and would yarn about his former days working in the mountains. Fifty years prior to my time, Roy was mustering large mobs of sheep and cattle in the mountains and so was not short of a good yarn. He would tell me of the time he was mustering on Macpherson Plains and realized he had lost his watch. The feller riding next to him said, "Don't worry about that; you might find it this time next year." Anyway, twelve months came and went and Roy was back in the mountains mustering again alongside the same feller. Then suddenly Roy yelled "There she is!" and jumps off his horse and picks up the watch. The other feller says, "Does it work?" and Roy says, "It does! What's the time?" The other feller looks at his watch and says, "Three o'clock." And Roy says, "Fancy that, it has not missed a beat." Now this other feller must have been a bit suspicious of Roy's comments and said, "How could that be so? You need to wind the thing up every day and it has been here for a year and right through winter." Roy said, "You see that old ant trail? Well those buggers have been walking over the winder of the watch every day for the last year and kept the time up." With that, old Roy would laugh and start another yarn about his days in the mountains. Another story was about chasing bucks [wild horses] in country south of the Maragle Range, carrying a bottle of rum. After a tiring gallop, the few riders sat by a small creek that was just trickling out over a rocky surface and Roy brought out the bottle of rum. Then they realized they did not have any pannikans [cups]. So Roy told them all to put their snouts [mouths] to the tiny trickle of water flowing out of the spring, and then poured the bottle of rum upstream to them. As it ran down into the water and over the rock, he yelled, "Now drink up boys!" and they did.

One great thing about a desperate situation is that your mind goes into overdrive, and you come up with ideas and take actions that you might otherwise not attempt. This has been the case with most situations I have been in life. **Turn a negative situation into a positive one.** In this particular case, I wondered how on earth I was going to turn this disaster into anything positive; I had a broken leg, no income and had lost a lot of cattle due to drought and bad hay and the urea mix. Although the urea and molasses protein supplement mix was below recommendation, a few animals had been accidently poisoned. I had just finished reading one of my many books, an autobiography of a drover, and he had said, **"One who has never experienced anxiety, despair and failure will never succeed in life. They will be shackled by fear alone. Fear creates a stable work force but never a happy one."** This was so true. As with all the sayings I have taken on board in life, this – plus the fact I was desperate - was all I needed to turn things around.

During my time working at Boral timber, there arose a huge problem: production was slowed down due to the lack of dry mill battens [stickers], a specially cut to size piece of timber that is placed between boards to dry the timber in the kilns. The timber mill had by then become one of the largest mills in the southern hemisphere, and the price of stopping production due to the lack of stickers was extremely costly to the company. As well as this, there were thousands of cubic meters of hard wood timber taking up many acres of the mill site, and yet the site was now a pine only mill. There was no way of 'value adding' *taking a basic product and transform it into something more useful in a specific way] the hardwood as the mill now was designed for soft wood. I had discussed this situation with the management for a long period of time, but any ideas I or others working there had fell on deaf ears. This is the way with a master-servant relationship. Ian Snowden was appointed as a new manager for the green mill, and he had been in the timber game all his life and had common sense. We had discussed the idea that all this stock should be value added, and the making of stickers should be out sourced. Now was the time for me to take action and I put together a feasibility study. I planned to build an entire timber mill on my free hold property and produce dry mill battens as well as value adding other types of timber that had been placed aside. It was common knowledge that the cost per batten was $1.50 when under Dunlop Pacific; yet when Boral took over, the cost was $1.35. That was still expensive and production stopped due to the lack of available battens. I believed I could manufacture the battens at a much cheaper cost and guarantee they would not run out. I would also mostly use their de-valued timber (the stocks of hardwood), thus producing a batten that would last longer and therefore reduce costs further. A meeting was arranged with the management and we discussed the whole idea of a timber mill on my property using value added timber from Boral. There was no cost to Boral whatsoever, and I was able to pick up some old saws from Boral that had scrap value only and build the timber mill on my own. I would employ my own people and have the timber freighted to my property by private freight carriers. The management of the Tumbarumba mill got the go ahead by Boral, and I negotiated a price of $0.70 cents a batten, plus other rates for different types of value added timber, such as floor boards, stud and webbing, etc.

I employed Gaven Willis, who had worked with me at the timber mill a few years prior. We had become mates and he was having a tough time with his cattle property and needed some off-farm income. I also employed Phil Cussons, who was my foreman at the Boral timber mill, and also a neighbour. An ex bull rodeo rider, saddler and stockman, he lived on his cattle and horse property but had left the mill due to the bureaucratic system there. I knew and trusted both of these men. With the snow still lying on the ground, we started building the mill with four upright poles made of stringy bark trees with a tarp over the top for shelter. I had gravel delivered and laid for the floor, and along the track in areas to get trucks in and out. I had to hire a fork lift, as I had limited capital. In fact, I hardly had any capital at all and relied on an agreement with Boral to be paid as soon as I invoiced them. I hired a huge 80 kva generator from Wrek Air, a machinery lease company. We needed this grunt for a multi saw for the batten manufacture. As with all businesses, it took some time to sort out the start up bugs. I was still on crutches and would sit on a 44 gallon drum (as it allowed me to roll slightly) and push timber through to whoever ran the saws. The other person stacked and strapped packs, ready to be invoiced out. I had put in a development application to the council and had contended with a few minor conditions. Then I had problems with some absentee land holders who complained about the prospect of a timber mill creating noise problems. I had to have an acoustic report prepared to prove you could not hear – or even see - the mill from any of the boundaries of the property. I was also required to maintain the road at my own expense which I did.

The mill was inspected by a representative of the council, a locum who was there on a temporary basis. After a friendly visit, I received a notice in the mail requesting I close down the mill due to the fact that I was not complying with the council's conditions. It was alleged that I did not have a fire break around the timber mill. The fact that it was in the middle of a grazed down paddock covered in green grass, and was impossible for any fire to get going due to conditions being wet with the odd snow falling never mattered. They also alleged that I did not have a registered business name and that a Work Cover Certification should apply.

I appeared at the local council meeting and stated my disgust over the notice to close the mill. The reasons behind the notice were absurd. Grazed down wet green grass is a fire break. The department of fair trading only requires a registered name if you use another name different to your own. For instance, I was A. J. MacLeod - that was my name and trading name and had been for years. It was not a legal requirement to have it registered. As for a work cover certification at a cost of thousands of dollars; I did not see why a local government would require this, as all my employees were insured under work cover and all machinery and safety procedures complied with work cover. I also told them that if I was not allowed to commence operation of the timber mill by the morning, I would have no alternative but to tell the several people who were now employed by me that they did not have jobs. I explained that this had hardship would carry on to their families, so dozens of people would be affected if the mill was going to cease. It would be fair to say Boral timber would then outsource their timber to be value added outside the community.

Within an hour the councillors had approved the continuation of my timber mill and I also was able to get the road to the mill into the council maintenance program. All this happened to the dismay of the locum from Sydney who had created this whole situation. Thank God for the local council representatives. This is the reason for local government: to represent the best interests of the community. It amazes me the amount of stories from people in business about dealing with bureaucracy and red tape, which in a lot of instances, destroys people's businesses simply due to some upstart trying to justify their own existence.

As the mill became more profitable, we developed the site into separate working areas. The first was a large trucking bay where all the timber would be off loaded, ready to be value added. The timber was placed onto large logs by a fork lift where the straps were cut and the timber physically pushed onto rollers and docked by a saw. Another person then would place the pieces into a stack and strap and wrap them in plastic before being sent out. We prepared timber for the multi saw in this area, and also docked for webbing or studs. The other area also had a docking saw, but on the other end of the docker there was a large multi saw whereby several battens would be created when timber pieces were pushed through. We would then stack the timber into a pack of hundreds of battens. All packs of timber where invoiced with the precise cubic meter recorded, or in the case of the packs of battens, the precise number. There was a dispatch area where the timber was loaded and trucked out, with a truck hired full time to load several times a day.

When the public liability insurance became unavailable to horse riding operations, my horse riding operation came to an end. The change became a nightmare for businesses across Australia that operated either horse, rope or water activities. It meant that 'Wangarra High Country Retreat' had to close after five years of guiding hundreds of people into the high country. I had ridden Redgum for an estimated 5,000 kilometres. But now this timber mill was an extremely viable business. On the days we were not cutting timber, the last thing I wished to do was to take people out for less pay than what I made running the timber mill. In fact, taking a brief look at the return on the timber mill: if I sold dry mill battens at $0.70 cents, and produced 4000 battens a day, that was $2,800 a day. Not bad money in anyone's language.

In the beginning, we towed the fork lifts out of wet bogs with our 4x4 vehicles. As the mill became larger we had an all-weather gravel road built through the property to the mill, and a large gravel base of about an acre at the main area of the site with cement floors, and canopies overhead that protected us from the weather. Electricians wired up the site so we could work after dark. We made up large sawdust bins with exhaust fans to take the dust from the work areas. I arranged for the saws to be sharpened by a crowd from Wagga and they were freighted out every week. The machinery repair work shop was at home in the converted saddle shed. I picked up machinery everywhere, from the local area to Sydney, not to mention at the odd clearing sale.

Two 4 x 4 vehicles that I had used on the farm were now solely used for taking away timber cuttings. We disposed of the off cuts by placing them up against old logs at Wangarra, and they kept a lot of families warm during the winter, as the lengths of hardwood were great for fire places. The bush accommodation hut had now become the work hut where we had the warmth of the pot belly stove and cooking facilities for lunch, with siestas on the bunks afterwards. During my union delegate days at Boral, I arranged a nine day fortnight after much negotiating. In this way, everyone who worked on the night shift was able to have a long weekend every fortnight by increasing their hours during the days. This worked well, as productivity increased, absenteeism was reduced and the plants cost was reduced. The employees cost was down as well, with one less day a fortnight to drive to work. From day one at my mill, we had a four day week with every weekend a long weekend. This gave me time for any repairs or upgrades if needed. The office was at home, 500 meters from the mill site. I was in daily contact with Sid Davey, the sales representative at Boral timber. The two of us arranged the whole supply of timber to Boral's site, as well as stud and webbing being trucked interstate. I was also asked to supply dry mill battens to Boral's second largest mill at Oberon. From then on the mill was a much larger concern. In one week, nine people were turning out over 200 tonnes of tim-

ber. Besides Gaven Willis and Phil Cussons, who were there from the start to the end, many others were employed over the two year period. In total, thirteen people worked there and after cut out on a Friday night, I would put on a few beers and we would all sit around a large fire and yarn about the week's event. There was great comradeship. I also started to develop the 456 acre forest block I had bought from the Reid's. I hired a bulldozer from Mal Reid and spent days clearing fence lines. When there were no timber orders, I fenced the bush property with Gaven and Phil. During this time, I employed a builder to start work on renovating the house. A property close to the home property came on the market, so I negotiated a price and had my bank manager come out to inspect the property as well as see the timber mill. He stood there and could not believe this industrial development that had been financed without the assistance of the banks. We discussed the financing of the property on the market and after several telephone conversations with the owner, an agreement on price was established. The next day I received a telephone call from the vendor who stated that there was another party willing to buy. He wanted the first one to sign a deal to get the property, saying that he had an obligation to an agent who had brought in a second buyer. I explained that we had an agreement on the purchase and the price and that the price was for now only. **I was not in the habit of playing second fiddle to anyone**, especially after we had agreed on the sale. The sale went through to the other party and I went ahead to develop the other properties further. A month later, I received another telephone call from the vendor, asking if I was still interested in the property as his deal had fallen through. I told him that I was, but now the price would be $40,000 less as the funds I had arranged to buy the property had been utilized in other areas. No deal was agreed to, and as it turned out once again it was not meant to be.

There came a new fear that Boral could close down their Tumbarumba facility. Another concern was over a new manager at the Tumbarumba plant. Since he had started, I had nothing but problems with having to chase money. We had an arrangement of 'payment once invoice received', but when the new manager started, there was call after call trying to get payment, and excuse after excuse blaming accounting departments. I believed it was all deliberate. I would have several invoices in and still be waiting on payment while I was covering all the costs with an open line of credit on the property. There were also other problems with the new manager involving the docking of timber. He notified me that he believed that the price I was charging for the docked timber was not viable for the company. I did not agree with this at all, and in fact I believed it was just a way for him to try to screw me over the price. There had been many occasions when he had tried to pull these types of stunts on me. I put my suspicions to the test and worked out the costs I had been charging Boral. I had charged about $75 dollars an hour for docking; and when equated to a lineal meter, it came out around $0.13 cents per lineal meter. I responded to his claim by giving him a price per lineal meter and I quoted them $0.19 cents. My quote was quickly accepted by him. It was hard to comprehend. There were other worries also. I had been informed by other sources within the company that Boral now were looking towards sheltered workshops to value add their timber. These were government subsidized and so were able to have their products value added at a very low cost. It would be totally impossible for any business like mine to compete with this; most of these sheltered workshops were running at a loss and large corporate companies like Boral would look at them as a means to reduce costs, but in the process destroy existing businesses. I held a meeting at my house with this manager and was told that Boral would continue to use my business. This was pure CRAP, as I received information after our meeting that the manager himself was arranging to undercut my operations, and had met with sheltered work shops prior to our meeting.

- Evils of the Family Law Court -

By January 2000, my marriage was over. I felt that I had no support throughout our entire relationship and I felt like I was treated like a stranger in my own home, by my wife, and also by her daughters from her previous marriage. I felt condemned by them when I entered into any of my business arrangements; and when things went wrong, as they do, I felt condemned for having a go. But when things went well and the money was rolling in, there was no 'well done' attitude over that success. Criticism is all I felt in the relationship, and it seemed she had a jealous negative nature towards anyone who had accomplished things in life. I have an overly positive attitude that sometimes gets me in tight situations, so these two opposites certainly clashed. In the late spring of 1999, we had both entered into an endurance ride and decided to take a couple of horses along. I completed the ride in good time and was vetted in. I was still recovering from my accident at the time and received a trophy and a round of applause from other competitors. Unfortunately my wife did not complete the ride and was vetted out. Also unfortunately for me, I was criticized for this and abused for entering the competition and was told "You always take the limelight!" That was one of many incidents of this kind and I could not continue this relationship any more. After trying to talk things out over a period of time, I told her that I was thinking of a divorce. I did try again to work things out for the sake of my son but I found it impossible, and we separated in January of 2000.

We had an arrangement that our son Brandon would live one week with her and the next week with me. We tried to agree on a property settlement, it being decided that I would remain at 'Wangarra' due to the fact I had owned it prior to meeting her and my mill was on the property. She had her own job working at the vineyard and she would move to town. She employed a solicitor but I did not get any legal representation at this stage, trying in vain to come to an amicable arrangement on a property settlement instead. But every time we came to an agreement, she would change her mind. When the day came for her move to town, it became a mad frenzy. She abused me in front of the children, and she encouraged her two girls to strip the house of items and told them not to speak to me. It was an appalling situation. But to be totally honest, it was a huge relief when I woke up the next morning. After she shifted into town with her two girls, Brandon stayed with me. Then it came to my attention that there was $1,000 being drawn every day from the business account via an ATM. That money was ear marked for the employees' superannuation and this had been going on for many days. I had no alternative but to cancel the re-draw. As a result, I was limited in obtaining funds needed for the running of the business. I rang my son while he was staying with his mother, only to be denied the right to speak to him. Sadly, this horrible game was to last many years. I would be continually abused during telephone calls and she demanded that I pay her a lump sum of $116,000, buy her a house in town plus give her the car. It all became a crazy situation. When I exercised my right to contact Brandon by telephone, I was threatened with a restraining order against me. For what reason, it was beyond me. Once while picking up my son from school at our arranged time, Brandon was extremely upset and told me his mother had told him not to go with me. Now I was in a situation that I had never been in before, torn between the love I had for my son and trying to keep my little boy's happiness intact. I received mail from an agency called Child Support, stating that my son lived with his mother 100% of the time yet this was not the case, as we had a 50/50 agreement. This was corrected but unfortunately within a short time even that agreement was terminated by the other party. It seemed like that at every moment there would be situations that would upset my son. Once while in town, my son tried to walk over to me while I was at the Post Office, only to be held back by his mother and told not to go to me. It was all extremely upsetting for him. If there was a time arranged for a pick up and her two girls were in the car, she would order them not to look at me. Then I witnessed my son and his mother drive straight past my property to stay with a neighbour, whom I knew very well, on his holiday property. He was married and his wife had just given birth and so that was the end of that marriage too. My son informed me that he was shown a photo of this new baby and was told by his mother: this is your new brother. It was all becoming bizarre to say the least and all of this took place within weeks of us separating.

In February, I had a sheriff serve me with an application by my son's mother for full custody of Brandon. I sought legal advice and was told by a family law solicitor that it would be highly unlikely a court would allow me full custody. After I had become familiar with a lot of the legalities of the family law court, I realized that it was an evil system, allowing whoever had custody of the child to win the biggest percent of the asset pool. I could not believe that children could be used as pawns by parents to obtain a financial gain, or that solicitors could fight for children to live with one parent in order to reap the rewards of the asset pool themselves. In my case, I could not see a reason why parents could not raise a child in a 50/50 living arrangement. But as I have been told by legal representativ'e and there were several over the next two years, that on many occasions the courts may not allow this if there are siblings, as they would want to keep the children together on a full time basis. Usually if the siblings are from a previous relationship then it is extremely difficult for the other parent to win full custody or even a 50/50 arrangement. The usual outcome would be an 'every second weekend' visitation. Once the child's arrangements have been established then the property settlement comes into play, and that is on a NEEDS VERSUS CONTRIBUTION basis. So need usually won over contribution, and although I had contributed the most towards the family pool, I was looking at a 70/30 deal, or in a worse case, 80/20.

During this whole ordeal the situation at the timber mill had become rocky, as Boral was limiting our timber supply. I was forced to put off most of the people I had employed and did not do any of the hands-on work myself, in order to leave work for Gaven and Phil as I felt ethically obliged to. Besides the worries of the pending family law court, I was frantically trying to come up with a market that we could get into to keep the mill going if Boral cut us out of operation. I looked at everything, from surveyor's pegs to tomato stakes, but all to no avail. In July 2000, I was told by the manager of the Tumbarumba site that he had engaged a sheltered work shop who could produce stickers at $90 per

1400 pieces; 6 cents each. As for all the other types of timber we were value adding for them, it had been given to other government subsidized businesses. This great business of mine was no longer. No income, court proceedings against me plus the legal costs, denied the right to raise my son, and a sell off of the assets with a best case 70/30 split scenario. I was in trouble again and it all took a big toll on me. How the hell could I turn this negative situation to a positive one? At this stage there had been some interim orders given whereby I had some of the weekends with Brandon. I sat up there on my property looking over the place where I had created three business operations, a home and two agricultural properties. Now everything was to be taken from me and the hard reality set in. What was it all for? How could it be that some people in society were legally able to destroy others lives with the stroke of a pen? Nothing at that point in my life seemed right, but I knew I had to stay strong, if not for myself, then for my son.

- Sales Consulting -

After a few weeks of finalizing the closure of the mill, I sent my cattle off to winter at Willigobung, turned my horses out over one hundred acres and went to Melbourne. I had to create an income and only returned for the weekend access with my son. On some occasions, I would drive the 500 kilometres out to Tumbarumba and return to Melbourne that night; spending the weekend showing Brandon what the city had to offer then returning him and driving back to Melbourne the same night: in total of 2000 kilometres and 22 hours of driving. As soon as I arrived in Melbourne I went out to find an income to survive and the next 10 months I worked for several companies in sales consulting work. I put together a résumé and applied for sales positions, and after several interviews I had several jobs to choose from, all on a commission basis. I knocked back a real estate position - which I later regretted - and took up the role of a sales consultant for a building company based in Footscray. It was a family concern that designed and built outdoor extensions and electrically operated 'open and shut' roofing. The owner employed three new consultants and we were given various areas of Melbourne to work in. We were all promised 20 leads a week obtained by an advertising campaign and the receptionist was to hand out the leads. I followed up my leads by ringing the inquirer and making a home visit. The consultation involved measuring up areas of the back yards for the proposed extension, carport or open roof system to be installed then returning to the office with my drawings to work out the costs from the company's material lists. Then I would return to the property to try to sell the proposed building. It was an extremely hard product to sell as the finished price was always well above any other builders who quoted the job. Trying to sell a luxury item like an electrically operated roof system in a traditionally blue collar area of the western suburbs was challenging. I did get a job for several roof installations from a company that was building a mansion at Caulfield, but out of the promise of 20 leads a week, we were only getting two. The owner had also promised us all a retainer of $400 per week that would last for the first 12 weeks but this cut out before the end of the 12 weeks due to the poor performance of his marketing and a very low lead generation.

I quickly took up a second position, selling window shutter roller blinds at a business in a northern part of Melbourne. The receptionist would ring me with a lead and I would head out to measure and sell this product on the spot. I sold many of these window shutters and I realized that I was also getting a fast, first hand experience in different types of businesses; how they operated, their marketing systems and selling techniques. I found out what the purchase price, selling price and profit margins were and quickly identified what type of problems, if any, were within their operation. Over a ten month period, I was given positions in twelve different companies. A lot of the sale roles, such as in the roller shutter company, had a huge turnover of staff, as leads were not qualified before driving out to the clients house. Most people were just getting a quote due to the ridiculous sales claim: "No obligation quote". I met up with this younger feller who had a contract to sell air coolers. He had set up an office in Collingwood and was doing advertising from there. I agreed to sell his coolers and he supplied me leads and so I was selling this type of a home product to home owners again.

I became very eager to learn about the running of different businesses and so I went for an interview with a company that operated an employment agency. They operated their company from an office in North Melbourne and I became employed as their sales consultant with a retainer plus commission. My role was to be out on the road, creating meetings with groups of employers and supplying them with man power. The employment agency employed the staff and sent them on to work for various industries as casual employment. The company had been experiencing hard times and larger employment agencies had taken their past markets. I realized that this was not their main problem but rather the fact they were not finding any new markets. They just gave me a business card and expected me to find work. No documentation of who we were, no mission statements or any type of material that would get our foot in the door of a potential business or recruit a potential client, except for a piece of paper that outlined a few brief statements, and this ridiculous quote: *We endorse the old Japanese quote: "It is safest to employ honest men, even though they may not be the smartest."* No wonder their business was going backwards; to insult their workers as well as telling potential clients that they employ dills?

It was a very interesting industry. Once I had lined up a vacancy with a cabinet maker which may have led to a full time job. I pulled this feller out of the employment company's employment list who was qualified, and arranged a meeting in my office. He appeared one hour late and told me that the job would be difficult for him to get to. I quickly got on the telephone and had arranged the transport, so that he would catch the train and then two busses to the work place. It took a while before it all was arranged and after the morning's interview and creating a timetable and a great hourly rate of payment offered, this person said to me, "Now I do not think it is worth it". He was on unemployment benefits and did not mind his current situation.

During several telephone calls prior to our meeting, he had been requesting a job, but it turned out the dole was more important.

I created a mission statement for the company and wrote up a description of who we were within the company and outlined the different industries of experience; as nearly every industry was covered with experience from the existing staff. I believed this was necessary to get our foot in the door of different industries. I had lined up potential work for us in a large plastics manufacturing plant, but not being able to leave a prospectus in the form of documentation was crazy. I was assisted with creating a prospectus by another sales consultant who had been working with the company for years. She told me that her retainer stopped once I arrived. It was just a penny pinching way of reducing costs but I could not get the thought out of my head that the other consultants' retainer went to me, and I found it all too unfair. The company was owned by two directors whom I had regular contact with and it was in trouble. I tried to have the supporting documentation created quickly but one of them had no interest in it at all. In fact he stated, "Your personality and a business card is all you need." Well you can't get a farrier to shoe horses with no tools, and you won't get a salesperson to sell without documentation. I had no choice but to leave, and it was not long before the company was no longer in operation.

I was given a job as a mortgage broker, selling American financed residential home loans. It was alleged that other brokers selling the same product were receiving a 100k plus per year income. The mortgage consultant process was initiated by telemarketers ringing homes. They would tell a potential client that they had a new loan product on the market and if they were already mortgaged, the company might be able to save them thousands of dollars. So if they were interested, a meeting was set up and a mortgage broker would go to their homes and sit down and compare their existing mortgage to this new American product. The new loan would be an open line of credit and they would have their incomes going into a loan account, reducing the principle and the client would then be encouraged to use a credit card and pay it off before the 30 day interest free period ended. Over a period of time the result can be savings in the tens of thousand dollars. The brokerage fees worked out to $4,000 and the figure was placed onto the total loan. Although it would cost $4,000 clients saved much more over a period of time. After a full-on week of training up in the skyscrapers of the C.B.D., I decided to give this job a pass. Consultants were supposed to relate the whole selling system word to word and the company demanded that you repeated only what you have been told to say like a COCKATOO. The time demands were too rigid as I needed to be able to take time off to see my son when I wished; the reason why I was only working commission jobs. But at that stage I was gaining knowledge rapidly. I attended all the property seminars and listened to their spruiking about investments. If ever there was an area where the word 'wanker' can be applied, it was at some of these sales seminars. Some were great and informative but others were just rip-off schemes. There were many potential jobs in the sales world that I had to say 'thanks but no thanks' to, as they were just one big con. I have never been able to accept any type of lying or misleading ways, but my learning experience during this time was very rewarding.

Another sales job came up in the Richmond area. I read an advertisement for a sales consultant and met this joker, spruiking about how to make a fortune by selling alarm installations and back to base monitoring. I was not keen, but received a call the following afternoon from the manager of the security company who asked me in for a meeting. I met the owner who also worked from this warehouse type of complex that bordered a railway line. They asked me if I was interested in selling this back to base security system. The money they offered in the contract was too good to pass, as I could make a good commission by signing people up to having the teams install an alarm system. I would have to generate my own leads as well as employ people. I started advertising and at this stage set up an office at my mother's place in Keilor East. I employed another person who I had met while selling outdoor extensions. He had also been doing the rounds, selling different products free lance. I paid him a commission and he went out door knocking at business premises. I advertised extensively, from newspaper adverts to leaflet drops at people's homes. I even asked a newspaper to write up an article and briefly mention my own home invasion experience. I created a logo of two hands shaking, with the words: A. J. MACLEOD SALES CONSULTANCY.

As I was allowing myself to freelance any other products that came my way, I set up displays in large shopping complexes where I would pay the management to have a stand in the hallways. I would have advertisements about home break and enters and the alarm systems themselves, and then I would generate leads from these sources, following them up by inspecting their homes and advising the alarm systems that suited their needs. My advertisement featured packages from as little as $795, installed. I would get most orders for this amount, as the company made their money on the back to base monitoring contract that lasted a 36 month period. The first few weeks were fantastic. The money came in quickly, then all of a sudden, every where I looked there were alarm systems being advertised from petrol stations to super markets. Different companies had door knockers targeting every suburb in Melbourne. You could not turn on the television without being bombarded with advertising alarms. So I started to look around for another product to sell.

One of the jobs I took on was spruiking in shopping centres, standing there with a microphone telling people what they should buy. I worked at Myers in the C.B.D. during a Levis jeans sale. I would say: "Now come on ladies, check what we have for sale today: Levis jeans 500s, and guess what? They're now discounted, down to $$$ and while you're here, pick up these tops at $$$!" I could not believe how a mass of people would flock and grab clothes in a mad frenzy. It is amazing what a flashing red light does when someone is telling them about a bargain. I spruiked everything from clothing to shoes to books. I had regretted turning down the real estate position that was offered to me when I first came to Melbourne. Then I noticed an advert in the paper for a property sales consultant to sell rural properties. I finally was about to find the product that I was comfortable selling and that, for me, was PROPERTY.

CHAPTER TEN
2000 – 2002

FEAR IS TEMPORARY REGRET IS PERMANENT

- Family law Case-

During the ten month period following the shut down of the timber operation and me working in a variety of sales jobs, **life was not all beer and skittles**. In fact it was a very stressful time. The legal action and the process of being dragged through the family law courts and the separation from my son had become extremely painful to me, to say the least. During this time, I was also advised that Boral possibly had acted illegally in cutting me out of the business for the value adding timber. I was lead to believe there may be a legislative act that did not allow big business to use government subsidized industries, such as sheltered work shops, to be able to cut out existing businesses. I arranged a meeting with a solicitor in the C.B.D. of Melbourne who specialized in industrial legalities. After a lengthy meeting researching law books, we came to the conclusion that the only action I was able to take would be against the sheltered workshop and I was sure that was not going to happen. I did have a telephone conversation with the main representative of Boral timber, who told me that he and the company had enough of the timber industry and Tumbarumba. He said that the company just wanted to get out of Tumbarumba and were trying in vain to sell off the site. They had a potential buyer and wanted to throw the keys over the fence to him as soon as possible. As I have found over the years, the larger the company becomes the less personal they are, and sadly there comes a time when there seems to be no moral obligation at all, as it was with this situation. So again it was time to move on and put it all behind me. The timber mill had been an extremely successful business for the two year period, and I had gained some priceless business skills.

I represented myself during the family law court proceedings and flew to Canberra. It was a crazy time; and a complete waste of time, trying to come to an agreement on a property settlement. My former wife seemed unable to come to an arrangement and when we finally agreed to a particular thing, she found it difficult to keep to the agreement. I was once ordered to appear at the family law court only to find the Registrar had given my former wife leave. It was explained to me it was too long a distance for her to attend, but there was no regard for the distance I travelled 400% further. We later would have court proceedings by telephone conference and these were great, as they were held in the court room and I was linked up by telephone broadcast to the court.

I was telephoned by the neighbours to my property at Tumbarumba, who told me that my former wife and her boyfriend had confronted them, requesting they give them the key to the premises. They refused and so my former wife with her boyfriend went onto the property and got into the home through a window and removed many items. There were no items of hers as we had already divided our personal property but that never seemed to matter. After that event, I had no alternative but to agree at a court hearing that I would pay for the interest payments on the property so to have a legal agreement stopping her from entering it. I had visions of her boyfriend and her moving into my home, a building I had owned prior to meeting her, and the huge legal ramifications that would occur. I decided on this costly measure as a way to stop this from happening. I also appointed a caretaker for the property, Shane, who would live at the house and look after the place in general. Shane had been in a bit of trouble in life and needed somewhere to reside and clear his head; he was working with the neighbours and seemed to be enjoying life. Unfortunately, Shane was dealing with his own demons and one night he took his own life. A lot in the bush call depression 'the black dog', and sadly I have known a few that have taken this drastic measure over the years. **If only they could look at the glass as half full rather than half empty.** There were many incidents over the years with my ex wife that I can only describe as deeply upsetting. During telephone conversations she would tell me, "I am going to be a thorn in your side the rest of your life," and call me a loser. "You have had three failed businesses and can't get over the shooting." To be totally honest, I had got to the stage where anything she said to me was like water off a ducks back, and I would try not to allow her to push my buttons. I had a court order that allowed me to ring my little boy at set times, yet these also became upsetting. The worst time occurred when I was speaking to my son and could hear him being punched repeatedly by his older sister. He was crying and I could hear his mother encouraging this behaviour, by trying to stop my little boy from speaking to me. The following weekend after this despicable event was my access weekend and my son was extremely upset from the continual mental and physical abuse he was receiving. He would tell me that he did not wish to go back to his mother. At the hand over on the Sunday evening, my son went to his mother then ran back to me at my vehicle and said, "Please daddy, please don't make me go back." I had a mate of mine with me at the time and he told my son, "You must, Brandon; you can't get your dad into trouble," knowing there was a court agreement in place. My son then went to his mother then again ran back to my vehicle and jumped in with me and refused to leave me. I could not force my son back to any situation that was so unhealthy. I took my son back to Melbourne, knowing very well that I was breaking the family law court agreement and there would be consequences for me, but my son's happiness was the only priority I had.

I took my son to a child psychologist and after he had spent a lengthy time there, I received a report stating that Brandon had alleged to the psychologist about events of physical and mental abuse. The psychologist's opinion was that my son should not be returned to his mother. I had another court case arranged for that week to discuss property settlement, and I flew up to Canberra while Brandon stayed with friends. I can only describe the proceedings as a total disgrace, akin to the Spanish Inquisition. I have never in my entire life been so intimidated. I appeared before the magistrate and my mother accompanied me, as Brandon and I had been staying at her home. My former wife's counsel tried to make out that no one knew where Brandon was. This was not true, as I had told my ex-wife by telephone. She had said to me, "You are playing into my hands", and when my son tried to speak to her she conveniently hung up the telephone. The magistrate briefly looked over the affidavits I presented to the court; all of which gave explanations of the event. I also offered the child psychologist's report that stated Brandon should not be returned to his mother. The magistrate seemed to scoff at this documentation and briefly looked them over before he ordered me to return my son to his mother by the end of the week. Words cannot describe my anger. Then the barrister started making false accusations about me as we quickly went from discussion on the well being of my son, to the property settlement. I told the magistrate that my son's welfare was at stake and that my duty was towards him, and that he was my only priority. I was glared at, not just by the magistrate and the barrister, but also this little old man who was the clerk of the courts. It seemed the entire court scoffed at my statements, as if to say, "How dare you speak your mind in our court?" Now all the discussion was about the values of the properties. I did not give a stuff about the financial side of things and I was gutted by all that had happened. There is a saying I use when my emotions are under threat: **"when the emotions go up, down goes the intelligence"**. These despicable proceedings really put that saying to the test; all I wanted to do was give the entire court a mouthful on what I thought of them, but all that would have achieved was guarantee me a night in the cells and a greater chance of being convicted for not obeying court orders. I somehow composed myself and proceeded in defending myself against the accusation of not assisting in the property settlement. I was able to produce evidence to the magistrate that I was misled on a valuation matter; and in fact that there had been an agreement that had been reneged on. The magistrate quickly looked over the documentation, and it seemed that his attitude quickly changed towards me. He saw I was not the so called rebel that I was meant to be and then turned his anger towards my exwife's legal defence, stating that I had been obviously mislead by them. I then tried in vain to further discuss the situation regarding my son, but the magistrate stated, "Mr. MacLeod, I have already made my decision on that matter." Then he asked me, in a very respectful way, to work within the system, explaining that a report would be compiled after a family law court appointed psychologist interviewed all concerned. He would then make his decision and if the decision was for my son to live with me then it would be arranged during the Christmas holidays, only a few weeks away. The magistrate again emphasized that he was giving me 'til Sunday to return Brandon and to work with in the system. I left the court not knowing what I was going to do and, believe me the thought of running off with my son and starting a new life overseas came seriously to my mind. I returned my son to his mother on the Sunday. He reluctantly went with her, without hugs or kisses, just her evil look.

- Nick the Rat -

When I returned to Melbourne, I quickly arranged a meeting with a solicitor to whom I will refer as Nick the Rat. I had spoken to him in the past regarding the custody arrangement as he had conveniently advertised in a 'fathers in grief' news letter, filled with stories about fathers being treated unfairly in the family law courts. I had been told by the solicitor I had employed at Wagga in the past that, due to the status quo of my son living with his mother most of the time, I would only ever get weekend visitations. But knowing my son's happiness was at stake and considering the magistrate's explanation of a family law court report, I had some hope of an outcome that would be in my son's best interests. I met Nick the Rat who was working for a solicitors firm in the south east of Melbourne. He took me out to lunch and we parted by way of me paying for the bill. These events took place across Melbourne on several occasions; he would arrange a meeting with me in the early morning in a hotel close to the law courts, and after he ordered a large meal I would be left with the bill. We also met at pancake parlours, where again he would order up and I would be left with the bill. He once asked me to attend a meeting in East Melbourne where he presented me with a photo album and asked if I would tell him what the items were in the photos, as he was not familiar with farming equipment. The photos were all of bric-a-brac that looked like it was left over from a clearing sale of junk items. They were things of no value, like rotten timber sleepers or rusted old iron farming implements. After I questioned him on why he wanted to know, he excitedly explained to me that he was representing this woman who had cleared out on her husband, and was taking him through the family law court. Nick was trying to create more of the pool of assets than what was really there. He said that this feller was a bridge builder and he was going to try to show the courts that the material in the photos had value, as they could be used in his bridge building, and so create a higher figure on the asset pool and increase this woman's stake in it. He pointed to a photo of a locked up railway container and said, "I want to get into this and see what's in there." I just could not believe what I was hearing, but I was getting first hand experience in what was in the mind of a family law court solicitor. Again I was left with the bill after that meeting.

I also paid a barrister for advice and arranged a meeting with him. This cost me $1,000 but it was worth every cent, as he was able to honestly explain to me how he made his fortunes through people becoming emotional. He showed me how the pool of assets was divided and the way a court would decide on custody.

In January 2001, I arrived at the Canberra family law court for the family law court report. What a joke; everyone had been interviewed and their concerns expressed, yet the counsellor told me just how unjust a report like this was, saying that she had only a brief meeting with us all to compile the report. How anyone could create a fair and reasonable report in one day, after briefly meeting parents and children, was beyond me. My son and I had not seen each other since I returned him to his mother, and conveniently all seemed to be fine with him back there. During the time leading up to the report from the family law court, the counsellor told to me, "Your son says he enjoys living with his mother. " She told me that, because he had been there since November, I should spend the lunch break with him and to have a talk, and that she would interview us both together after lunch, and ask my son that question again. During lunch with him, I did not know if I should discuss the proceedings with him or not. I decided against bringing them up, as I was against the thought of getting into my son's head. So I did not talk about the proceedings at all, and as a result the counsellor's report recommended my son to stay with his mother and then maybe live with his father at a later date.

It was pointless to contest the report, as I would be fighting a losing battle. The reports conducted by the family law court were from brief meetings on one day and that is what a magistrate worked from, so I decided not to contest the custody decision. But if Brandon refused to go back to his mother again, then again I would not force him.

I arranged with my solicitor, Nick the Rat, to obtain an agreement about Brandon spending school holidays with me, as now I lived in Melbourne. We again had our meetings at a coffee shop in Lygon Street in Carlton where Nick told me that he was unable to get the holidays. In fact, I was under the impression he was arranging conditions without my consent. He brought up wild accusations that I had $100,000 in cash funds and I am certain he believed this. He did not have documentation filed before the court in the time frame requested, leading to costs awarded against me. At some of my arranged meetings with Nick, I would arrive only to be left waiting for hours when he did not front.

The opposition was contesting my mothers' legal right to a third of the property at Wangarra. Prior to my marriage, I placed my mothers name on the title along with my wife's name and my name as equal shares. This was a fair situation, as all owned a third each. At the time my future wife and I had a son and she did contribute towards Wangarra financially, so we agreed her contribution would equate to a third of the value of the property. My mother had assisted me by guaranteeing her home for the borrowing of monies and as well as financing from my father's estate, hence her third. The second property was only in my former wife's and my name. My mother's home had been bought from the proceeds of the sale of my fathers and mothers home in Ascot Vale. Ascot Vale was bought with the proceeds of my grandfather's home, and those proceeds were from my great grandfather's home. So I found it only fair to have the Wangarra property divided in this way.

I had no idea at the time of conveyance of the huge power of one person - a magistrate - in the family law court; that a legal title could be struck off by a pen if it was believed that the title was created in another persons name to avoid legal action. This was the argument against me: that I had placed my mothers name on the title to avoid paying money; for instance, if a divorce occurred. Now this just proved to me that the system was a total joke, and was just a free meal ticket for lawyers who profited from the misery of others. At this particular meeting with Nick the Rat, he told me, "I have got you part of the holidays," as if he had made a great accomplishment. I said, "That is not good enough. I am not contesting residency, so at least have a court order stating I have holidays with my son." After an argument, he blatantly said, "I am not going to try for that." It was obvious he had agreed to issues behind my back. He also tried to put fear into me by telling me "Your mother could lose her house," and that it was not possible to win her third in the family court. Previous to that meeting, Nick the Rat had arranged for my mother to meet a solicitor friend of his. It was supposed to be a no-fee meeting, as Nick just wanted my mother and me to get a clear picture of the situation. His mate's advice was that it was not possible to obtain the third. That meeting was very suspicious. I realized later that Nick the Rat was leaving his current firm and moving to this other jokers' solicitors firm, and was trying to get my mother to have this solicitor as a legal representative. We both declined his suggestion. I said, "It will not be necessary."

Then I tried to engage another family law court solicitor, and after our meeting she said that she would not be able to represent me, as her work load did not permit it. As documentation had not been filed with the courts in the due time by Nick the Rat, she urged me to go back to Nick and get him to get his act together. I was billed several hundred dollars for this meeting and it was simply an interview to see if I was able to get legal representation from her. Nick and I met up again, and by this stage I was certain this solicitor had led me up the garden path. He was in my office at Keilor looking through all the documentation that he had requested, when it then dawned on me that he honestly believed the crap that I had $100,000 stashed away. After I had shown him evidence of how the other party had created this blatant lie, his attitude changed and he continually told to me, "You think I am a rat." I did, and he proved to me beyond doubt that he was. But what I thought of this person did nothing to fix my situation. I was to be on trial for a three day sitting at the Federal Magistrates court in a week's time. Legal documents had not been filed, I was up for costs and fines against me and then Nick the Rat refused to appear in Canberra, as he said he was not experienced enough. He convinced me to hire a barrister from Canberra, so he and I spent a frantic two days preparing a brief for the new barrister.

The barrister I employed was a very decent type of person. He went all over the brief and after building rapport with him he advised me on the case, stating, **"We just have got to get this monkey off your back."** He also suggested I had a case regarding the professional conduct standards of my so-called solicitor. He had received an affidavit that had been printed up by Nick the Rats other solicitor mate, that requested my mother sign. My mother had not made this affidavit and so it quickly was disposed of. The case was adjourned, like most court cases I have been involved in, as negotiation took place for nearly a whole day. The outcome from the negotiation was to sell the properties and decide on a percent figure at the next court case. The case was adjourned to June so there was time to arrange buyers.

The opposition insisted on placing the selling of the properties with an agent in Wagga Wagga, but those agents did not sell in Tumbarumba and had no intention to do so. I gave the marketing to a local agent, but after many weeks with only one inspection I realized that to sell it I was going to have to do all the marketing myself. I placed advertisements in rural papers outlining a description of the properties and posted or faxed details to potential buyers and arranged inspections by telephone. Nick the Rat was again arranging meetings with me in pubs or coffee shops and not turning up to the particular place he had arranged to be. Once he insisted that we must meet to finalize documentation to be filed. He was attending court and insisted we meet at 5 p.m. on a Friday at his hotel near the Melbourne courts. That particular weekend was my access weekend with my son, so my mother drove the 1,000 km return trip to collect him for me and guess what? Nick the Rat did not turn up or answer his calls. Maybe he forgot. The last meeting I had with him was in Lygon Street in Carlton. I had already paid him for his work in brief preparation, etc., but to my astonishment, he was trying to get me to pay monies towards his lawyer mate that had created an affidavit on behalf of my mother without her consent. So much for the promised free advice. Nick continued to put fear into me, saying that my mother could lose her home. He now had joined his mate in a different legal firm, owned by the other rat. I was disgusted by these solicitors and wondered whose interests they were representing beside their own. I told him about my disgust in him and his offsider, and decided then and there to represent myself and my mother's interests, even though all these solicitors had said I had no chance of retaining my mother's third share. Besides the pathetic legal representation, it was a commercial decision. My former wife was to receive 65 to 80%, being a 'person of needs' with the children. After I calculated the huge costs over the year and the interest that I was to pay from my side of the pool, there would be nothing left. In fact, if I paid thousands of dollars for a barrister and a solicitor for a three day trial, I would come out owning nothing and deep in debt. So in my mind I had no choice but to conduct my own case. I was very angry and frustrated with the whole legal system. I found it hard to accept that I could work, scraping and saving for nearly twenty years, and have it all taken away from me along with the right to raise my son. How could all these other people, whom I would describe as not of a fit and proper character, be legally allowed to deceive me to make financial gain?

I was afraid of becoming bitter about life over this whole event, and I did everything I could think of to stop this happening. I also did not want my son to have a father who was bitter from life's experiences. I was extremely interested in the story of Tibetan Buddhists, who experienced atrocities at the hand of a Chinese invasion and went to live in exile, but still showed compassion to others and seemed to have a great perspective on happiness. I read up on their culture and visited a Buddhist temple where I met a monk who had lived in the snow for many days meditating during the invasion of his country. He had stories of horrible brutality yet the people still did not let those negative influences affect him. In fact the monks somehow used the experiences to be positive in their journey of life. Although I did not continue to study their religion (or maybe it was the fact that I could not meditate) I did gain an understanding and admiration for anyone who can create this powerful mind set.

- *Frog and the Scorpion* -

I have always had trouble with anyone who is deceitful. I am forever beating myself up about the question of WHY deceitful people come into my life. I try to defuse my questions when I cannot find reason for others actions, with a story that was told to me about a frog and a scorpion.

You see, there was this frog swimming from side to side in a river, and this scorpion came along and said, "Hey Mr. Frog, can I hop on your back? You can take me to the other side of the river because I can't swim." The frog looked at him very reluctantly and said, "I don't know if that's a good idea. You're a scorpion and I am a frog and you might sting me and I would die." The scorpion said, "Now why would I do that? You're a frog and you can swim, I am a scorpion and I can't swim. If I sting you, you will die but then I will drown and what would be the point of that?" The frog thought for a moment and said, "That's true; there would be no reason for you to sting me. Hop on, Mr. Scorpion and I will take you to the other side." Once the duo had reached the centre of the river the frog felt this terrible pain, and realized the scorpion had stung him. The frog turned to the scorpion and said "Why did you do that? We will both die now." **The Scorpion said, "I know we will both die, but it was in my nature."**

- *Running My Own Legal Case* -

I drove to Canberra with my mother to defend myself and my mother's interests. My brief was at the chambers of a barrister whom I had employed in the past. I contacted his assistant and arranged to pick it up prior to the case that afternoon. When I arrived at his chambers, I was shocked to find out that the barrister had sent the entire brief back to Melbourne months earlier, to the legal firm where Nick the Rat used to work. I contacted them straight away and one of the Principles of the firm refused to post it back to me, in case there was money owed. There was not, as I had already paid Nick the Rat for work done but it was too late now. Luckily, when I was preparing the brief with Nick and a secretary during a two day ordeal, I ran another copy off for myself, but it did not contain certain information that I needed. Now I had no choice but to use it as there was not a hope in hell that I would have the case adjourned. I just wanted the whole legal thing over. So I went into the court with what I would regard as a part brief, but I had more than a brief; I had a great memory. All that I had written in affidavit was the truth, so I had nothing to worry about. I had no experience at all at running my own case, not to mention representing my mother's interests, and was up against a barrister of many years experience but I did not allow this to daunt me. I had the mind set to stay focused and not to let anyone intimidate me. Like my mate Pete Blackman said to me: **"Play the game mate, become a solicitor; take the emotion out of it."** And that is what I did when I walked through those doors into the horrible world of the family law court; in my mind I became a solicitor.

The opposition consisted of a solicitor sitting down and handing documentation to the mouthpiece, the barrister. My former wife sat there alongside her boyfriend, while they conducted their case against me. The magistrate was the same magistrate who had ordered me to return Brandon and also reserved the costs that Nick the Rat had caused for me. It was a long three days; I was cross examined about how I had built the pool of assets. They asked questions and I was able to give them precise details of how I bought the properties and about how I funded the different enterprises. They made out that I had deliberately not helped in the selling of the properties. I corrected the barrister and proved to the magistrate that it was in fact the opposition's counsel who wanted a real estate agent in Wagga to sell the properties, which they were unable to do, due to location. I pointed out that in fact I had marketed the properties myself and had buyers for them both. They told me that they had not been notified of this. I stated that both the agreements had only just occurred, and that we could agree or disagree to the price that day. The prices I gave for both properties were very quickly agreed to. These prices were a huge reduction from what they had claimed those assets to be worth, which made a mockery out of their previous demands. We agreed to the buyers; one was a mate of mine. Every time the barrister came up with something he thought was untrue, he would try in vain to discredit me. I was always able to prove his allegations incorrect. He was the type of person that would get extremely personal when he failed to prove his claims. For instance he would refer to the mill as 'another failed business'. It is beyond me how a profitable timber mill could be called a failed business. Even the magistrate stated that the timber mill by all accounts was a profitable venture. The magistrate also stated in my defence, "It seems Mr Macleod has never sat on his behind," when this barrister was trying to discredit me. You would think I was Alan Bond and the pool was worth millions; yet the fact was I knew I was to come out with nothing at all. Their past wild claims had been about the value of items such as specialized mill machinery, which was now worth nothing, but now all the value was in the sale price of the properties. After they had tried to grill me in the witness box, it was time for me to cross examine. I invited my former wife into the witness stand and cross examined her. Everything was based on what was stated in the affidavit, and after reading over my former wife's statements, I was able to pull it to shreds. For instance she had stated that there was only an empty shed when she first moved into the property. In fact I had built a comfortable living area with a bathroom prior to her and her girls moving in. She stated that she could not remember if there was a bathroom or not, but the magistrate assisted me by asking her, "You brought two of your children there and you cannot remember whether there was a bathroom or not?" It did not take long before I felt I had the magistrate on side. As she sat in the witness box, I questioned her on many discrepancies in her affidavit. She had made a wild accusation that it was she that Boral timber had approached to build a timber mill. I pointed out to her, "Is it true you do not have any timber experience prior to our timber mill? Why would they approach you?" The reason she gave was that we owned a forest property. It was all coming together for me, and the magistrate just shook his head in disbelief.

She stated that the property was unfenced when she moved there, but how could I have kept cattle and horses there if it was not? Another obviously blatant lie. She stated she did not receive any benefits after the separation, but there was evidence she had taken thousands of dollars via a teller machine from the business account, money ear marked for employees' superannuation. She stated that she also had sole responsibility for all accounts, and that she herself built the timber mill. It was all becoming quite unbelievable. I could hear her counsel sitting next to me making noises under their breath, as if to say, "Oh no, what is she saying?" She stated that my mother, who had spent three months at Wangarra assisting the household when I broke my leg, did nothing to contribute; and that her third share should be eroded, even though there was evidence my mother had provided her home as collateral for the financing.

Besides all of these untruths that I considered totally unbelievable accusations, the best was yet to come. As there was no stone left unturned, every cent had been accounted for over the years, and there was evidence of thousands of dollars gone for my defence in the shooting incident court case several years ago. In an affidavit, she now stated that the shooting incident had not involved protecting her as alleged. She claimed that the person shot was a neighbour who had simply verbally assaulted her husband at the front door. I had become accustomed to not allowing her to push my buttons, but this was different. I questioned her, "A criminal, who neither of us had ever seen in our lives, attacks us in our own home, now is a neighbour and you claim I did not protect you as alleged?" Words cannot explain my disgust with her. There was complete silence in the court while she sat there with this smug look on her face. It proved to everyone present, and emphasized to me again, what type of person she truly was. I stated, "It does not cease to amaze me what lengths you will go to for financial gain." I admit I did become emotional at that point, because the fact was this known criminal was shot in protecting her.

Here is a newspaper report from The Daily Advertiser from the time of the shooting trial, April 1995, six years prior.

Woman feared for life, jury told

The defacto wife of a Tumbarumba farmer charged over the shooting of a man near the town on Easter Sunday last year yesterday told a Wagga District Court jury she had feared for her life when two men confronted her husband at the front door of their home.

Ms<<. giving evidence on the second day of the trial of Alistair John MacLeod, 29 of Allawah Road, Tumbarumba, who has pleaded not guilty to a charge of maliciously inflicting grievance bodily harm with intent to inflict grievance bodily harm.

MacLeod is accused of shooting 20 year old Christopher Godfrey in the leg, causing serious injury, during an incident at MacLeod's farm south of Tumbarumba, at about 9 p.m. on April 3, 1994.

"I was terrified - I was frightened - we feared for our lives," Ms. <. told the jury of seven men and five women.

Ms. <. testified that her and MacLeod, who operate a tourist horse trail-riding service into the Kosciusko National Park, had returned home at about 6.30pm after a 2 day trail ride, involving an overnight stay away from home.

Being exhausted from the trip, she had gone to bed at about 8 p.m. and had fallen asleep immediately, Ms <. said.

Ms. <.. told the jury she was later awoken by dogs barking and engines revving. She could hear yelling and screaming and saw lights of a motor vehicle going backwards and forwards outside the house, she said.

Ms. <.. said she could also hear horses on the property rushing about, as if frightened.

MacLeod was worried, she said, and asked her to get the shot gun, which was kept under her side of the bed, broken down into three pieces.

Ms<< said that from the bedroom window she could see a vehicle come through the front gate of the house yard. 'Lights were moving around the yard, wheels were spinning and gravel and stones were being thrown up," she said. "I would call it 'hooliganising'."

Ms. << said Macleod turned on the verandah light and went to the front door.

He had the shot gun in his hands, pointed towards the ground, she said.

Macleod said to the two men: "Why are you terrorizing us?" Ms. <<. told the court.

She said she heard a voice say, "We are going to get you guys - we're here to get you."

Alistair kept trying to reason with them, but they kept saying things like, 'We're going to get you, you're dead" and "You're history," she said.

Ms. << said she saw a man's arm and shoulder come through the door, throwing punches at Macleod. Macleod jumped back, she said, stumbling on a boot stand in the foyer of the house. Ms.

<.. said he hit the wall with his shoulder; the gun discharged, hitting the alleged victim Christopher Godfrey in the leg.

Ms. <.. said she applied first aid to Godfrey's leg and tried to stop the bleeding.

Under cross examination by counsel for Macleod, Robert Jovanovic and his de facto wife, <<., who went to McLeod's farm with Godfrey, denied they had gone there to steal from the property yesterday. The trial will continue today.

The major issue in the family law court trial was my mother's third share in the property. The opposition's argument was it should be eroded as it was not a legitimate third ownership and that I had only placed my mother's name on the title as a form of asset protection, to avoid a claim. My argument was that it was a valid third interest. When my former wife contributed to the property financially some 18 months after being there, she insisted on being on the title, and we all agreed at the time that her contribution amounted to a third of the value of the property. My mother had previously assisted us in many ways, and also she had used her own home as collateral for our borrowing on all the business ventures. Therefore I said that my mother's third must not be part of the pool of assets to be distributed.

The last day of the trial was the hardest. I thought about how I was going to summarize all of the evidence and to put the final case before the magistrate. I was very worried as the opposition's barrister rose from his chair and started arguing his case on precedent, 'Mary smith versus Joe Blow'. I, who had no idea on past precedent, could not know how to close my case this way. All of a sudden this barrister said, "Your worship, statistics state that a child costs in the vicinity of $200 per week, and my client Ms<<. will have the care of Brandon for a further 12 years." So his argument for 'need versus contribution', was based on the needs factor being a higher ratio, possibly 80%. The barrister concluded by stating my mother's third was not a legitimate third and should not be taken out of the pool of assets, closing with all the associated legal jargon. He also stated, "As a lay person Mr. Macleod has shown exceptional ability in running his own legal defense," and the Magistrate agreed with this comment. The barrister was not praising me but was grasping at straws, trying to show that I was a capable person and was not in need of the pool of assets as his client was in need.

The magistrate then asked for my closing statement, and I sat there not knowing what to say, slowly standing to address the court. My mind was in overdrive, as everything achieved in the past three days of court proceedings relied on my closing. What the hell was I going to say? I wondered, as I rummaged through my notes. As I looked down at what I had scribbled down of the barrister's closing statements, I became clear in my thinking.

"Your worship, I agree with the opposition." The Magistrate looked over his glasses and said, "Mr. Macleod?" I said, "Your worship, I agree that the figure the opposition has given as $200 per child a week is correct. Therefore when you consider that I provided for two children that were not my own over a period of seven years - and it has been proven here in this court room that the financial contribution towards the family came mainly from me - we have two children at $200 per week; that makes $400. Multiply that by 52 weeks of the year and we have $20,800; and over a seven year period that is $145,600, your Worship. When we take into account 'contribution versus needs', my contribution has been considerably higher."

The magistrate, with a smile on his face, stated, **"Those who live by the sword will die by the sword."** After going over his notes, the magistrate stated that he would come to a decision about dividing the asset pool and decide whether my mother's third would be removed from it. At one stage, he also told me, "Mr. Macleod, what you and I believe is morally right may differ from the legal decision." This concerned me but whatever the outcome, I was glad I had represented myself. I walked out of the court room knowing that I would be penniless, and if I lost the third of mum's share, well, a bit more than penniless, but I felt a huge sense of accomplishment.

Due to the work load of the family law courts, it was to be many months before the magistrate would hand down his findings. I waited as the orders came through via a fax machine in Melbourne. And there it was in writing: my mother's third was to be retained by my mother. I had done it, protecting her third of the assets despite numerous solicitors telling me I couldn't. The split in the pool was 60/40. I knew this was coming, due to the one with needs always beating the one who contributed. But considering the end result was less for my former wife than what I had offered her prior to the case and the fact she would have legal fees to pay from this made it all the more crazy. It was a huge weight off my mind and so time to move on, to continue my business ventures.

Very soon after the family law court order, my former wife handed over her two children from her previous marriage to their father on a full time basis. I knew it would not be long before my son would be living with me. The Rat's solicitor mate was billing my mother and was threatening interest of 11.5 %. He took legal action against my mother and she was ordered to appear at a local court in Moonee Ponds, Melbourne. I appeared at the court with her and the

Rat's mate was waiting at the entrance before we went in. He approached my mother and said, "Mrs. Macleod, we can settle this here by you paying my fee." I told him that there was not a chance in hell that we were going to pay him. It had been his business associate, Nick the Rat, who had insisted on my mother and I listening to his opinion, and it was to be a free consultation about my mother's third interest, something both of them claimed could not be won. In fact, I had represented my mother's interests and now had a family law court order stating my mother's third was valid. The court then opened and the clerk of the courts called us in, repeating our names. The solicitor rat said, "Well I will adjourn the hearing and we can discuss this further." I said, "We won't be adjourning anything. I will be walking through the doors and explaining to the magistrate you created a false affidavit without my mother's consent, and I will have you reported to the professional standards board." With that, the solicitor rat called us terrible people and scribbled on the bill, withdrawing his request for payment, and stormed out of the court. I was starting to enjoy playing lawyer.

CHAPTER ELEVEN
2001 – 2006

HAPPINESS LIES IN THE JOY OF ACHIEVEMENT AND THE THRILL OF CREATIVE ENERGY

- Property Consultant -

Not long after the family law court proceedings were over, I started seeing a woman of Polynesian origin. It was hard getting my head around the fact that I was selling Wangarra. She told me about her grandmother, an indigenous person, who had told her as a child that when anyone walks, only leaving a footprint behind them, then others shall have the right to place their feet in those footprints. This was the same philosophy as Chief Seattle's environmental statement about the web of life that I have always kept in my offices. I was going to have to accept the philosophy that **we are only custodians to the land and never really own it.** This simple belief helped me let go of not just my first property, but also enabled me to reject materialistic thoughts of property possession. Being able to do so assisted me in my career as a property developer. I noticed an advert in the Sun newspaper that had a position for a property consultant in the sales of rural properties. I applied for the job and got the position. It was with Vic Properties, owned and operated by Livio Cellantee and his sons. They were well known property developers who were supposed to have been Rural Victoria's biggest developer. It was rumoured that he had fallen in hard times during the recession and owed millions, but now was back on his feet, starting again, developing and selling properties. My position was to market properties with a sales team consisting of six people. We would create adverts and place them in numerous magazines and newspapers and take in calls, arrange inspections and negotiate the selling of properties. We also prepared section 32's and contracts and signed up buyers. The company also offered vendor finance so we qualified people to see if they could afford the repayments. I had just marketed and sold my own property arranging for a neighbour to show the buyers around. I took to what the job entailed like a duck to water. The vendor term structure was also familiar to me, as I had negotiated properties in the past on a vendor term arrangement and the product - properties in rural Australia - well, that was a product I felt comfortable with. It was on a commission basis. The office was in Templestowe a suburb in the north east of Melbourne. I worked with other dynamic salespeople. Angelo Lamantia and I teamed up to sell properties. We created this system that we called the 'Solicitor Barrister approach'. Angelo would take calls, and arrange for me to meet with the potential buyers. He did the telephone selling and arranged the meeting and inspections. I met the prospective buyers at the property, and tried to close the deal. It worked extremely well, as properties usually sell themselves anyway, and I just had to illuminate the positive aspects. For instance, we could sell on the vendor finance or a long settlement. The company's position would very rarely move on price; if anything, prices would increase over time to cover holding costs. So I negotiated a time frame with the buyer, saving him money in interest and securing his dream property.

I finally was enjoying life again, and the time I spent with my son was 100% quality time. He would even come out with me selling properties. During this time, I had arranged for my former wife's solicitor to attend to the settlement of the properties. I had organized my mate to buy the second property having a court order to do so, but it was agreed to by the opposition that I buy the property instead as they wanted their money sooner than later. I then arranged a loan to finalize it, as this forest property of 456 acres had huge potential.

I sold properties across Victoria and a couple of houses but mostly parcels of land from acreage consisting of blocks in excess of 100 acres at Alexander in north eastern Victoria, to ten acre blocks at the base of Mount Macedon. I sold bush blocks in Wedderburn and Ballarat region, Heathcote, and near Horsham. All told, there were dozens of properties across the state that I took people to, or directed them to by telephone.

In the years following my separation, I was adamant not to become a man with an 'anti-woman attitude' that I had seen so many fellers become after going through the family law court system. During the few years after my separation, I dated many women. I hadn't realized that Melbourne women were so friendly. I do not apologise for one moment for my actions, as I met and enjoyed the company of many women over these few years.

- *To beat a conviction* -

During an access weekend with my son, I arrived in Tumbarumba to find my son had not been at school that day. I had a great relationship with the school he was attending that made life easier for the both of us, since keeping to prior arrangements seemed to be an impossible task for my former wife. On this particular occasion, I had made the six hour drive but he was not there for me to pick up as per the court order. He arrived back to school on the Monday following, and later explained to me that his mother and her boyfriend had forced him into their car and had taken him to Sydney that weekend. They had ignored my calls and, while I stayed in the township during the week, my son and I were denied the right to see each other. The friends I stayed with in the town just happened to be the next door neighbours of my former wife. When I called for my son he was physically stopped from seeing me, and despite me ringing him, I was even denied speaking to him. I made contact with him at the school and during one of these visits the local sergeant came to speak to me, since my former wife had filed an Apprehended Violence Order against me, and I was now supposed to appear at the local magistrate's court.

I was held up for a week in town waiting for my case to be heard. I appeared before a magistrate and the police prosecutor stated that I had 'use of a carriage in an offensive manner'. Apparently there is a law that states that you can not use a carriage (referring to the old days of carriages as a way of transferring a statement -- this means the telephone today) in an offensive manner. I was to be charged on the day in court with the criminal charge due to a claim of Apprehended Violence order placed on me: that my son's mother feared for her life. I had thought I had heard it all, but what a load of crap! I explained to the magistrate that I was exercising my rights under the family law court orders to see my son, and that my former wife had broken those orders by taking my son away with her boyfriend on my access weekend. She had continued to break those orders by refusing to let me to speak to my son although I had court orders stating I was allowed telephone calls. (It was during this time that I had supposedly used the telephone in an offensive manner.) The magistrate adjourned the case to a later date, and the prosecution tried to get an interim order against me but failed. So I left the court only to return at a later date. That later date came around and I was hopeful to have this ridiculous charge thrown out, as I believed the magistrate could see through the whole situation. But to my disbelief, there was a different magistrate on the day and he was what I can only describe as a person of no common sense and should never have been made a magistrate. The prosecution had previously produced a tape recording from an answering machine that allegedly contained statements by me that my former wife was an evil, despicable person who played with a little boy's mind and his happiness, and also had a few more words that she regarded as offensive. I was refused the right to listen to the tapes. The prosecutor's argument was that I could erase them if handed the recording while in court. How absurd, but they had a police officer to listen instead and although he admitted he could not make out some of the words of the brief recording, he wrote down what he thought was said. Now I do admit that what was allegedly said were words that I could have said under the circumstances, but I cannot say I said them. The prosecution produced transcripts from the previous court hearing and stated, "You admitted to saying this in the witness box." It did not make any difference to the magistrate that I was denied the right to listen to them to ascertain if I had said the alleged words or not. What was more alarming was the fact the family law court order had been continuously broken yet he did not even take that into account. He convicted me of the crime and had then the audacity to impose a fine as well as well as the Apprehended Violence Order. I stated my disgust at his decision and assured him that I would appeal the conviction, which I did. It would take several months before I would appear at the Albury district court before Judge Morgan, a female judge. The prosecution's case was that the entire case had already been proven and therefore the conviction should stand. But that was nearly all the prosecutors case contained, and it seemed he thought it was as ridiculous as I did; I just needed to have the Judge think so. I only said a few things while requesting that the conviction should be dismissed, and gave emphasis to the circumstances. To my delight the Judge dismissed the conviction and dismissed the fines. Another win. I walked out of the court on cloud nine.

The commission structure that Vic Properties paid on the selling of the properties was 3%. Although 3% is regarded as good commission, most of the properties were only low value rural blocks, so I negotiated a higher amount with Livio. It was no small feat; in fact the negotiations took many days before I was able to convince him to an increase to 5% commission. I also was given his potential development properties: for instance, Sandstone Island, an island property in Western Port Bay just off Hastings. Also there was a subdivision at Wandong and at Broadford and another property known as Pylong Park, near the small township of Pylong, central Victoria. I arranged a meeting with real estate agents in East Melbourne and gave them a presentation on the viability of the properties. I networked many people like that over a period of time and met with potential developers and drive them out to the properties for inspection. I was able to find a buyer for the Pylong property and had the contract prepared and put conditions in the contract to be able to subdivide the property into 2.5 acres blocks as per the surveyors plans. I had the 10 % deposit placed into a trust account with the real estate group that introduced me to the buyers. Then I was contacted by their legal representative who stated that, after due diligence, they were under the belief that the property was not able to be subdivided into anything under 5 acres, certainly not the proposed 2.5 acre subdivision as planned. I contacted the local government in that area and it was confirmed to me that it was not possible to subdivide it into the small amounts. Integrity to me is everything. To be fair to Livio Cellantee in this matter, he insisted that he was also under the belief you could subdivide into the planned smaller lots. But all of my research showed it was impossible and I had wasted many months working on selling this development. So I arranged to have the deposit returned to the buyers to save my integrity. Although I was annoyed at the end result of this project, overall it was a very enjoyable time working as a property consultant for 12 months. Now it was time for me to operate my own businesses again and be in control of my own destiny. By now I had arranged a loan to buy out the 456 acre forest property and to settle the whole family law dispute and I was champing at the bit to get back into my business ventures. I had a wealth of experience and I had now had put in place a business plan, a structure that would emphasis the growing of my net worth, and it would all happen through the property development. One of the greatest things I learned by being dragged through the family law court was at the end of the day, all that matters is your net worth and the agreed value of it. Assets minus liabilities gives you a net figure that is called equity, and that was going to be my focus: on equity and how to build wealth more quickly than ever before. It took me 18 years to build what I had, but only two years to lose the lot so in principle I should be able to make it all back within two years with a written plan of just how to accomplish it, and that's exactly what I did. **He who fails to plan, plans to fail. He who succeeds by the plan, planned to succeed.**

- A. J. MacLeod Property Development -

On the 10th of July 2008, A. J. MacLeod Property Development was registered. I went into hospital and had my knee operated on with money that I had borrowed, as I was not under any health insurance. I bought myself a Toyota Landcruiser 4 x 4 and set up office at the Keilor East house, and then headed off back into the bush to make my fortune again. I made camp in a State Forest called Witchytella in the north east of the state. I had been searching for properties that I could buy with limited funds and be able to quickly develop to increase the overall value. After networking people via lengthy telephone calls, I came up with a few properties around the Wedderburn district, which explains why I was camped out in the bush. I had my dog Rusty by my side, cooked out on the open fire and had the swag in the back of the vehicle. At this point in my life, calculating my assets minus my liabilities, my net worth was a stone cold $0. But I had arranged an open line of credit with a loan of $180,000. I sat at night in this secluded bush camp and realized that I had literally lost everything I had ever worked for. I had started like this, with a 0 net worth, 19 years ago. I thought I should be sad or depressed, thinking about the capital I had lost. In fact I felt quite the opposite. I felt great. **I had finally realized that I had the greatest type of capital in the world: knowledge.** It now was up to me to put it to the test with a plan and persistence.

"My greatest assets have always been my memories"

I inspected a few houses around Wedderburn and a small town called Korong Vale. The town was an ex-railway wheat distribution town. I inspected a few properties with an agent and bought an old Victorian house on a large block. I attended to all the legalities myself, as well as paying the stamp duty at the State Revenue and registered the titles at the titles office. Then I returned to this old Victorian house and commenced work. It was a bigger job than I had thought.

I put in a new hot water service and painted the outside with heritage colours, totally repainted the inside, replaced broken windows and placed a new large window looking into the backyard. I replaced the veranda floor boards and opened up the once covered lead lit windows. It was a huge clean up. I even found pot plants in the ceiling where a plant growing system had been. I completed the project and sold the house on terms, and more than doubled my money on the books.

At the same time as developing this property, I bought a former cropping property of 40 acres for what I can only describe as a song, dealing with a real-estate agent. The Calder Freeway was being built at that time and the area was about to experience its own property boom. I had studied the area intensively and realized there were properties on the market that I believed were well under value. The 40 acres were made up of two Crown allotments and I marketed and sold the property on terms for a higher figure, always at least doubling my return on investment. I prepared the section 32's and the contract for sale myself when selling properties, and attended to all the settlements when purchasing. During the time at Korong Vale, I became friends with the person who owned the Post Office: Gil Williams. He showed potential buyers the properties while I went back into the mountains to develop the 456 acre open forest property. The basic principle in my mindset for development was this: if I was to invest $20,000, for example, and through property development double that, then I would only have to do this six times to make a million dollars. Return on your investment means focusing on a large return but at the same time not being too highly geared; and to have access to your equity in the form of loans. It is like the fact that if you take a $1 coin and double it 20 times, you would have turned a dollar into a million dollars. Most people cannot grasp that simple philosophy, but I have found **it is the philosophy that drives the business structure to success.**

It was great to be back in the high country. Now I had the goals to complete my dreams and to put a cattle grazing operation together. I had bought a 16 foot caravan when I was in Bendigo and had towed it onto the property, which was called MacLeod's Run. At this stage I was seeing a woman, Evie, from Sunbury. She would catch up with me on many weekends. I arranged a camp in the spot where I had taken the horse treks to a few years prior. Over the summer, the year was declared the worst drought in Australia's history, and then the thing everyone dreaded most actually happened: a lightening strike on the northern side of the mountains created a bush fire. As the mountains were the driest in known history, the entire Kosciusko Park went up in smoke and the fire did not stop until it hit the sea, hundreds of kilometres away. I stayed put for those weeks as I only had my horses at the time, but I was fortunate not to have the fire come through my place. It went through the Tumut Gorge taking everything in its path. I rode up on horse back with Barry Patton not long after it went through, and it was completely devastated, leaving behind one huge black deathly landscape.

I bought a generator as my power source and in the beginning all the water was carted from the creek. I placed a bush shower outside and contracted a bulldozer to clean up all the old timber windrows and regrowth. I built a large multi-purpose shed of 50 x 30 feet. On one side all the farm tools were stored and the other was a living area equipped with a bathroom and kitchen. The walls were lined and rooms carpeted throughout with a large fireplace for heating. Next to the multi-purpose shed, I built a generator shed and had a few generators installed over the next four years. I also built a hayshed and contracted the bulldozing of numerous fence lines and put a large dam on the southern side of the property. I had materials trucked in and fenced off kilometres of country, subdividing it into 10 paddocks with dozens of gateways. When all the 'dozed fallen timber was in rows, I burnt the country. It lit up the entire valley and you could see the glow for miles. Cattle yards were put together with a loading ramp and I bought a 90 horse power Belarus tractor with front end loader and cabin to assist in developing the property.

I had a contractor dig into one of the numerous springs with an excavator to create a spring fed dam, and rolled poly pipe from the spring to the office area for my water supply. I continued the pipe over to the holding paddocks for a water supply for the stock.

- Belted Galloway Cattle -

Over the years I had been involved with numerous breeds of cattle, but had not had anything to do with the Galloway breed. After research, I realized that they were ideal for the property, originating from the highlands of Scotland. They were renowned for their doing ability, being known as a great foragers in cold country, browsing as opposed to select grazing. The main trait of this breed was the fact it had a double coat, equal to the American bison, protecting it during the harsh winter months and reducing its need to eat to keep warm. The meat was naturally marbled and the breed had won many 'hoof and hook' competitions. The only problem was there were hardly any numbers about. The Belted Galloway had traditionally been a hobby farmers breed, as they looked attractive being black with a huge white band around the body. Most of the information I received about the breed was from Europe or the States, and even those countries had only small herds of 50 head or so. I bought my first few cows from Murrumbatmen outside of the A.C.T. and from a breeder at Dalton N.S.W. The worst drought in 100 years had been declared and I had received reasonable rains in the mountains and just needed the warm days of late spring to kick off the grass growth. I arranged a delayed settlement whereby I produced a contract and paid a deposit and balance payable on pick up within the next couple of months, which saved me feeding costs. My first truckload arrived late spring 2003, and I measured their progress by bringing them in and weighing them to measure their weight gains, and to study the breed over a period of time to see if the claims made about this beast were correct.

Besides doing the hands-on development of the 456 acre property, I negotiated and inspected properties throughout Victoria. I had the telephone lines put in to the property at MacLeod's Run and so was able to have internet access, now crucial to my business. I drove to Horsham and purchased a former school on two acres that was situated not far from the Grampians at a place called Nurrabiel. In fact, that was all there was at Nurrabiel; the school. It was a historical site; the school had the black boards in one major room and another smaller room that had been used as a kitchen when the past owners had lived there. There was a septic tank outside and shelter sheds and a great garden made up of native trees that had been planted 30 years earlier and now were all mature. There was an old bore on the property as well. I bought it for a song and planned to return at a later date to do a makeover on it, but due to the development in N.S.W. it was left for a period of time.

- Out Back Trip -

Winter was truly on us in the mountains, and the snowy conditions in the mountains were nothing to be desired. So Brandon and I packed up and made a trip out to the desert country. We headed to the Darling River, camping out in our swags every night. I had just bought two new blue heeler pups, Ned and Kelly: no prizes for guessing games on our name selection! We visited the towns of Wilcannia and White Cliffs and while there met a feller who had been opal mining most of his life; a real eccentric. He showed us around his mine and reckoned he came to the conclusion many years ago that if there were big seams of opal left then all the major mining companies would have taken up mining rights. So instead of digging for opals, he dug out all the old back filled dirt and started showing people around the mine for a couple of dollars. Then we visited Milpirinka and spent a couple of days gold detecting. On the old gold mining sites, there were many old graves - nearly all of children who had died of illnesses in that harsh environment. We explored the Strezlicki desert in South Australia and since the country had just experienced good rains, feed was everywhere; the water courses full of beautiful legumes and native clovers. We camped at Innaminka on the Coopers Creek, then travelled over to Queensland and to the famous 'dig tree', where Burke and Wills perished in the 1800's on their heroic attempt to traverse this country from south to north only to perish. They had tried to return to where their supply party had left only that morning after waiting months for their return, and had placed supplies in the ground with the word 'dig' carved into the tree.

We returned back to the mountains and, as with most of the trips I have made away in these remote parts of the country, I came back with a renewed appreciation of life, and that helps to create the passion for one's endeavours. My asset and liability statement was looking pretty good. In fact, my net worth was more than when I was married. In fact, I had made every thing back that I once had and more, in just over a 12 month period with the start of A.J.MacLeod Property Development. That was in half the time of my original plan. I had people close to me who knew of this little success in my life, and told me that I should go out and buy something for myself. I know a lot of people would buy a new car or a similar thing, but I arranged for my mother to have a boat trip and a tour of Tasmania, as it was a place she had always wanted to visit. It was lucky that I did, as in a few years later she had a major stroke. I have never been interested in splashing out for myself, but I did buy myself a leather jacket and I even was able to negotiate 10% off the price. I loved entertaining people on my properties or taking people out for dinner, but I have never been into the gifts for myself. **I have always had what I need in life; what I want is only a bonus.**

- Buying Up Grazing Country -

I purchased a 100 acre property, south of Macleod's Run with a natural high plain in the middle of the block, and a permanent spring that flowed even through the drought. Ironically, it was the property that Tony Digrande and I had ridden across all those years before when I unfortunately staked a horse looking for brumbies. Spraying the blackberries and burning off the place was the only development I did. Otherwise I walked cattle through the bush to the property and used it as a paddock in conjunction with the rest of the property. I funded the purchase of this property with the equity from other properties and monies coming in from the sales of the properties on term agreements. As it was so isolated, I left it unencumbered as I knew it would be hard for evaluators to find comparable sales and therefore be difficult to find financing for it.

Mal and Karen Reid had had enough of the farming industry and approached me to see if I was interested in buying the rest of their property. They were in no hurry to sell the entire place but were up for any ideas for me to purchase all or part of it. We entered into an agreement whereby I could purchase three titles immediately on terms. Then I would develop the properties and build a reasonable herd of cattle. It made up of a 244 acre title and another 145 acre title, there was also a small 2 acre title. We entered into a contract of sale for this and at a later date the option to purchase the rest of the country, made up of another 1,000 acres. There was a no obligation agreement and down the track, a pine plantation company bid for the Reid's remaining 1,000 acres. I encouraged Mal to accept the offer as it was higher than what I was able to pay. In hindsight it worked out well, as the drought was not going to break; in fact the worst was yet to come. My mind set of being immune to fear and blind to failure was going to be put to the test.

I put together 1,000 acres of grazing country in total, made up of four properties, which made up its own valley running along the upper reaches of the Maragle Creek. I went to work over the next couple of years, spraying blackberries over the properties, and then burning off all the old timber windrows. I had a bulldozer create a road for 2.5 kilometres and had gravel pushed up by the bulldozer at a location on one of the properties, and hired an old tip truck. With the tractor and front end loader, I would bucket up gravel to the truck and drive to the road areas and tip out the gravel. I repeated this until I had built a road through the property, and then hired a grader to level off the gravel. I fenced areas of the new property, bought iron and welded up road grids, as opposed to having to open gates along the three kilometre drive through the property.

- Father and Son Pack Horse Adventure -

Over the years I had ridden into the mountains more times than I can remember, covering thousands of kilometres on horse back. Redgum alone had taken me on 5,000 kilometres. I rode with literally hundreds of people, guiding them into the mountains, and also made many lone trips as well. But the most memorable of these would have to be when Brandon, aged nine, and I headed off for a few days in April 2004. We packed up our old faithful pack horse Metro, Brandon rode his favourite Tiny and I was on Redgum. We left our property and headed up into the Maragle Range and brought along a video camera to film the entire trip. We had enough supplies for several days but on the trip feasted on apples from trees at the old mining sites from the gold mining era. Our first night was spent camping on the side of Mount Black Jack's range in a mountain ash forest. We climbed up onto the higher altitude which is snow covered in winter and looked back deep down into the Tumut Gorge. Then we moved onto Emu Plains, crossing the area and climbing up onto Fifteen Mile Spur, camping anywhere we wished, with the horses hobbled at night and tied around snow gum trees in a taped off area. We carted our swags on the top of the pack horse and lay out in them at night, talking about the adventurous day that had just past and the excitement of what lay ahead as we rode further into the mountains. It was great up on the high plains with the sweet smell of alpine grasses and views towards the highest mountain range: Mount Kosciusko and the main range. We decided to ride down the Tumut River Gorge where the bush fires had been through the year before and had decimated the alpine ash forests in the valleys. Although it was the most disastrous fire the mountains had experienced, it opened up the mountains and made horse riding through the area more accessible, not to mention the available feed for horses. The mountain grasses grew back with vigour and the horses were well fed for the whole trip. The descent into the gorge tended to move the pack saddle, and I would be forever adjusting the rigging. Once we arrived at the river, we crossed with our horses and made the climb up the other side for many kilometres. I was somewhat concerned when our pack horse Metro walked very near to the side of the track; one slip and a horse would fall and plummet to his death. We reached the high plains of Happy Jacks Plain after a long climb. Metro was allowed to walk freely during most of the trip and now and then we would have to whistle to him and he would run to catch up to us. Most of the old cattlemen's huts in the area that had stood the test of time had been sadly lost in the fires. We camped one night on a small hill overlooking the high plains on the North east side of Mount Jagungal. The frosts had set in at night and we had a roaring fire going in between the snow gums to keep warm. At dawn we awoke to find our horses were gone. We had not heard them break loose. We stood on the hill and could just see them in the far distance. It was not the first time that our horses had broken away at night, but this time it would be a few days walk home if we could not catch them. Luckily we caught one still with hobbles on, and once saddled I rode after the other two. I found that one had busted the hobbles and the other had lost the entire hobble set totally.

We rationed out our food supplies and after we had eaten half the rations we turned and headed back, again down into the Tumut Gorge and across the river. There was once a steel and timber bridge there that had been burnt out in the fires. The blaze was so fierce that it killed everything in that valley, and I believe no one would have had any chance of survival if caught in those fires. Once we climbed up out of the gorge, we made camp on the eastern side of Fifteen Mile Ridge in an opening amongst the snow gums. The eastern side looked towards Table Top Mountain and the west looked out to the low country and we experienced a fantastic sunset. There was a cold front moving through and a fair bit of cloud cover was forming and as the sun was slowly going down it seemed literally below us; this huge red ball falling away in the cracks of the mountains, creating a reddish evening light that lit up the whole high country; it was truly spectacular. The fear of approaching wet weather and the guarantee of snow with it put the pressure on us, to return home before the front hit. That night we tethered the horses, and I ran a string out along two trees, so the horses could freely move with their lead ropes along the length of tape.

At dawn we were up and decided to make a fast trek out, keeping to the tracks of the mountains; back over Emu Plains and up over Mount Manjar and the descent down into the Maragle Range. The sky was black by the end of the day and down it came, only a few kilometres from home and with it came the ice. We arrived back in the dark and brought our horses onto the veranda to unsaddle. Another great horse trek into the mountains was over. My son had ridden a couple of hundred kilometres throughout the remote high country at only nine years of age and not once whinged about the journey.

- Cattle buy up -

I had borrowed finance from a rural lender for the development operation and planned to borrow $200,000 for further developments, and to purchase cattle to increase the breeding herd. It was extremely difficult to obtain finance on rural properties as most lenders would not go more than 50 % of the properties' value. I always had access to funds in the way of a re-draw facility with the banks, and tried not to go below 10% of my total liabilities. But in a lot of cases things get close to the bone. By the time finance was approved many weeks later, it was not what I had originally applied for: no open line of credit. This rural finance group then insisted on approval on all redraws. As it was difficult to obtain rural finance, I accepted their offer and settlement took place, with them having a mortgage over the 457 acres plus insisting on having a mortgage on the cattle that I planned to purchase as well. I would call this a double dip. I contacted them after settlement as I could not access funds. They stated that they now wanted a copy of my business certificate and I was told that if I did not supply it, they would not allow me access to the funds. The certificate was in the Melbourne office and that was another week in the delay of the funds. This was just the start to a very bad financial relationship.

Once I had access to the funds, I went out buying Belted Galloway cattle from across Southern Australia. I had now started developing my seventh property. **I had gone from broke to owning seven properties in 24 months.** I inspected cattle from the South Australian border to the A.C.T. and eventually purchased an entire breeding herd from Strathbogie, Victoria. I bought cattle at Beaufort Victoria, Leongattha in Gippsland and I also bought cattle at Flinders on the Mornington Peninsula. I bought bulls from Walwa, Victoria.

All the cattle had to have come from a hard type of country and not be too long in the tooth for guaranteed longevity. I did not purchase cattle from soft country and none from any herd that I believed was pampered. All cattle had been through the drought in the last few years, and I never paid more than the market price. I would use b doubles [double deckers and trailer] to reduce my freight costs, as in a lot of cases the cattle would be freighted hundreds of kilometres. The mountains were looking good, due to recent rains and the drought looked to be well and truly over; or so I thought.

In December 2004, Tony Digrande and I made a trip to Western Australia. We flew over and explored the south west coast, spun the coins in the casino and checked out the property market over there. Not a week went by when I was not researching the property market in all areas across Australia.

- My Son with Me -

The past four years had been bedlam trying to arrange access to my son despite having a court order. There were times when I was simply denied access in an arranged time; or when trying to speak to him by telephone (again at a court order time), to be denied and or an excuse made; or my former wife's boyfriend picking up the phone and refusing to let me to speak to my son. Brandon's school became the place where we made contact beside my weekend access. The principle was very supportive of me and my son during this time and encouraged me to visit him during school times. While spending time with me, Brandon would tell me that he was not happy with his mother and did not want to go back, and that he wanted me to go back to the courts. But I was not going to go back to the courts until I was sure that my son was adamant in his decisions; I had to believe he would not be easily led by others - a lot to expect for a nine year old boy. But in January 2005, when I picked up my son for the school holidays, we made the decision to never ever return him to his mother to live. He told me he was not going to go back and live with his mother, and told me about all the emotional abuse he alleged he had received, such as being denied speaking to me on the telephone. He showed me a cut on his arm where he alleged, he had nails dug into his skin. Words cannot describe my disgust and anger. I explained to my son, then and there, that he would never ever have to go back there to live; never ever, if that is what he wished to do. He wanted to know what would happen if the courts made him and I explained the courts would not make him; and even if they did, that I would never ever allow him to go back there to live as long as he did not want to. I then got legal advice on the matter from a new lawyer and this time I was not charged for the advice. I wrote a letter to my former wife stating my disgust and that I would not be returning Brandon to live with her. She could issue recovery order if she wanted and if that was to be the case, then I would have a family law court report conducted on what my son had said he had experienced and she then would have to deal with the consequences of that.

Within a few weeks, my former wife had legal aid representation, and a telephone conference was held, lasting for 3.5 hours. It was agreed that we would have consent orders, whereby Brandon would live with me and visit his mother. This was to be interim and final orders would be made at a later date. I made it clear that my son could visit his mother any time he wanted, **but hell would freeze over before I forced my son to go back there to stay.** So after four years of trauma, my son finally came back to live with me.

- Ballarat Property -

Besides developing a cattle property in the Snowy Mountains, I was always on the look out for another property. I found a 5 acre block at Snake Valley, west of Ballarat. At the time I was extremely limited in funds and so another person came into the deal with me. I knew him via a mutual friend and he also wanted to start developing properties. He had recently had an accident, in which he had crashed his semi trailer on the Hume Highway and so did not want to continue driving;

instead wishing to go into the development business. He asked if I would go into a property development with him and as I had my hands full develop-

ing a 1,000 acre cattle operation, I agreed, and we purchased a 5 acre property together on which we planned to build a large steel shed to increase the overall value. The property was purchased well under the market value. In fact we quickly snapped it up at a bargain price after it had only been on the market a few hours. **You make the money when you buy.** The agreement was that I was to arrange all the settlements and building plans, etc., and all that was required from my co-developer was to pay for half of the property, half of the building costs and to be onsite to arrange the building of the shed. We arranged a long settlement so as to have ample time to arrange funds. I also paid the co-developer to do a paint job on my school house. When settlement day came, I drove to Melbourne for the settlement and the co-buyer was not to be found. In fact, he had done a runner on the day of settlement. I was left paying 90% of the purchase price not to mention dealing with the contracts that had arrived for the building. I also had to make all due diligence with the council for the building. I visited the solicitor's office that was representing the Vendor and extended the settlement. I finally met up with my co-buyer, who explained he was now not capable of buying the property. So I bought the property outright to save my integrity. Although it would have been easier to walk away from the deal, I had put too much work into it and integrity to me is everything. I was rewarded at a later date for this decision, as I had the property valued by the banks at 70% more than what I paid for it and I later sold the property on vendor terms. Selling properties on term opened up the market for me and I always was able to sell for the price I asked. In all cases, I would offer an interest free deal between three months to sometimes twelve months, depending on the amount of properties I was marketing. After the interest free period, there would be an interest payment and contracts would be drawn up for two years to three year terms. This interest free deal created a win-win situation. I would also have an agreement with the purchasers that, as long as they never fell into arrears, they were able to on sell the property as long as I received my money from that sale. In the beginning I would put together my own contracts of sale and at a later date, when the net value increased and I was in no need to penny pinch, I employed lawyers to compile the contracts. The Australian Tax Office looked at these sales as a loan, and I employed solicitors for insurance reasons only.

I visited the school house and my co-buyer had not even finished the painting, so I had to make the 1600 kilometre trip again at a later date to complete it, and then sold it on vendor finance.

- *The Catch* -

During those four years I had also noticed items going missing from the properties. Firstly from Wangarra, then MacLeod's Run. It was becoming worse over the last two years, ever since I moved to the Run. I experienced car keys disappearing from the vehicles. I had book work stolen, tax records, a diary, even a Valentines Day card from a Melbourne girlfriend who would visit me. Many farm tools vanished. Rusty my dog went missing while chained up and never seen again. The generator that was in a dry shed was found full of water on several occasions. Sugar also was found in the generator on different occasions, as well as in the tractors' fuel. I had an employee nearly hurt by collapsing hydraulics and we discovered that they had been tampered with. A carved sign went missing from a gateway.

I had contacted the police over the last couple of years and there was a huge list of all these incidents. My close group of friends in the Tumbarumba district all believed they knew who it would be. I also knew beyond any doubt who was behind this. My son also believed he knew. The police advised me not to take the law into my own hands and try to catch the culprit in the act. Then a neighbour driving down the remote power line road that runs on the eastern side of the property passed a vehicle known to us all and the person who was driving the vehicle was the person we all believed was behind these acts. The tyre tracks indicated he was parked, hidden behind a treed area where he was able to see me drive out to pick my son from Scouts, leaving my home vacant. There was an agreement in place whereby my son would be picked up by his mother and taken to Scouts and they would spend an hour together. Then I would collect Brandon after Scouts had finished. By the time I went to town and returned, it would be a 1.5 hour trip. I believed this person would drive all the way from town, an 80 kilometre return trip, sometimes in snow, along a slippery track that ran along the eastern side of the property. The entrance to the property was on the western side on a totally different road. I was sure he waited there for me to leave, then would sneak down to my office and vandalize or steal my belongings. I arranged for several people to keep an eye on his movements and I would be telephoned over a period of time on his location. I also had two of my mates to take turns in watching the property. They stayed at the property conducting surveillance in the hope of catching this person in the act.

Mal Reid conducted the first surveillance shift. It was his idea to take turns watching the place and he had said he would be there as many times as it took to catch the culprit. Phil Daly drove to the property to watch the place on the second shift while I was going to town to pick my son up from Scouts in my usual routine that time of the week. Phil had been a great mate of mine since the Union days of Boral timber. He has been referred to as one of Tumbarumba's toughest on the rugby field. Honest as they come, but with the looks of a person not to be messed with: a bald head, over 6 feet tall and a picture of Ned Kelly tattooed on his arm. I was telephoned by two separate people who believed this person had driven up towards my property. At the same time there were two others on the property: a dingo trapper with the National Park and a pest controller with the pasture protection board. I quickly explained the situation to them and they drove off the property. At this stage, we believed the culprit was hiding up on the range watching who drove out. Phil had hidden his car out of sight and placed himself in a caravan watching the office and living area. I gave Phil a video camera and a quick lesson on how to use it. I then hopped in the 4 x4 and drove out of the property to town. I stopped at Pete and Ruth Blackmans and when I walked into their home, the mobile telephone rang. It was my office number and I answered, asking Phil, "What is he doing, going into the office?" thinking that he, Phil, would be seen by the culprit. Phil said, **"I got him, you better get out here!"** That was music to my ears. I quickly arranged for Brandon to be picked up and Pete and I drove out there. When we arrived, Phil was sitting on a log outside the office and, standing there dressed in camouflage gear, was who we all expected: my former wife's boyfriend. Phil, who was supporting an injury to his eye, explained how he was sitting in the caravan when this creep appeared, walking around the office/living area. He was wearing camouflage gear and a camouflage wig, the same as a soldiers' head wear during war. Phil explained how the culprit then went into the tool shed. Phil had briefly filmed this and then had run straight to the tool shed. The culprit had two of my boots in his hands. Phil made a comment like, "Don't you usually steal one at a time?" The culprit said, "I've been set up!" and charged at Phil as Phil was trying to close the door to the shed. Phil copped an eye gouge and, in self defence head butted the culprit and they both wrestled a bit until Phil persuaded him to give up. I looked at this pathetic person who was showing obvious signs of nervousness and unable to stand still. I said to him, in an abusive way, that I had put up with this for five years. I was furious to see my mate, who had caught this pathetic human being, with an eye injury. It was unbelievable that a person would drive a return trip of 80 kilometres sometimes in terrible weather, hide his vehicle and walk through the bush to a remote property to cause damage or rummage through personal belongings. He quickly ran off into the bush as I contacted the local sergeant of police. Phil told to me that as he was talking with him, he had continually asked Phil, "How does Al do it, get all this together?" meaning my property developments. He seemed to be a very obsessed person. The police came out and within the next couple of days the culprit was charged with a wide variety of offences. It was a period of 12 months before he stood trial, and to be honest, it was an exciting court case. Phil, Pete and I appeared for the entire three days to give evidence and watch the proceedings. Ironically, the police prosecutor was the same prosecutor that had me convicted for the use of 'carriage in an offensive manner', the charge that I had appealed and had thrown out. Now he was playing a theatrical role in prosecuting this person. The excuse the man gave while under cross-examination was comical to say the least, explaining how he just happened to decide to go bush walking, hence the camouflage gear, and was only placing things away in the tool shed to clean up on my behalf. His testimony must have been totally embarrassing for his legal counsel, and the magistrate even stated that, if there was evidence of a mental condition, he may have not even convicted him.

CHAPTER TWELVE
2005 – 2007

MONEY WILL NOT BRING HAPPINESS BUT BAD STEWARDSHIP OF MONEY WILL STEAL HAPPINESS

-Utopia -

It was an incredible time in the summer and autumn of 2005. I had my boy with me after years of trauma and he was now as happy as any kid could be. We had several properties and hundreds of head of Belted Galloway cattle and it felt amazing to be out in our entire valley of which we were now custodians. Mustering our own cattle on our horses with our dogs barking, moving the large mob along the valley, with the sounds of cows bellowing as we pushed the mob along to the yards; cracking our stock whips with the sounds echoing through the ranges like rifle shots. This moment was what I had dreamed of since I was a small child, and now I had achieved my dreams; my own cattle operation in the mountains. **It does not get better than this**. The remarkable thing was that I had financially achieved this, going from being penniless to owning several properties within a short period of time: just 33 months. It made all the anxiety, despair and feelings of failure that life had thrown at me over the years as worthwhile. I had a feeling of being rewarded; not so much for the accomplishment of owning the properties, but for the more important reason: what I had endured. I had turned all the events that at the time I found crippling into rewarding experiences as I looked back over those events. They enabled me to achieve my dreams, and to have the great feeling of accomplishing my ambitions. I had created a plan, a business model, of exactly how I could accomplish what I wanted, and I did not try and reinvent the wheel along the way but added to the plan as I found a better way of going about things. I had no idea then that this success was going to be short lived, as the drought was not over and the worst was yet to come. In fact, I was now like every other person on the land; about to witness the biggest drought in history and a cattle crash that was going to send many people to the wall.

'When the dream becomes a reality It no longer is a dream'

I arranged for my yearlings to be sold through the sale yards at Wagga Wagga. The agents were also from the same rural finance company that financed the cattle purchase. I was told that the Galloways would return an estimated $1.85 to $2.15 a kilogram. To my disgust they were sold for $1.48 a kilogram; the return was thousands of dollars short of what I expected. I had had enough of the entire sale yard process. How crazy to send your livestock into these yards and be paid a pittance, while people down the chain profited. I decided to value add my own beef, bringing it from the paddock to the dinner plate, and so embarked on a long term business plan to value add. It would be nearly twenty months before I would have animals ready for slaughter as I had sold most of my weaners through the yards. Over the next year I had arranged for a feed lot to finish my yearlings off. I relied on growing them out at home to a certain kind of condition then having the feed lot finish them off to what is described as 'butcher trade'. I arranged with an abattoir to kill my beasts and to have them divided into quarters, which would be freighted to a meat packaging plant in the northern region of Melbourne. I then negotiated a price whereby the quarters would be broken down into a variety of cuts and arranged into a beef pack, all cuts being individually packaged to suit the freezer. Then I arranged a price for a contractor to deliver these packs to the door of people's homes. I created the advertising flyers with ten reasons to buy a Macleod's Beef Pack.

"Low in fat, high in flavour, due to the breed's unique two layer coat system, which keeps the cattle warm in winter, and reduces the need for a large fat cover. More meat, less fat from an ancient breed renowned for juicy, tender, flavoursome beef. Free range grazed, bred in the Snowy Mountains in a natural environment at Macleod's Run, a 1,000 acre high country property. No growth promotants, antibiotics or genetically modified material is used on Macleod's Run. An all natural product. Save $ by purchasing straight from the producer @ discount price. Delivery free. Variety of beef cuts. Porterhouse-beef for stir fry, rump beef for kebabs, roasts, beef for stew, T-bone, mince and BBQ. Individually snap frozen, retaining all the goodness and freshness to suit every freezer option. Suits all, ideal for the large family and the single person."

I planned on producing 100 steers a year through this system and the profit margin would have been satisfactory, as I needed 5 % return minimum after costs as a yield off the property, not to mention the 10% capital growth. This was part of my development policy. I created the logo and continued developing the property and the beef herd.

My romances continued and I was seeing Lisa from East Keilor, whom I had known for many years. These weekend get togethers lasted nearly three years.

- *Winter Drought - 2005* –

The drought that most of us thought had broken was in no way over. I had hay delivered to the property which, due to winter conditions, would have to be brought in during the early hours of the morning while the road was solid with ice. If it melted then we would have to wait for the road to dry out or refreeze during the next night to drive the truck out. Many times I would tow the truck with the tractor. Every second morning I was out with Brandon, feeding cattle from the back of the trailer. We also would mix up molasses and urea. It was a terrible winter trying to keep cows alive. I lost a few over this period, as they had been through the drought over the past few years and had become very vulnerable. It was a winter of all winters, with open night skies creating freezing conditions. I would be out with an axe breaking the ice off the top of the water troughs. Brandon was able to walk on the top of the iced up dam. Melting down the urea was a task. We had large 44 gallon drums in which I would carefully melt the urea in boiling water, and mix with the appropriate amount of molasses. Then I poured the contents into several plastic roller licks that the cattle would feed from. Over this period I had become a slave to my cattle, unable to be away for too long due to having to feed them. Brandon and I headed to the coast of Mallacoota for a brief break. I arranged to have a flying lesson. **When was the last time you did something for the first time?** It was great, flying out to sea, hoping to spot whales. Brandon sat behind me as the pilot directed me in flying the plane. Then it was the long drive back to continue trying to keep our cattle alive. As soon as we drove onto the property, there they were, bellowing, demanding their feed. The cattle had become so well behaved that I could just ride out on my horse, open a gate and count them through without any trouble. The exception was a few young strays that were out in the bush and Brandon and I had a lot of fun trying to catch the rogues out there. On occasion, brumbies would get into the high plains property and we would both ride our horses to run these wild horses out. Watching my ten year old son galloping up to the side of a brumby stallion had my heart in my mouth a few times.

- *Final Court Case* -

The court orders I had were for residency on an interim order and it had been planned for them to be reviewed within six months. This period came around quickly and a telephone conference was arranged. My former wife had a solicitor at this conference representing her, and after a lengthy conference, again she was unable to agree. My son did not wish to go with her if her boyfriend was around. This was not a problem as she never had her boyfriend present when seeing her son. This creep had emotionally abused my son on many occasions, and considering his bizarre ways and the proven event at my property, there was no way I was going to allow my son to be around this per-

son. I stated that I did not want set times for when a mother could see her own son, but wanted her and Brandon to have open access. It was up to the two of them to arrange to see each other, and to restore their relationship, so I could see no reason why there should be set times. But the ex and her solicitor would not agree. I do not even know what they really wanted; in my opinion it was just playing games. So as a result of no agreement being reached, I was requested to appear at the magistrates courts in Wagga Wagga, instigated by my former wife and her solicitor.

I appeared at the courts, and again waited ages for my case to be heard. To my surprise, my former wife did not appear and neither did her solicitor. I stood up and explained the situation to the magistrate. The magistrate suggested that she was able to make the orders final there that day, but was unable to change the conditions to allow open access or the condition about her boyfriend, so we agreed to have the conditions heard at a later date and a notice was sent out for my ex-wife and her solicitor to appear again at the local magistrates court at Wagga. The final orders were stamped, and I received a copy by mail. Again I attended the magistrate's court and this time my former wife and her solicitor were present. Our case was called and I requested the conditions to be placed on the final orders. The magistrate asked both parties to be mediated for an hour in the court mediation rooms, and then return to her within the hour. We sat there, and all that my former wife asked was, "So did you like your son's new earring?" She was laughing while she said it to me. On the previous visit with her, Brandon had come back with an earring. It was quickly removed and never worn again by him, as he does not like earrings. I am 'old school' and my son wearing an earring at such a young age was unacceptable to me. So there I was, trying to allow her to have open access at anytime to her son, on the condition that her fruitcake boyfriend was not around during this time. Again, she was unable to make a decision; her solicitor took her into another room, all whispers, and returned to tell me, "We do not have an option but to place this before the Family Law Court in Canberra." I knew exactly where this solicitor was coming from. She would be paid by the Legal aid Commission and to railroad this to the Family Law Court would guarantee her a pay packet. As for what reason my former wife would want to go there, as she was not requesting any additional conditions whatsoever, was beyond me. So the solicitor and my former wife stormed back into the court room. I was about to deliver a nice surprise for them. The solicitor told the magistrate that an agreement was unable to be made and we had no choice but to take this matter to the Family Law Court of Canberra. I then stood up and addressed the magistrate, explaining that what this solicitor said was incorrect. The fact was that I was seeking a change to the order, allowing my son's mother to have open access with no restrictions, and I also wanted a condition that her current boyfriend, who at that stage had several criminal charges pending over his unlawful entry into my premises, would not be around during the access times. The fact that we were unable to reach an agreement was no reason to take it to the Family Law Court as it would be wasting the courts time as well as our own. When the solicitor started to make reference to the orders being interim, I explained that the orders now had been stamped and were final, saying that this had happened at the previous court hearing that they did not appear, and that this was where we now shall leave things. The magistrate looked into the orders and explained to the solicitor that these orders were made final at the last hearing when both she and her client did not show. Case was dismissed. **If you do not have a plan of your own you will be part of someone else's.**

I decided to on-sell the school. I went about marketing the property; again I tried to use real estate agents and had no success whatsoever. Then I marketed the property myself by placing adverts on the internet as well as in newspapers. I offered vendor terms to open my market up. After a period of time with no bites, I was inundated with people wanting this quaint little school near the Grampians. Some of the adverts read: "School's in. A former school house on two acres of native garden." Two girls from Melbourne bought it on a term contract. Again I created a win-win situation by giving them an interest free period and a contract for three years.

Back to the livestock: I was frantically trying to keep cattle alive through the horrible winter drought. Every night I prayed that the short days would be over and we would have warmer weather to create growth. Spring just seemed so far away, and spring in the high country comes much later than anywhere else due to the higher altitude. On the 10th of August 2005, it was the coldest day recorded since the '70s and my cattle and I felt it. Then the warmth in the air started, spring came and the frozen ground became damp and wet and the warm weather caused the grass to grow. It was beautiful with lush green feed covering the whole 1,000 acre property. The cattle walked away from the hay and only ate this new green feed that came through. Then disaster struck and the cows started to fall over. Every day I was losing a cow, some days more. I could not put it down to anything but pregnancy toxemia. But that was not it: they had gone through years of drought, and now were heavily in calf and eating this new green pick; it just rolled them over. I had experienced something of a similar nature with ewes lambing at Stonyhurst after the drought of '83 broke. But here I was, with my cows dying, trying everything I could come up with but it was to no avail. I searched all my books, got advice, tried to keep them on the hay, but the harsh droughts had taken their toll. I knew about other cattlemen that were experiencing the same problems, and there were reports of large losses. I had a beautiful large cow that had produced twins in the past, and one morning after I counted the herd while they were on the feed, I went looking for the one missing and there she was. She had walked into a spring to eat all the new growth and gotten stuck. Although she had been in there overnight, she was still alive and I was in the bog for ages, trying to physically drag her out, which I finally did. I was exhausted as I sat there with her lying next to me. Then I looked at her and realized she had stopped breathing; another loss. It was nearly all too much to bear. Only livestock producers who have experienced this can relate to the horrible anxiety one goes through for months on end trying to keep animals alive and, by the fate of nature, when you think you have got through it, they fall over on you.

Some of the cows had rotten teeth. I realized that these had come from a property that had given them sugar lollies from a sweet factory in an effort to give them energy, and a few years later this was the effect. The biggest percent of cows lost came from the one property. Although I had selected cattle from hard country, they had been supplying them with a daily balance of nutrients for years, so even good hay was not enough and the trauma of years of drought and high country grazing took its toll. My tractor had broken down and I was feeding by 4 x 4 and trailer, making life extremely difficult without the front end loader. I needed to refinance to obtain funds to keep going, as well as settle on the 244 acre property I had bought under terms. I had huge difficulties obtaining finance for a rural grazing property. I placed an application to the rural finance company that had loaned me money for the 456 acre property. The original application was for 60% of the value of the 456 acres; then at a later date, 60% of the value of the 244 acres. They had been given the date when the funds were needed for settlement but it took months to process the application. In fact settlement came and went and I had not heard from them, despite my requests.

It seemed no one was interested in lending to someone with live stock during a drought. I finally had the Westpac Bank agree to lend me 60% of the value. This now allowed me to have access to funds as well as get settlement for the property, as I had increased the value substantially due to the development. The bank requested I pay their valuer for the report, which I did, and the value came out at the exact price as I said it was now worth. But then the bank did not go through with the loan. They gave no reason whatsoever, so I had wasted money on the request for a valuer. Then I extended settlement and obtained a loan through a second tier finance group at a higher interest rate and a very low LVR at 50%, so surplus funds were limited. Then, weeks after the settlement, the rural finance company sent me a letter of an offer; weeks too late.

One positive thing about the situation was the cattle herd I had was fantastic. The old natural selection process had given me a great tough mob of cows. Unfortunately my leg was giving me trouble from my accident in '98 and all the work going into developing the property and feeding out took its toll on me physically. I went to Melbourne and was diagnosed with extreme arthritis and was told to retire. I was also told that my knee was bone on bone and I would need a knee replacement in the future. I went back home to the Run and soldiered on. Although I had achieved my goals, I was determined to make this cattle operation profitable. The drought was surely over as we had had a reasonable spring, but that was short lived and old Mother Nature was about to show me how really tough she was going to get. **My attitude was: bring it on.**

The people who I had sold the old Victorian house to stopped paying and did a runner. They had up to ten people living in the house and trashed it. I employed people in the town to clean up the place and I heavily advertised the property for sale, and sold it for the second time for what the original people owed me for it.

'Brick walls are there to make sure you are still keen on what you want in life'

This was a period when I was asking myself: do I still want to be a cattleman? More and more reports were coming in from leading scientists around the world, stating that it was not a drought but a climate change, and this new level of rainfall was to be as good as it gets. I thought that even with a drop in rainfall I would still have close to the 40 inches a year but this was not the case. We were only getting rainfall of 20 odd inches; terrible winters, dryer summers and no autumn breaks. Therefore there was only a small window of growth for the year in spring and that was limited. It was very alarming. The mountain region had become totally unviable for producing cattle as the high cost of buying feed and freight took any profits. My business plan did not allow me to operate at a loss unless there was a huge capital growth in a year on the properties, such 15% per year. I believed it would only be 10%, and with the seasons as they were and if this was to be permanent, I believed I would be returning no yield at all, and in fact risking a debt for the year and working for nothing.

Due to the poor season, our calving rate was extremely low. After a bit of a spring, summer was on us and feed became scarce again. The water situation in the mountains was starting to be of a concern. Most of the springs had dried up and the creeks were only a trickle as we went into a very dry autumn. In April of 2006, I moved all the cows to the Mannus Valley to Gaven Willis' property. He was to agist the cows there and I had arranged for hay to be cut there as well; good quality hay that I freighted home where I fed all the weaners, yearlings and bulls. This drought never seemed to end. I planned to subdivide the property as a second option if things did not turn around. I put in a development application for two subdivisions; one being the 456 acres and the other the 244 acres; combined they would give me 700 acres. I applied for 7 x 100 acre lots, and had the application approved with minimal conditions. It was going to be two years before I would have this development complete. Most of the lots had creek frontage and views. The property down the creek from the Run was sold for $400,000 being only 122 acres. So as a farmlet, the value with a subdivision now increased the overall value. That was fantastic as capital growth goes, but to get a yield from cattle in this drought was becoming impossible. I had to decide if I was going to cut my losses on the livestock side of things, or gamble for another year, and hope it will finally rain. It was a very hard decision to make; a lifetime of working towards a dream and to achieve it, and now I had to re valuate it all and decide to sell the entire herd and the properties. The steers I had in the feedlot were brought home when the feedlot ran out of feed. Feed prices were increasing and, although I had plenty of feed arranged, it would only last for the winter. On top of the dry winter we were having, there now was a chance we would not get a spring. If that was the case, then I knew I might have to wait for another year for the next spring growth. I did not think it was guaranteed we would get a break in the summer or autumn, going by recent years. Cattle numbers in Australia had reached the 26 million mark and with a huge switch from wool growers to beef and then the drought, I believed the beef industry was in trouble. I had been making regular trips to Melbourne during this time to escape the horrible drought. During one of this trips I met and became involved with a woman, Susan, from the Sunshine area. Another week end relationship started and continued for over a year.

I decided to sell the entire herd, as to hold on would have been economic suicide. If we did not get spring rains, I would have to feed hundreds of cattle though another year, and this was not going to happen. The reality was that hay would be as scarce as hen's teeth with no hay production possible for spring. I advertised everywhere I could think of, from internet sites to newspapers; but no buyers. In desperation, other cattlemen were trucking cattle to yards to offload them before they died in the paddocks. Gaven Willis had my herd out on the road getting what feed was left and there was still no rain in sight. I arranged to the sell the herd through the sale yards, and I was advised by an agent from the same company that I had borrowed from (who had the mortgage on the stock as well) to sell at Moss Vale. After he inspected the cattle he believed that we might get around $650 per cow, as they were in demand for small farmers. I arranged for three 'double deckers' to cart the cattle to Sydney and loaded them at Mannus Gaol yards. It now was October: no rain. The country had run out of feed, and water was becoming scarce. Up to this point I was very concerned with the cattle dropping in condition. They held on, but they were loaded not a day too soon. I even contemplated going on the road with the mob; horses, caravan and dogs, but now the reality was that this was the worst drought in living memory and now, for the first time, water was scarce. I really had no choice; I had to off load. It was a sad day, loading the cattle into the trucks; they could be handled with little effort now. The agents had arranged advertisement in the rural papers, but to my amazement the advert came out only a day prior to the sale. I did not attend the sale, as this really was not a wish of mine to sell, but purely an economic decision. The night after the sale, the telephone rang and my agent read out the prices I received. I could not believe what I heard: my entire breeding herd was sold for pittance; in fact they equalled to $.50 cents a kilogram. All told, I had lost well over $100,000 dollars that afternoon. I was expecting poor prices but this was disgusting. The same week black cows received 27 cents a kilogram in Wodonga and Wagga. It was a CATTLE CRASH, a result of the worst drought in history and unfortunately I experienced it first hand. I definitely would have taken all the cattle on the road if I thought, or was told by my agent, that I was to receive those prices. One of the most alarming reports was coming out that a farmer was committing suicide every three days. I tried to create the attitude of how good is the loss, **I never thought three years ago I would have 100 thousand dollars to lose.**

As all this disaster due to the drought was taking place, I was having difficulty in refinancing the properties. Over this time I literally had contacted dozens of lenders or brokers. Low Documentation loans, development loans, you name it; I inquired and on many occasions was misled or taken up the garden path by lenders who stated that they would give me 60 or 70% of the value of the properties. Once the valuer was paid, it then would become 50%. There are dishonest people who mislead you in all industries but those in the finance sector are equal to solicitors and car salesmen. One lender, whom I had made the 1,000 kilometre trip to see, insisted that along with the application that they would give 70% on the projected sale. I had a value done and paid thousands of dollars for the multiple lots, only to then be offered 50% LVR. I even hired a valuer who had valued the property a year previously. He told me what type of value he would place on it, but once the account was paid prior to the report (as requested), the value came out below the valuation a year ago. The comparables did not even work out; neither did his reason for giving a value under his previous value before development. It seemed that it all had become a fruitless task.

I quickly sold the 5 acre property at Ballarat on terms over a 3 year period, but money was short. I then sold the rest of the cattle herd and all the weaners that I had on the run. The creek stopped flowing and eventually I only had a small water hole that had enough water for our five horses. The spring dam that fed our living area ran out of water, and even the Paddy's River falls stopped flowing. If I had not sold, I would have been in the terrible situation of having no water for my stock at all. There was to be no growth for a year so I had made the right decision even though I had lost a lot of money. Brandon and I had visited many places that we might move to, and decided to have a sea change. We had visited the western port bay region of Victoria and decided to move there. I would run the office, marketing the properties on the subdivision as well as arranging the next lot of developments into residential. Just prior to Christmas 2006, we packed up the 4 x4 and trailer with our personal possessions, put our two working dogs in the vehicle and turned out our five horses over the 1,000 acres. Horses can get their teeth closer to the ground and so are better able to survive and get a feed in the bush, more so than cattle. This was a better option than selling them as they were all old so to be turned out to live the remaining days of their lives free had merit. Then we drove off and away from our home and our beloved high country, to start a very different lifestyle to what we had become accustomed. It was the end of a dream that had taken 31 years. It should have been a sad day, leaving the land, but to be honest it was a relief. My mindset was: I have lived my boyhood dreams. I have gained knowledge that is priceless. I have succeeded in reaching my goals. I have survived the drought, and stopped throwing good money after bad. I will eventually profit from the property, through the development of properties and my business model.

My son and I moved to the coast for six months then moved to Melbourne, completed the Snowy Mountain subdivision and made the development a huge success. We formed a development company and now have purchased city residential development sites for subdivision and construction. We also made a trip into the remote regions of Papua New Guinea exploring the Highlands, the Sepik River country, the coasts and islands; experiencing this last frontier, its people traditions and customs. It does not get better than this. A mate of mine would say to me many times over the years, when I was adamant about living a dream, if you fail or if you succeed one thing is certain, **"You will never die wondering"**.

SUCCESS

To laugh often, to win the respect of intelligent people and the affection of children, to earn the appreciation of honest critics and endure the betrayal of false friends, to appreciate beauty, to leave the world a bit better, whether by a healthy child, a garden patch or a redeemed social condition, to know even one life has breathed easier because you have lived: this is to have succeeded.

INSPIRING SAYINGS

The book Never Die Wondering is the journey of Alistair MacLeod who has overcome seemly insurmountable obstacles to succeed in living his dreams and accomplishing his ambitions, here are 100 sayings that are in the book or had assisted him in his life's journey. They come from greats like Churchill, Gandhi, Emerson, Mandela, Chief Seattle, RM Wiliams and many other unknown philosophers.

1. "Learn more to earn more"

2. "Hardest lessons leave the biggest impact"

3. "Most people are two pay packets away from bankruptcy"

4. "Have goals and measure yourself against them"

5. "Riches do not respond to wishes they respond to definite plans"

6. "Every failure brings with it the seed of an equivalent advantage"

7. "If you can not control your own mind you will not control anything else"

8. " A winner never quits a quitter never wins"

9. "Amateurs compete/ professionals create"

10. "The only thing I can't afford is to do the same thing twice"

11. "Plan the work then work the plan"

12. "In times of change the learners shall inherit the earth while the learned themselves equipped with a world that no longer exists"

13. "People are always blaming circumstances for what they are, I do not believe in circumstance"

14. "If you understand what is happening you will no what to do"

15. "It's pointless going down stream and pulling people out, go upstream and find why they fell in"

16. "The golden rule, he who has the gold makes the rules"

17. "Luxury once enjoyed becomes a necessity"

18. "Imagination is more important then knowledge"

19. "A millionaire and pauper both have the same hours in a day"

20. "Let time be your Ally and patience your friend"

21. "People who order their lives rightly an all areas, are kept in poverty because they lack gratitude"

22. "Every one is richer in Australia today, than the richest people in the world 200 years ago"

23. "When one winger's about their life, would they place their name in a hat and take a chance to swap with someone else through out the world"

24. "Accept responsibility of where you are today, or you will be powerless to change"

25. "Lack of money is a temporary condition, being poor is a state of mind"

26. "No one can go back and make a brand new start, anyone can start from now and make a brand new ending"

27. "The deal of the decade comes along once a week"

28. "Great minds must be ready not only to take opportunities but to make them"

29. "Power goes to the person who controls the land"

30. "If you could never sell it, would you be happy to own it forever"

31. "To not succeed is not an option"

32. "The future depends on what we do in the present"

33. "Think laterally there is always another option"

34. "A real mate is someone that walks in when the rest of the world walks out"

35. "A mate is someone who believes in you when you cease to believe in your self"

36. "It is only risky if you do not know what you are doing"

37. "Ventures are only risky if you do not create an option"

38. "Just because you failed does not make you a failure, just because you succeeded does not make you a success"

39. "600 million people in the world live on less than $3.50 a day how dare we complain"

40. "If you only do what you know, you will not do much"

41. "Positive mind set = success"

42. "No problems only challenges"

43. "Take the knowledge and apply it"

44. "Its not the size of the dog in the fight that counts, it's the fight in the dog that counts"

45. "Deal with life what ever it brings with strength, humanity and integrity"

46. "Its more important to have access to money than making money"

47. "If you chase two rabbits one will escape"

48. "Property is not for people to own, it should be treated as a loan"

49. "If you can not measure it you can not manage it"

50. "A successful person fails more times than an unsuccessful person"

51. "Our greatest glory is not by falling, but rising every time we fall"

52. "A person is not old until regret takes place of dreams"

53. "Go out on a limb that is where the fruit is"

54. "There is only two times in life, right now and too late"

55. "Common sense is not common.

56. "Live life like there is no tomorrow, but learn as much as you can as if you where to live forever"

57. "Biggest regrets in life are the things we don't do, not the things we do"

58. "A pessimist sees difficulty in every opportunity an optimist sees opportunity in every difficulty"

59. "Brick walls are there to make sure you are still keen on what you want in life"

60. "When was the last time you did something for the first time"

61. "Immune to fear blind to failure"

62. "Happiness lies in the joy of achievement and the thrill of creative energy"

63. "Fear is temporary regret is permanent"

64. "Money wont buy happiness but bad stewardship of money will steal happiness"

65. "Embrace your fears and turn them into positive energy"

66. "Success is a journey not a destination"

67. "I have everything in life I need, what I want is only a bonus"

68. "A journey of a thousand miles must begin with a single step"

69. "What would life be like if we did not have the courage to attempt anything"

70. "A great sailor does not become great by sailing on calm waters"

71. "Successful people make quick decisions and rarely change their mind, unsuccessful people delay making decisions and always change their mind"

72. "He who fails to plan plans to fail"

73. "We are only custodians of the land"

74. "Wealth is made along time before any money is made"

75. "Never measure a man by his destination he has reached but the journey he has made along the way"

76. "Healthy stock and healthy land makes you wealthy"

77. "Never allow the fear of change or failure to stop you from succeeding of what you wish to do"

78. "The best time to buy is now"

79. "You have to go the extra yard in life to achieve anything"

80. "Integrity is everything"

81. "Contaminate your bed and you will one night suffocate in your own waste"

82. "No point having friends in the good times if they are not there in the bad times"

83. "No point of worrying what people think of you, if you only realized how little time they do think of you"

84. "The best place to be is here and the best time to be here is now"

85. "It is better to deal with an honest man with the shake of a hand than a signed contract with a crook"

86. "One who has never experienced anxiety, despair or failure will never succeed in life, they will be shackled by fear alone, fear creates a stable work force, but never a happy one"

87. "When emotions go up, down go the intelligence"

88. "I have the greatest capital in the world, I have knowledge"

89. "You make the money when you buy"

90. "It does not get better than this"

91. "If you do not have a plan you will be part of someone else's"

92. "If you can dream it you can live it"

93. "You do not have to see the whole stair case to make the first step"

94. "My greatest assets have always been my memories"

95. "A life spent making mistakes is not only more honorable, but more useful than a life spent doing nothing"

96. "One mans fear becomes another mans opportunity"

97. "Allowing grievance and resentfulness is like drinking poison and thinking it is going to kill your enemy"

98. "The difference between a successful person and others is not the lack of strength, not the lack of knowledge, but rather the lack of will"

99. "Tough times never last but tough people do"

100. "A man builds a huge house, and now he has a master, and a task for life, he is to furnish it, watch it, show it, and keep it in repair the rest of his days"

Order the book Never Die Wondering online www.neverdiewondering.com.au

About The Author

Alistair MacLeod has continued his adventurous life exploring some 20 countries across three continents. He has written short stories on these adventures. Along with his second book Son of a Highlander published in 2015.

He started sailing after retiring from horseback riding, with a small mono yacht, learning to sail on Port Phillip bay and then moved to the Gippsland Lakes on the Victorian coast for four years were he bought and prepared a 33 foot Crowther catamaran along with completing a property development what is now known as Seafarers Rest accommodation at Metung Victoria.

In 2018 Alistair sailed the entire East coast of Australia mostly solo, living full time on his vessel, sailing the swells of Bass strait and the Tasman sea in Winter, along the Coral coast into the Torres Strait and then into the Gulf of Carpentaria and then back to Cairns in 2019, some 4,000 nautical miles on the vessel he affectionately named NEVER DIE WONDERING.

"An adventurer, a free spirited person must never conform to other people's expectations. It is essential to live your dreams, to explore and to discover. Anything less would eventually lead to a life of regret. Pursue the ultimate goal to NEVER DIE WONDERING."

Alistair J MacLeod

SON OF A HIGHLANDER

Son of a Highlander is the true story of the author, a third-generation Australian of Scottish Highland descent discovering his ancestral history over eight generations, from father to son.

This is a search for authenticity of a verbal story handed down over a two hundred-year period, along with a 1797 penny coin and a collection of photos and correspondence that are one hundred years old, which were from his late grandfather's old tattered leather case.

The author descended from the Clan MacLeod—Clan meaning "Children in Scottish Gaelic," Mac meaning "son in Gaelic," and the Leod derived from the Viking era; it basically means "children of the son of Leod." The family originated from a small two-acre semisubsistent existence on the Isle of Skye in far western Scotland. The MacLeod Clan was once a warrior race that feuded with neighboring clans in the most bloodiest of warfare.

A clan system of traditions and culture that lasted hundreds of years that eventually came to an end with the notorious Highland Clearance, whereby thousands of people were evicted from their lands and replaced by sheep. With the mass exodus of people, some forcibly while others left in desperation.

This book is the history of one Highland family who survived a dangerous sailing journey to Australia only to continue their struggle against adversity on foreign soil. A search for the whereabouts of a Gaelic-speaking great-great-grandfather to discover he was sent to an island off the Australian coast, where he eventually died and was buried in a pauper's grave along with 8,500 souls, whose only crime was that they were poor.

This book is a must read for anyone wishing to trace their own ancestral history. It will inspire you and encourage you toward your own personal voyage of discovery.

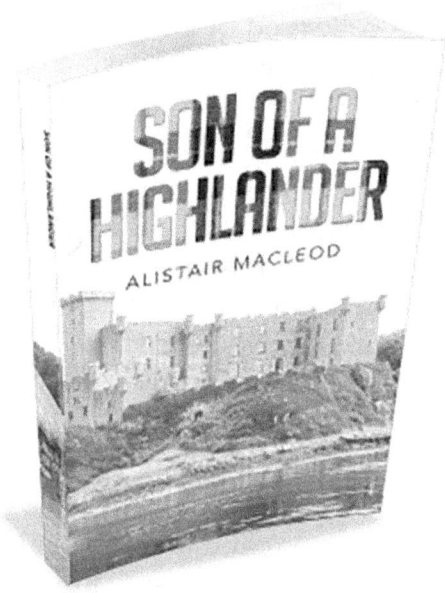

Go to www.neverdiewondering.com.au

ORDER A BOOK ON LINE

Never Die Wondering
Alistair MacLeod story

www.neverdiewondering.com.au

www.ingramcontent.com/pod-product-compliance
Lightning Source LLC
Chambersburg PA
CBHW050306010526
44107CB00055B/2123